STATISTICAL METHODS FOR RESEARCH WORKERS

STATISTICAL METHODS FOR RESEARCH WORKERS

BY

Sir RONALD A. FISHER, SC.D., F.R.S.

Fellow of Cornville and Caius College Cambridge Foreign Associate United States National Academy of Sciences and Foreign Honorary Member American Academy of Arts and Sciences ; Foreign Member of the Royal Swedish Academy of Sciences; Formerly Galton Professor, University of London; Arthur Balfour Professor of Genetics, University of Cambridge

ISBN: 978-93-5128-658-5

First Published in 1925
Indian Reprint in 2017

Published by

Kalpaz Publications
C-30, Satyawati Nagar,
Delhi – 110052
E-mail: kalpaz@hotmail.com
Website: kalpazpublications.com
Ph.: +91-9212142040

Cataloging in Publication Data—DK
Courtesy: D.K. Agencies (P) Ltd. <docinfo@dkagencies.com>

Fisher, Ronald Aylmer, *Sir,* 1890-1962, **author.**
Statistical methods for research workers / by Sir Ronald A. Fisher (SC.D., F.R.S.).
pages cm
"First published in 1925"—Title page verso.
ISBN 9789351286585

1. Statistics. 2. Biometry. I. Title.

HA29.F57 2017 DDC 519.5 23

CONTENTS

TABLES

EDITORS' PREFACE

The increasing specialisation in biological inquiry has made it impossible for any one author to deal adequately with current advances in knowledge. It has become a matter of considerable difficulty for a research student to gain a correct idea of the present state of knowledge of a subject in which he himself is interested. To meet this situation the text-book is being supplemented by the monograph.

The aim of the present series is to provide authoritative accounts of what has been done in some of the diverse branches of biological investigation, and at the same time to give to those who have contributed notably to the development of a particular field of inquiry an opportunity of presenting the results of their researches, scattered throughout the scientific journals, in a more extended form, showing their relation to what has already been done and to problems that remain to be solved.

The present generation is witnessing "a return to the practice of older days when animal physiology was not yet divorced from morphology." Conspicuous progress is now being seen in the field of general physiology, of experimental biology, and in the application of biological principles to economic problems. Often the analysis of large masses of data by statistical methods is necessary, and the biological worker is continually encountering advanced statistical problems the adequate solutions of which are not found in current statistical text-books. To meet these needs the present monograph was prepared, and the early call for the second and later editions indicates the success attained by the author in this project.

F. A. E. C.
D. W. C.

I

INTRODUCTORY

1. The Scope of Statistics

THE science of statistics is essentially a branch of Applied Mathematics, and may be regarded as mathematics applied to observational data. As in other mathematical studies, the same formula is equally relevant to widely different groups of subject-matter. Consequently the unity of the different applications has usually been overlooked, the more naturally because the development of the underlying mathematical theory has been much neglected. We shall therefore consider the subject-matter of statistics under three different aspects, and then show in more mathematical language that the same types of problems arise in every case. Statistics may be regarded as (i) the study of **populations,** (ii) as the study of **variation,** (iii) as the study of methods of the **reduction of data.**

The original meaning of the word "statistics" suggests that it was the study of populations of human beings living in political union. The methods developed, however, have nothing to do with the political unity of the group, and are not confined to populations of men or of social insects. Indeed, since no observational record can completely specify a human being, the populations studied are always to some extent abstractions. If we have records of the stature of 10,000 recruits, it is rather the population of statures than the population of recruits that is open to study. Nevertheless, in a real sense, statistics is the study of populations, or aggregates of individuals, rather than of individuals. Scientific theories which involve the properties of large aggregates of individuals, and not necessarily the properties of the individuals themselves, such as the Kinetic Theory of Gases, the Theory of Natural Selection, or the chemical Theory of Mass Action, are essentially statistical arguments, and are liable to misinterpretation as soon as the statistical nature of the argument is lost sight of. In Quantum Theory this is now clearly recognised. Statistical methods are essential to social studies, and it is principally by the aid of such methods that these studies may be raised to the rank of sciences. This particular dependence of social studies upon statistical methods has led to the unfortunate misapprehension that statistics is to be regarded as a branch of economics, whereas in truth methods adequate to the treatment of economic data, in so far as these exist, have only been developed in the study of biology and the other sciences.

The idea of a population is to be applied not only to living, or even to material, individuals. If an observation, such as a simple measurement, be repeated indefinitely, the aggregate of the results is a population of measurements. Such populations are the particular field of study of the **Theory of Errors,** one of the oldest and most fruitful lines of statistical investigation. Just as a single observation may be regarded as an individual, and its repetition as generating a population, so the entire result of an extensive experiment may be regarded as but one of a possible population of such experiments. The salutary habit of repeating important experiments, or of carrying out original observations in replicate, shows a tacit appreciation of the fact that the object of our study is not the individual result, but the population of possibilities of which we do our best to make our experiments representative. The calculation of means and standard errors shows a deliberate attempt to learn something about that population.

The conception of statistics as the study of variation is the natural outcome of viewing the subject as the study of populations; for a population of individuals in all respects identical is completely described by a description of any one individual, together with the number in the group. The populations which are the object of statistical study always display variation in one or more respects. To speak of statistics as the study of variation also serves to emphasise the contrast between the aims of modern statisticians and those of their predecessors. For, until comparatively recent times, the vast majority of workers in this field appear to have had no other aim than to ascertain aggregate, or average, values. The variation itself was not an object of study, but was recognised rather as a troublesome circumstance which detracted from the value of the average. The error curve of the *mean* of a normal sample has been familiar for a century, but that of the *standard deviation* was the object of researches up to 1915. Yet, from the modern point of view, the study of the causes of variation of any variable phenomenon, from the yield of wheat to the intellect of man, should be begun by the examination and measurement of the variation which presents itself.

The study of variation leads immediately to the concept of a **frequency distribution.** Frequency distributions are of various kinds; the number of classes in which the population is distributed may be finite or infinite; again, in the case of quantitative variates, the intervals by which the classes differ may be finite or infinitesimal. In the simplest possible case, in which there are only two classes, such as male and female births, the distribution is simply specified by the proportion in which these occur, as for example by the statement that 51 per cent. of the births are of males and 49 per cent. of females. In other cases the variation may be discontinuous, but the number of classes indefinite, as with the number of children born to different married couples; the frequency distribution would then show the frequency with which 0, 1, 2 . . . children were recorded, the number of classes being sufficient to include the largest family in the record. The variable quantity, such as the number of children, is called the **variate,** and the frequency distribution specifies how frequently the variate takes each of its possible values. In the third group of cases, the variate, such as human stature, may take any intermediate value within its range of variation; the variate is then said to vary continuously, and the frequency distribution may be expressed by stating, as a mathematical function of the variate, either (i) the proportion of the population for which the variate is less than any given value, or (ii) by the mathematical device of differentiating this function, the (infinitesimal) proportion of the population for which the variate falls within any infinitesimal element of its range.

The idea of a frequency distribution is applicable

either to populations which are finite in number, or to infinite populations, but it is more usefully and more simply applied to the latter. A finite population can only be divided in certain limited ratios, and cannot in any case exhibit continuous variation. Moreover, in most cases only an infinite population can exhibit accurately, and in their true proportion, the whole of the possibilities arising from the causes actually at work, and which we wish to study. The actual observations can only be a sample of such possibilities. With an infinite population the frequency distribution specifies the fractions of the population assigned to the several classes; we may have (i) a finite number of fractions adding up to unity as in the Mendelian frequency distributions, or (ii) an infinite series of finite fractions adding up to unity, or (iii) a mathematical function expressing the fraction of the total in each of the infinitesimal elements in which the range of the variate may be divided. The last possibility may be represented by a frequency curve; the values of the variate are set out along a horizontal axis, the fraction of the total population, within any limits of the variate, being represented by the area of the curve standing on the corresponding length of the axis. It should be noted that the familiar concept of the frequency curve is only applicable to an infinite population with a continuous variate.

The study of variation has led not merely to measurement of the amount of variation present, but to the study of the qualitative problems of the type, or form, of the variation. Especially important is the study of the simultaneous variation of two or more variates. This study, arising principally out of the work of Galton and Pearson, is generally known under the name of **Correlation,** or, more descriptively, as **Covariation.**

The third aspect under which we shall regard the scope of statistics is introduced by the practical need to reduce the bulk of any given body of data. Any investigator who has carried out methodical and extensive observations will probably be familiar with the oppressive necessity of reducing his results to a more convenient bulk. No human mind is capable of grasping in its entirety the meaning of any considerable quantity of numerical data. We want to be able to express all the *relevant* information contained in the mass by means of comparatively few numerical values. This is a purely practical need which the science of statistics is able to some extent to meet. In some cases at any rate it *is* possible to give the whole of the relevant information by means of one or a few values. In all cases, perhaps, it is possible to reduce to a simple numerical form the main issues which the investigator has in view, in so far as the data are competent to throw light on such issues. The number of independent facts supplied by the data is usually far greater than the number of facts sought, and in consequence much of the information supplied by any body of actual data is irrelevant. It is the object of the statistical processes employed in the reduction of data to exclude this irrelevant information, and to isolate the whole of the relevant information contained in the data.

2. General Method, Calculation of Statistics

The discrimination between the irrelevant information and that which is relevant is performed as follows. Even in the simplest cases the values (or sets of values) before us are interpreted as a random sample of a hypothetical infinite population of such values as might have arisen in the same circumstances. The distribution of this population will be capable of some kind of mathematical specification, involving a certain number, usually few, of **parameters**, or "constants" entering into the mathematical formula. These parameters are the characters of the population. If we could know the exact values of the parameters, we should know all (and more than) any sample from the population could tell us. We cannot in fact know the parameters exactly, but we can make estimates of their values, which will be more or less inexact. These estimates, which are termed **statistics**, are of course calculated from the observations. If we can find a mathematical form for the population which adequately represents the data, and then calculate from the data the best possible estimates of the required parameters, then it would seem that there is little, or nothing, more that the data can tell us; we shall have extracted from it all the available relevant information.

The value of such estimates as we can make is enormously increased if we can calculate the magnitude and nature of the errors to which they are subject. If we can rely upon the specification adopted, this presents the purely mathematical problem of deducing from the nature of the population what will be the behaviour of each of the possible statistics which can be calculated. This type of problem, with which until recent years comparatively little progress had been made, is the basis of the tests of significance by which we can examine whether or not the data are in harmony with any suggested hypothesis. In particular, it is necessary to test the adequacy of the hypothetical specification of the population upon which the method of reduction was based.

The problems which arise in the reduction of data may thus conveniently be divided into three types:

(i) Problems of **Specification**, which arise in the choice of the mathematical form of the population.

(ii) When a specification has been obtained, problems of **Estimation** arise. These involve the choice among the methods of calculating, from our sample, statistics fit to estimate the unknown parameters of the population.

(iii) Problems of **Distribution** include the mathematical deduction of the exact nature of the distributions in random samples of our estimates of the parameters, and of other statistics designed to test the validity of our specification (tests of **Goodness of Fit**).

The statistical examination of a body of data is thus logically similar to the general alternation of inductive and deductive methods throughout the sciences. A hypothesis is conceived and defined with all necessary exactitude; its logical consequences are ascertained by a deductive argument; these consequences are compared with the available observations; if these are completely in accord with the deductions, the hypothesis is justified at least until fresh and more stringent observations are available. The author has attempted a fuller examination of the logic of planned experimentation in his book, *The Design of Experiments*.

The deduction of inferences respecting samples, from assumptions respecting the populations from which they are drawn, shows us the position in Statistics of the classical **Theory of Probability**. For a given population we may calculate the probability with which any given sample will occur, and if we can solve the purely mathematical problem presented, we can calculate the probability of occurrence of any given statistic calculated from such a sample. The problems of distribution may in fact be regarded as applications and extensions of the theory of probability. Three of the distributions with which we shall be concerned, Bernoulli's binomial distribution, Laplace's normal distribution, and Poisson's series, were developed by writers on probability. For many years, extending over a century and a half, attempts were made to extend the domain of the idea of probability to the deduction of inferences respecting populations from assumptions (or observations) respecting samples. Such inferences are usually distinguished under the heading of **Inverse Probability,** and have at times gained wide acceptance. This is not the place to enter into the subtleties of a prolonged controversy; it will be sufficient in this general outline of the scope of Statistical Science to reaffirm my personal conviction, which I have sustained elsewhere, that the theory of inverse probability is founded upon an error, and must be wholly rejected. Inferences respecting populations, from which known samples have been drawn, cannot by this method be expressed in terms of probability, except in the trivial case when the population is itself a sample of a super-population the specification of which is known with accuracy.

The probabilities established by those tests of significance, which we shall later designate by t and z, are, however, entirely distinct from statements of inverse probability, and are free from the objections which apply to these latter. Their interpretation as probability statements respecting populations constitute an application unknown to the classical writers on probability. To distinguish such statements as to the probability of causes from the earlier attempts now discarded, they are known as statements of **Fiducial Probability.**

The rejection of the theory of inverse probability was for a time wrongly taken to imply that we cannot draw, from knowledge of a sample, inferences respecting the corresponding population. Such a view would entirely deny validity to all experimental science. What has now appeared is that the mathematical concept of probability is, in most cases, inadequate to express our mental confidence or diffidence in making such inferences, and that the mathematical quantity which appears to be appropriate for measuring our order of preference among different possible populations does not in fact obey the laws of probability. To distinguish it from probability, I have used the term "**Likelihood**" to designate this quantity *; since both the words "likelihood" and "probability" are loosely used in common speech to cover both kinds of relationship.

3. The Qualifications of Satisfactory Statistics

The solutions of problems of distribution (which may be regarded as purely deductive problems in the theory of probability) not only enable us to make critical tests of the significance of statistical results, and of the adequacy of the hypothetical distributions upon

* A more special application of the likelihood is its use, under the name of "power function," for comparing the sensitiveness, in some chosen respect, of different possible tests of significance.

which our methods of numerical inference are based, but afford real guidance in the choice of appropriate statistics for purposes of estimation. Such statistics may be divided into classes according to the behaviour of their distributions in large samples.

If we calculate a statistic, such, for example, as the mean, from a very large sample, we are accustomed to ascribe to it great accuracy; and indeed it will usually, but not always, be true, that if a number of such statistics can be obtained and compared, the discrepancies among them will grow less and less, as the samples from which they are drawn are made larger and larger. In fact, as the samples are made larger without limit, the statistic will usually tend to some fixed value characteristic of the population, and, therefore, expressible in terms of the parameters of the population. If, therefore, such a statistic is to be used to estimate these parameters, there is only one parametric function to which it can properly be equated. If it be equated to some other parametric function, we shall be using a statistic which even from an infinite sample does not give the correct value; it tends indeed to a fixed value, but to a value which is erroneous from the point of view with which it was used. Such statistics are termed **Inconsistent** Statistics; except when the error is extremely minute, as in the use of Sheppard's adjustments, inconsistent statistics should be regarded as outside the pale of decent usage.

Consistent statistics, on the other hand, all tend more and more nearly to give the correct values, as the sample is more and more increased; at any rate, if they tend to any fixed value it is not to an incorrect one. In the simplest cases, with which we shall be concerned, they not only tend to give the correct value, but the errors, for samples of a given size, tend to be distributed in a well-known distribution (of which more in Chap. III) known as the Normal Law of Frequency of Error, or more simply as the **normal distribution.** The liability to error may, in such cases, be expressed by calculating the mean value of the squares of these errors, a value which is known as the **variance**; and in the class of cases with which we are concerned, the variance falls off with increasing samples, in inverse proportion to the number in the sample.

Now, for the purpose of estimating any parameter, such as the centre of a normal distribution, it is usually possible to invent any number of statistics such as the arithmetic mean, or the median, etc., which shall be consistent in the sense defined above, and each of which has in large samples a variance falling off inversely with the size of the sample. But for large samples of a fixed size the variance of these different statistics will generally be different. Consequently, a special importance belongs to a smaller group of statistics, the error distributions of which tend to the normal distribution, as the sample is increased, with the least possible variance. We may thus separate off from the general body of consistent statistics a group of especial value, and these are known as **efficient** statistics.

The reason for this term may be made apparent by an example. If from a large sample of (say) 1000 observations we calculate an efficient statistic, A, and a second consistent statistic, B, having twice the variance of A, then B will be a valid estimate of the required parameter, but one definitely inferior to A in its accuracy. Using the statistic B, a sample of 2000 values would be required to obtain as good an estimate as is obtained by using the statistic A from a sample of 1000 values. We may say, in this sense, that the statistic B makes use of 50 per cent. of the relevant information available in the observations: or, briefly, that its **efficiency** is 50 per cent. The term "efficient" in its absolute sense is reserved for statistics the efficiency of which is 100 per cent.

Statistics having efficiency less than 100 per cent. may be legitimately used for many purposes. It is conceivable, for example, that it might in some cases be less laborious to increase the number of observations than to apply a more elaborate method of calculation to the results. It may often happen that an inefficient statistic is accurate enough to answer the particular questions at issue. There is however, one limitation to the legitimate use of inefficient statistics which should be noted in advance. If we are to make accurate tests of goodness of fit, the methods of fitting employed must not introduce **errors of fitting** comparable to the **errors of random sampling**; when this requirement is investigated, it appears that when tests of goodness of fit are required, the statistics employed in fitting must be not only consistent, but must be of 100 per cent. efficiency. This is a very serious limitation to the use of inefficient statistics, since in the examination of any body of data it is desirable to be able at any time to test the validity of one or more of the provisional assumptions which have been made.

Numerous examples of the calculation of statistics will be given in the following chapters, and, in these illustrations of method, efficient statistics have been chosen. The discovery of efficient statistics in new types of problem may require some mathematical investigation. The researches of the author have led him to the conclusion that an efficient statistic can in all cases be found by the **Method of Maximum Likelihood**; that is, by choosing statistics so that the estimated population should be that for which the likelihood is greatest. In view of the mathematical difficulty of some of the problems which arise it is also useful to know that *approximations* to the maximum likelihood solution are also in most cases efficient statistics. Some simple examples of the application of the method of maximum likelihood, and other methods, to genetical problems are developed in the final chapter.

For practical purposes it is not generally necessary to press refinement of methods further than the stipulation that the statistics used should be efficient. With large samples it may be shown that all efficient statistics tend to equivalence, so that little inconvenience arises from diversity of practice. There is, however, one class of statistics, including some of the most frequently recurring examples, which is of theoretical interest for possessing the remarkable property that, even in small samples, a statistic of this class alone includes the whole of the relevant information which the observations contain. Such statistics are distinguished by the term **sufficient** and, in the use of small samples, sufficient statistics, when they exist, are definitely superior to other efficient statistics. Examples of sufficient statistics are the **arithmetic mean** of samples from the normal distribution, or from the Poisson series; it is the fact of providing sufficient statistics for these two important types of distribution which gives to the arithmetic mean its theoretical importance. The method of maximum likelihood leads to these sufficient statistics when they exist. By a further extension, also depending on a special, but not uncommon, functional relationship, the advantage of sufficient statistics, namely **exhaustive** estimation may be gained by using **ancillary** statistics, even when no statistic sufficient by itself exists.

While diversity of practice within the limits of efficient statistics will not with large samples lead to inconsistencies, it is, of course, of importance in all cases to distinguish clearly the parameter of the population, of which it is desired to estimate the value from the actual statistic employed as an estimate of its value; and to inform the reader by which of the considerable variety of processes which exist for the purpose the estimate was actually obtained.

4. Scope of this Book

The prime object of this book is to put into the hands of research workers, and especially of biologists, the means of applying statistical tests accurately to numerical data accumulated in their own laboratories or available in the literature. Such tests are the result of solutions of problems of distribution, most of which are but recent additions to our knowledge and have previously only appeared in specialised mathematical papers. The mathematical complexity of these problems has made it seem undesirable to do more than (i) to indicate the kind of problem in question, (ii) to give numerical illustrations by which the whole process may be checked, (iii) to provide numerical tables by means of which the tests may be made without the evaluation of complicated algebraical expressions.

It would have been impossible to give methods suitable for the great variety of kinds of tests which are required but for the unforeseen circumstance that each mathematical solution appears again and again in questions which at first sight appeared to be quite distinct. For example, Helmert's solution in 1875 of the distribution of the sum of the squares of deviations from a mean, is in reality equivalent to the distribution of χ^2 given by K. Pearson in 1900. It was again discovered independently by "Student" in 1908, for the distribution of the variance of a normal sample. The same distribution was found by the author for the index of dispersion derived from small samples from a Poisson series. What is even more remarkable is that, although Pearson's paper of 1900 contained a serious error, which vitiated most of the tests of goodness of fit made by this method until 1921, yet the correction of this error, when efficient methods of estimation are used, leaves the form of the distribution unchanged, and only requires that some few units should be deducted from one of the variables with which the Table of χ^2 is entered.

It is equally fortunate that the distribution of *t*, first established by "Student" in 1908, in his study of the probable error of the mean, should be applicable, not only to the case there treated, but to the more complex, but even more frequently needed problem of the comparison of two mean values. It further provides an exact solution of the sampling errors of the enormously wide class of statistics known as regression coefficients.

In studying the exact theoretical distributions in

a number of other problems, such as those presented by intraclass correlations, the goodness of fit of regression lines, the correlation ratio, and the multiple correlation coefficient, the author has been led repeatedly to a third distribution, which may be called the distribution of z, and which is intimately related to, and indeed a natural extension of, the distributions introduced by Pearson and "Student." It has thus been possible to classify the necessary distributions covering a very great variety of cases, under these three main groups; and, what is equally important, to make some provision for the need for numerical values by means of a few tables only. Tables needed for a wider range of problems, with illustrations of their use, have since been published separately.

The book has been arranged so that the student may make acquaintance with these three main distributions in a logical order, and proceeding from more simple to more complex cases. Methods developed in later chapters are frequently seen to be generalisations of simpler methods developed previously. Studying the work methodically as a connected treatise, the student will, it is hoped, not miss the fundamental unity of treatment under which such very varied material has been brought together; and will prepare himself to deal competently and with exactitude with the many analogous problems which cannot be individually exemplified. On the other hand, it is recognised that many will wish to use the book for laboratory reference, and not as a connected course of study. This use would seem desirable only if the reader will be at the pains to work through, in all numerical detail, one or more of the appropriate examples, so as to assure himself, not only that his data are appropriate for a parallel treatment, but that he has obtained a critical grasp of the meaning to be attached to the processes and results.

It is necessary to anticipate one criticism, namely, that in an elementary book, without mathematical proofs, and designed for readers without special mathematical training, so much has been included which from the teacher's point of view is advanced; and indeed much that has not previously appeared in print. By way of apology the author would like to put forward the following considerations.

(1) For non-mathematical readers, numerical tables are in any case necessary; accurate tables are no more difficult to use, though more laborious to calculate, than inaccurate tables embodying the approximations formerly current.

(2) The process of calculating a probable or standard error from one of the established formulæ gives no real insight into the random sampling distribution, and can only supply a test of significance by the aid of a table of deviations of the normal curve, and on the assumption that the distribution is in fact very nearly normal. Whether this procedure should, or should not, be used must be decided, not by the mathematical attainments of the investigator, but by discovering whether it will or will not give a sufficiently accurate answer. The fact that such a process has been used successfully by eminent mathematicians in analysing very extensive and important material does not imply that it is sufficiently accurate for the laboratory worker anxious to draw correct conclusions from a small group of perhaps preliminary observations.

(3) The exact distributions, with the use of which this book is chiefly concerned, have been in fact developed in response to the practical problems arising in biological and agricultural research; this is true not only of the author's own contribution to the subject, but from the beginning of the critical examination of statistical distributions in "Student's" paper of 1908.

The greater part of the book is occupied by numerical examples; and these have steadily increased in number as fresh points needed illustration. In choosing them it has appeared to the author a hopeless task to attempt to exemplify the great variety of subject-matter to which these processes may be usefully applied. There are no examples from astronomical statistics, in which important work has been done in recent years, few from social studies, and the biological applications are scattered unsystematically. The examples have rather been chosen each to exemplify a particular process, and seldom on account of the importance of the data used, or even of similar examinations of analogous data. By a study of the processes exemplified, the student should be able to ascertain to what questions, in his own material, such processes are able to give a definite answer; and, equally important, what further observations would be necessary to settle other outstanding questions. In conformity with the purpose of the examples the reader should remember that they do not pretend to be discussions of general scientific questions, which would require the examination of much more extended data, and of other evidence, but are solely concerned with the critical examination of the particular batch of data presented.

5. Historical Note

Since much interest has been evinced in the historical origin of the statistical theory underlying the methods of this book, and as some misapprehensions have occasionally gained publicity, ascribing to the originality of the author methods well known to some previous writers, or ascribing to his predecessors modern developments of which they were quite unaware, it is hoped that the following notes on the principal contributors to statistical theory will be of value to students who wish to see the modern work in its historical setting.

Thomas Bayes' celebrated essay published in 1763 is well known as containing the first attempt to use the theory of probability as an instrument of inductive reasoning; that is, for arguing from the particular to the general, or from the sample to the population. It was published posthumously, and we do not know what views Bayes would have expressed had he lived to publish on the subject. We do know that the reason for his hesitation to publish was his dissatisfaction with the postulate required for the celebrated "Bayes' Theorem." While we must reject this postulate, we should also recognise Bayes' greatness in perceiving the problem to be solved, in making an ingenious attempt at its solution, and finally in realising more clearly than many subsequent writers the underlying weakness of his attempt.

Whereas Bayes excelled in logical penetration, Laplace (1820) was unrivalled for his mastery of analytic technique. He admitted the principle of inverse probability, quite uncritically, into the foundations of his exposition. On the other hand, it is to him we owe the principle that the distribution of a quantity compounded of independent parts shows a whole series of features—the mean, variance, and other cumulants (p. 73)—which are simply the sums of like features of the distributions of the parts. These seem to have been later discovered independently by Thiele (1889), but mathematically Laplace's methods were more powerful than Thiele's and far more influential on the development of the subject in France and England. A direct result of Laplace's study of the distribution of the resultant of numerous independent causes was the recognition of the normal law of error, a law more usually ascribed, with some reason, to his great contemporary, Gauss.

Gauss, moreover, approached the problem of statistical estimation in an empirical spirit, raising the question of the estimation not only of probabilities but of other quantitative parameters. He perceived the aptness for this purpose of the Method of Maximum Likelihood, although he attempted to derive and justify this method from the principle of inverse probability. The method has been attacked on this ground, but it has no real connection with inverse probability. Gauss, further, perfected the systematic fitting of regression formulæ, simple and multiple, by the method of least squares, which, in the cases to which it is appropriate, is a particular example of the method of maximum likelihood.

The first of the distributions characteristic of modern tests of significance, though originating with Helmert, was rediscovered by K. Pearson in 1900, for the measure of discrepancy between observation and hypothesis, known as χ^2. This, I believe, is the great contribution to statistical methods by which the unsurpassed energy of Prof. Pearson's work will be remembered. It supplies an exact and objective measure of the joint discrepancy from their expectations of a number of normally distributed, and mutually correlated, variates. In its primary application to frequencies, which are discontinuous variates, the distribution is necessarily only an approximate one, but when small frequencies are excluded the approximation is satisfactory. The distribution is exact for other problems solved later. With respect to frequencies, the apparent goodness of fit is often exaggerated by the inclusion of vacant or nearly vacant classes which contribute little or nothing to the observed χ^2, but increase its expectation, and by the neglect of the effect on this expectation of adjusting the parameters of the population to fit those of the sample. The need for correction on this score was for long ignored, and later disputed, but is now, I believe, admitted. The chief cause of error tending to lower the apparent goodness of fit is the use of inefficient methods of fitting (Chapter IX). This limitation could scarcely have been foreseen in 1900, when the very rudiments of the theory of estimation were unknown.

The study of the exact sampling distributions of statistics commences in 1908 with "Student's" paper *The Probable Error of a Mean*. Once the true nature of the problem was indicated, a large number of sampling problems were within reach of mathematical solution. "Student" himself gave in this and a subsequent paper the correct solutions for three such problems—the distribution of the estimate of the variance, that of the mean divided by its estimated standard deviation, and that of the estimated correlation coefficient between independent variates. These sufficed to establish the position of the distributions of χ^2 and of t in the theory of samples, though further work was needed to show how many other problems of testing significance could be reduced to these same two forms, and to the more inclusive distribution of z. " Student's " work was not quickly appreciated (it had, in fact, been totally ignored in the journal in which it had appeared), and from the first edition it has been one of the chief purposes of this book to make better known the effect of his researches, and of mathematical work consequent upon them, on the one hand, in refining the traditional doctrine of the theory of errors and mathematical statistics, and on the other, in simplifying the arithmetical processes required in the interpretation of data.

II

DIAGRAMS

7. The preliminary examination of most data is facilitated by the use of diagrams. Diagrams prove nothing, but bring outstanding features readily to the eye; they are therefore no substitute for such critical tests as may be applied to the data, but are valuable in suggesting such tests, and in explaining the conclusions founded upon them.

8. Time Diagrams, Growth Rate, and Relative Growth Rate

The type of diagram in most frequent use consists in plotting the values of a variable, such as the weight of an animal or of a sample of plants against its age, or the size of a population at successive intervals of time. Distinction should be drawn between those cases in which the same group of animals, as in a feeding experiment, is weighed at successive intervals of time, and the cases, more characteristic of plant physiology, in which the same individuals cannot be used twice, but a parallel sample is taken at each age. The same distinction occurs in counts of micro-organisms between cases in which counts are made from samples of the same culture, or from samples of parallel cultures. If it is of importance to obtain the general form of the growth curve, the second method has the advantage that any deviation from the expected curve may be confirmed from independent evidence at the next measurement, whereas using the same material no such independent confirmation is obtainable. On the other hand, if interest centres on the growth rate, there is an advantage in using the same material, for only so are actual increases in weight measurable. Both aspects of the difficulty can be got over only by replicating the observations; by carrying out measurements on a number of animals under parallel treatment it is possible to test, from the individual weights, though not from the means, whether their growth curve corresponds with an assigned theoretical course of development, or differs significantly from it or from a series differently treated. Equally, if a number of plants from each sample are weighed individually, growth rates may be obtained with known probable errors, and so may be used for critical comparisons. Care should of course be taken that each is strictly a random sample.

Fig. 1 represents the growth of a baby weighed to the nearest ounce at weekly intervals from birth. Table 1 indicates the calculation from these data of the absolute growth rate in ounces per day and the relative growth rate per day. The absolute growth rates, representing the average actual rates at which substance is added during each period, are found by subtracting from each value that previously recorded, and dividing by the length of the period. The relative growth rates measure the rate of increase not only per unit of time, but also per unit of weight already attained; using the mathematical fact, that

$$\frac{1}{m}\frac{dm}{dt} = \quad (\log_e m),$$

it is seen that the true average value of the relative

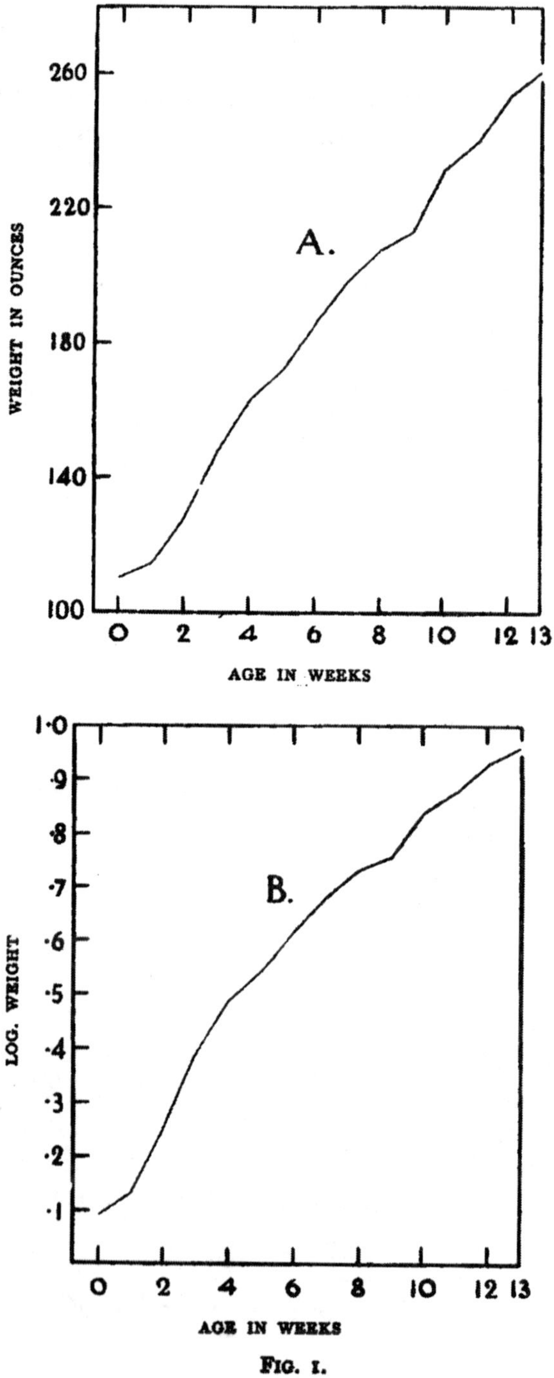
WEIGHT IN OUNCES
260
220
180
140
100
A.
0
2
4
6
8
10
12
13
AGE IN WEEKS
LOG. WEIGHT
1·0
·9
·8
·7
·6
·5
·4
·3
·2
·1
B.
0
2
4
6
8
10
12
13
AGE IN WEEKS

FIG. 1.

growth rate for any period is obtained from the natural logarithms of the successive weights, just as the actual rates of increase are from the weights themselves.

TABLE 1

Age in Weeks. $\frac{t}{7}$	Weight in Ounces. m	Increase. δm	Growth Rate per Day (Oz.). $\frac{\delta m}{\delta t}$	Natural Log of Weight. $\log \frac{m}{100}$	Increase. $\delta \log m$	Relative Growth Rate per cent. per Day. $\frac{\delta}{\delta t} \log m$
0	110			·0953		
		4	·57		·0357	·51
1	114			·1310		
		14	2·00		·1159	1·66
2	128			·2469		
		19	2·71		·1384	1·98
3	147			·3853		
		16	2·29		·1033	1·47
4	163			·4886		
		9	1·29		·0537	·77
5	172			·5423		
		14	2·00		·0783	1·12
6	186			·6206		
		12	1·71		·0625	·89
7	198			·6831		
		10	1·43		·0493	·70
8	208			·7324		
		5	·71		·0237	·34
9	213			·7561		
		19	2·71		·0855	1·22
10	232			·8416		
		8	1·14		·0339	·48
11	240			·8755		
		14	2·00		·0567	·81
12	254			·9322		
		7	1·00		·0272	·39
13	261			·9594		

Such relative rates of increase are conveniently multiplied by 100, and thereby expressed as the percentage rate of increase per day. If these percentage rates of increase had been calculated on the principle of simple interest, by dividing the actual increase by the weight at the beginning of the period, somewhat higher values would have been obtained; the reason for this is that the actual weight of the baby at any time during each period is usually somewhat higher than its weight at the beginning. The error introduced by the simple interest formula becomes exceedingly great when the percentage increases between successive weighings are large.

Fig. 1 A shows the course of the increase in absolute weight; the average slope of such a diagram shows the absolute rate of increase. In this diagram the points fall approximately on a straight line, showing that the absolute rate of increase was nearly constant at about 1·66 oz. per diem. Fig. 1 B shows the course of the increase in the natural logarithm of the weight; the slope at any point shows the relative rate of increase, which, apart from the first week, falls off perceptibly with increasing age. The features of such curves are best brought out if the scales of the two axes are so chosen that the graph makes with them approximately equal angles; with nearly vertical, or nearly horizontal lines, changes in the slope are not so readily perceived.

A rapid and convenient way of displaying the line of increase of the logarithm is afforded by the use of graph paper in which the horizontal rulings are spaced on a logarithmic scale, with the actual values indicated in the margin (see Fig. 5). The horizontal scale can then be adjusted to give the line an appropriate slope. This method avoids the use of a logarithm table, which, however, will still be required if the values of the relative rate of increase are needed.

In making a rough examination of the agreement of the observations with any law of increase, it is desirable so to manipulate the variables that the law to be tested will be represented by a straight line. Thus Fig. 1 A is suitable for a rough test of the law that the absolute rate of increase is constant; if it were suggested that the relative rate of increase were constant, Fig. 1 B would show clearly that this was not so. With other hypothetical growth curves other transformations may be used; for example, in the so-called "autocatalytic" or "logistic" curve the relative growth rate falls off in proportion to the actual weight attained at any time. If, therefore, the relative growth rate be plotted against the actual weight, the points should fall on a straight line if the "autocatalytic" curve fits the facts. For this purpose it is convenient to plot against each observed weight the mean of the two adjacent relative growth rates. To do this for the above data for the growth of an infant may be left as an exercise to the student; twelve points will be available for weights 114 to 254 ounces. The relative growth rates, even after averaging adjacent pairs, will be very irregular, so that no clear indications will be found from these data. If a straight line is found to fit the data, the weight at which growth will cease, supposing the law of growth continues unchanged, is found by producing the line to meet the axis.

9. Correlation Diagrams

Although most investigators make free use of diagrams in which an uncontrolled variable is plotted against the time, or against some controlled factor such as concentration of solution, or temperature, much more use might be made of correlation diagrams in which one uncontrolled factor is plotted against another. When this is done as a dot diagram, a number of dots are obtained, each representing a single experiment, or pair of observations, and it is usually clear from such a diagram whether or not any close connexion exists between the variables. When the observations are few a dot diagram will often tell us whether or not it is worth while to accumulate observations of the same sort; the range and extent of our experience is visible at a glance; and associations may be revealed which are worth while following up.

If the observations are so numerous that the dots cannot be clearly distinguished, it is best to divide up the diagram into squares, recording the frequency in each; this semi-diagrammatic record is a correlation table.

Fig. 2 shows in a dot diagram the yields obtained from an experimental plot of wheat (dunged plot, Broadbalk field, Rothamsted) in years with different total rainfall. The plot was under uniform treatment during the whole period 1854-1888; the 35 pairs of observations, indicated by 35 dots, show well the association of high yield with low rainfall. Even when few observations are available a dot diagram may suggest associations hitherto unsuspected, or what is equally important, the absence of associations which would have been confidently predicted. Their value lies in giving a simple conspectus of the experience hitherto gathered, and in bringing to the mind suggestions which may be susceptible of more exact statistical or experimental examination.

Instead of making a dot diagram the device is sometimes adopted of arranging the values of one variate in order of magnitude, and plotting the values of a second variate in the same order. If the line so obtained shows any perceptible slope, or general trend, the variates are taken to be associated. Fig. 3 represents the line obtained for rainfall, when the

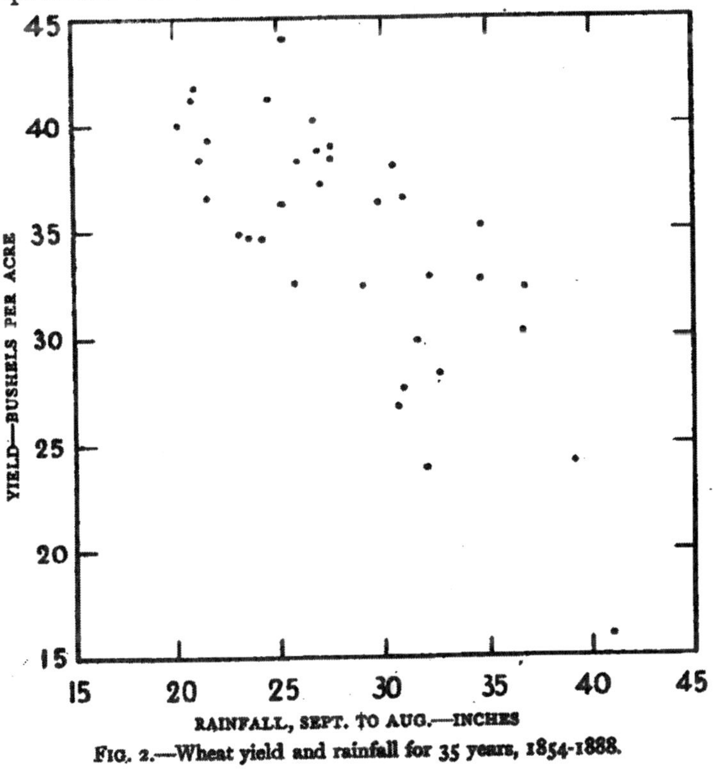

FIG. 2.—Wheat yield and rainfall for 35 years, 1854-1888.

years are arranged in order of wheat yield. Such diagrams are usually far less informative than the dot diagram, and often conceal features of importance brought out by the former. In addition, the dot diagram possesses the advantage that it is easily used as a correlation table if the number of dots is small, and easily transformed into one if the number of dots is large.

In the correlation table the values of both variates are divided into classes, and the class intervals should be equal for all values of the same variate. Thus we might divide the value for the yield of wheat throughout at intervals of one bushel per acre, and the values of the rainfall at intervals of a 1 inch. The diagram is thus divided into squares, and the number

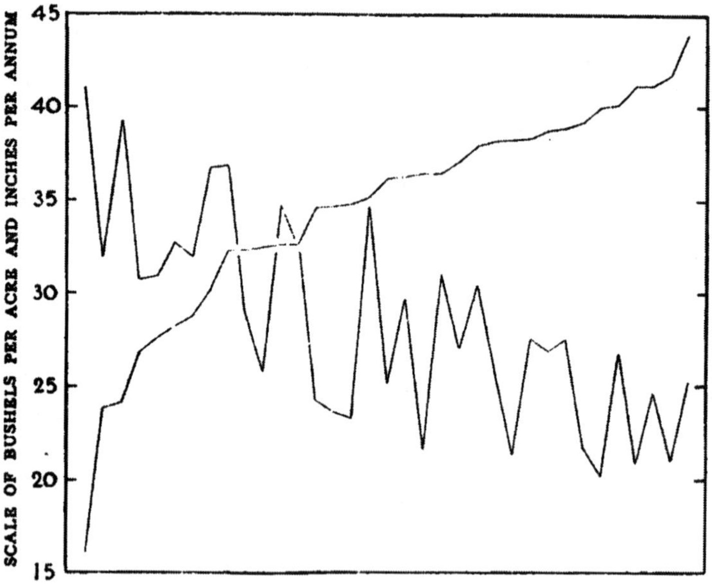

FIG. 3.—Rainfall and yield of 35 years arranged in order of yield.

of observations falling into each square is counted and recorded. The correlation table is useful for three distinct purposes. It affords a valuable visual representation of the whole of the observations, which with a little experience is as easy to comprehend as a dot diagram; it serves as a compact record of extensive data, which, as far as the two variates are concerned, is complete. With more than two variates correlation tables may be given for every pair. This will not indeed enable the reader to reconstruct the original data in its entirety, but it is a fortunate fact that for the great majority of statistical purposes a set of such twofold distributions provides complete information. Original data involving more than two variates are most conveniently recorded for reference on cards, each case being given a separate card with the several variates entered in corresponding positions upon them. The publication of such complete data presents difficulties but it is not yet sufficiently realised how much of the essential information can be presented in a compact form by means of correlation tables. The third feature of value about the correlation table is that the data so presented form a convenient basis for the immediate application of methods of statistical reduction. The most important statistics which the data provide, means, variances, and covariance, can be most readily calculated from the correlation table. An example of a correlation table is shown in Table 31, p. 178.

10. Frequency Diagrams

When a large number of individuals are measured in respect of physical dimensions, weight, colour, density, etc., it is possible to describe with some accuracy the *population* of which our experience may be regarded as a sample. By this means it may be possible to distinguish it from other populations differing in their genetic origin, or in environmental circumstances. Thus local races may be very different as populations, although individuals may overlap in all characters; or, under experimental conditions, the aggregate may show environmental effects, on size, death-rate, etc., which cannot be detected in the individual. A visible representation of a large number of measurements of any one feature is afforded by a frequency diagram. The feature measured is used as abscissa, or measurement along the horizontal axis, and as ordinates are set off vertically the *frequencies*, corresponding to each range.

Fig. 4 is a frequency diagram illustrating the distribution in stature of 1375 women (Pearson and Lee's data modified). The whole sample of women is divided up into successive height ranges of 1 inch.

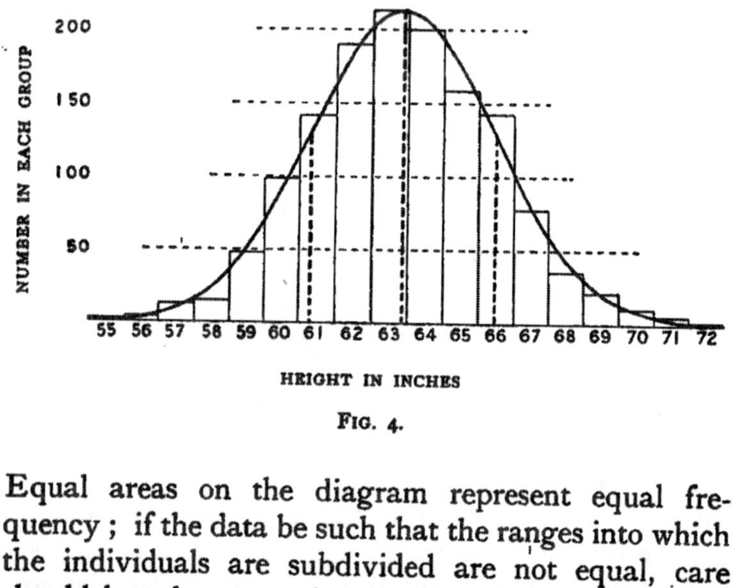

FIG. 4.

Equal areas on the diagram represent equal frequency; if the data be such that the ranges into which the individuals are subdivided are not equal, care should be taken to make the areas correspond to the observed frequencies, so that the area standing upon any interval of the base line shall represent the actual frequency observed in that interval.

The class containing the greatest number of observations is technically known as the modal class. In Fig. 4 the modal class indicated is the class whose central value is 63 inches. When, as is very frequently the case, the variate varies continuously, so that all intermediate values are possible, the choice of the grouping interval and limits is arbitrary and will make a perceptible difference to the appearance of the diagram. Usually, however, the possible limits of grouping will be governed by the smallest units in which the measurements are recorded. If, for example, measurements of height were made to the nearest quarter of an inch, so that all values between $66\frac{7}{8}$ inches and $67\frac{1}{8}$ were recorded as 67 inches, all values between $67\frac{1}{8}$ and $67\frac{3}{8}$ were recorded as $67\frac{1}{4}$, then we have no choice but to take as our unit of grouping 1, 2, 3, 4, etc., quarters of an inch, and the limits of each group must fall on some odd number of eighths of an inch. For purposes of calculation the smaller grouping units are more accurate, but for diagrammatic purposes coarser grouping is often preferable. Fig. 4 indicates a unit of grouping suitable in relation to the total range for a large sample; with smaller samples a coarser grouping is usually necessary in order that sufficient observations may fall in each class.

In all cases where the variation is continuous the frequency diagram should be in the form of a histogram, rectangular areas standing on each grouping interval showing the frequency of observations in that interval. The alternative practice of indicating the frequency by a single ordinate raised from the centre of the interval is sometimes preferred, as giving to the diagram a form more closely resembling a continuous curve. The advantage is illusory, for not only is the form of the curve thus indicated somewhat misleading, but the utmost care should always be taken to distinguish the infinitely large hypothetical population from which our sample of observations is drawn, from the actual sample of observations which we possess ; the conception of a continuous frequency curve is applicable only to the former, and in illustrating the latter no attempt should be made to slur over this distinction.

This consideration should in no way prevent a frequency curve fitted to the data from being superimposed upon the histogram (as in Fig. 4) ; the contrast between the histogram representing the sample, and the continuous curve representing an estimate of the form of the hypothetical population, is well brought out in such diagrams, and the eye is aided in detecting any serious discrepancy between the observations and the hypothesis. No eye observation of such diagrams, however experienced, is really capable of discriminating whether or not the observations differ from expectation by more than we should expect from the circumstances of random sampling. Accurate methods of making such tests will be developed in later chapters.

With discontinuous variation, when, for example, the variate is confined to whole numbers, the reasons given for insisting on the histogram form have little weight, for there are, strictly speaking, no ranges of variation within each class. On the other hand, there is no question of a frequency curve in such cases. Representation of such data by means of a histogram is usual and not inconvenient ; it is especially appropriate if we regard the discontinuous variation as due to an underlying continuous variate, which can, however, express itself only to the nearest whole number.

10·1. Transformed Frequencies

It is, of course, possible to treat the values of the frequency like any other variable, by plotting the value of its logarithm, or its actual value on loga-

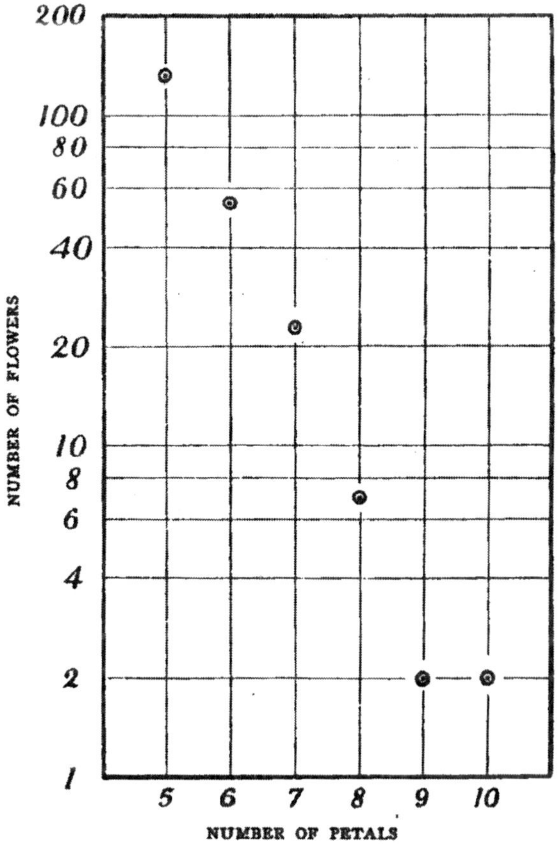

FIG. 5.

rithmic paper, when it is desired to illustrate the agreement of the observations with any particular law of frequency. Fig. 5 shows in this way the number of flowers (buttercups) having 5 to 10 petals (Pearson's data), plotted upon logarithmic paper, to facilitate comparison with the hypothesis that the frequency, for petals above five, falls off in geometric progression. Such illustrations are not, properly speaking, frequency diagrams, although the frequency is one of the variables employed, because they do not adhere to the convention that equal frequencies are represented by equal areas.

A useful form, similar to the above, is used to compare the death-rates, throughout life, of different populations. The logarithm of the number of survivors at any age is plotted against the age attained. Since the death-rate is the rate of decrease of the logarithm of the number of survivors, equal gradients on such curves represent equal death-rates. They therefore serve well to show the increase of death-rate with increasing age, and to compare populations with different death-rates. Such diagrams are less sensitive to small fluctuations than would be the corresponding frequency diagrams showing the distribution of the population according to age at death; they are therefore appropriate when such small fluctuations are due principally to errors of random sampling, which in the more sensitive type of diagram might obscure the larger features of the comparison. It should always be remembered that the choice of the appropriate methods of statistical treatment is quite independent of the choice of methods of diagrammatic representation.

A need which is felt frequently in Genetics and occasionally in other studies is to survey the evidence on some particular frequency ratio provided by a number of different samples, which may or may not be homogeneous in this respect. The classification of samples, such as progenies of plants or animals, according to the frequency-ratio they exhibit, and the homogeneity of the samples classified alike, are in such studies of critical importance, and the explicit tests of Chapter IV will usually be needed. A graphical survey of the evidence gives useful guidance as to what particular points should be tested, and is of further value, as a means of presenting the evidence most simply to the reader.

The frequencies observed of the two alternatives in each sample may be used as co-ordinates of a point, so that just so many points are shown as there are samples. In Fig. 5·1 the useful device has been adopted of plotting not the absolute frequencies, but their square roots. Points representing samples of n observations will then fall on a quadrant of a circle of radius $\sqrt{n}$. Samples showing a frequency ratio $p:q$, where $p+q=1$, will fall on a radius vector making an angle ϕ with the axis, such that

$$\sin^2\phi = p, \quad \cos^2\phi = q.$$

The device thus allows the diagram to exhibit a wider range of sample size, and a wider range of frequency ratio, than would otherwise be possible. Graph paper embodying this principle has been designed by F. Mosteller and J. W. Tukey and is now available.

Since, moreover, the standard error of random sampling of ϕ, for given n, is proportional to $1/\sqrt{n}$, and is independent of ϕ, it follows that the scatter of the observation points on either side of the radii to which they approximate is nearly equal in all parts of the diagram, and the eye is thus materially aided in recognising homogeneous groups.

In the material for *Lythrum salicaria* illustrated in Fig. 5·1, three classes represented by 1, 19 and 7 families respectively, appeared according to expectation. The one family of 41 plants all mid-styled, which evidently belongs to a fourth class, was un-

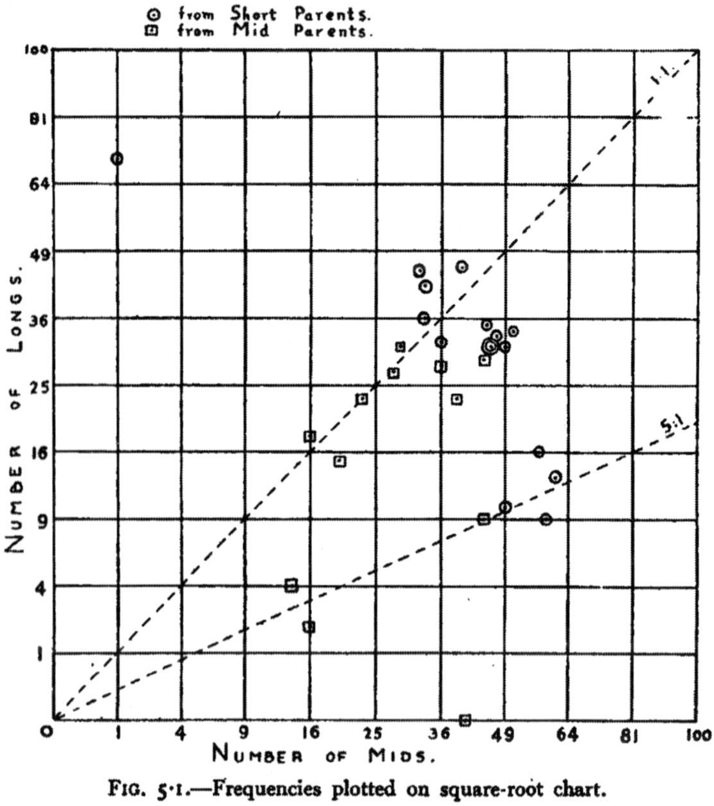

FIG. 5·1.—Frequencies plotted on square-root chart.

expected; later experiments showed it to contain three dominant genes for Mid, due to double reduction having occurred in the preceeding meiosis, and that by the same process it gave about 2 per cent. Longs in a more extensive test.

III

DISTRIBUTIONS

11. The idea of an infinite **population** distributed in a **frequency distribution** in respect of one or more characters is fundamental to all statistical work. From a limited experience, for example, of individuals of a species, or of the weather of a locality, we may obtain some idea of the infinite hypothetical population from which our sample is drawn, and so of the probable nature of future samples to which our conclusions are to be applied. If a second sample belies this expectation we infer that it is, in the language of statistics, drawn from a different population; that the treatment to which the second sample of organisms had been exposed did in fact make a material difference, or that the climate (or the methods of measuring it) had materially altered. Critical tests of this kind may be called tests of significance, and when such tests are available we may discover whether a second sample is or is not significantly different from the first.

A **statistic** is a value calculated from an observed sample with a view to characterising the population from which it is drawn. For example, the *mean* of a number of observations $x_1, x_2 \ldots x_n$, is given by the equation

$$\bar{x} = \frac{1}{n} S(x),$$

where S stands for summation over the whole sample

(this symbol is the one regularly used in our subject), and *n* for the number of observations. Such statistics are of course variable from sample to sample, and the idea of a frequency distribution is applied with especial value to the variation of such statistics. If we know exactly how the original population was distributed it is theoretically possible, though often a matter of great mathematical difficulty, to calculate how any statistic derived from a sample of given size will be distributed. The utility of any particular statistic, and the nature of its distribution, both depend on the original distribution, and appropriate and exact methods have been worked out for only a few cases. The application of these cases is greatly extended by the fact that the distribution of many statistics tends to the **normal** form as the size of the sample is increased. For this reason it is customary to apply to many cases what is called "the theory of large samples" which is to assume that such statistics are normally distributed, and to limit consideration of their variability to calculations of the standard error.

In the present chapter we shall give some account of three principal distributions—(i) the normal distribution, (ii) the Poisson series, (iii) the binomial distribution. It is important to have a general knowledge of these three distributions, the mathematical formulæ by which they are represented, the experimental conditions upon which they occur, and the statistical methods of recognising their occurrence. On the latter topic we shall be led to some extent to anticipate methods developed more systematically in Chapters IV and V.

12. The Normal Distribution

A variate is said to be normally distributed when it takes all values from $-\infty$ to $+\infty$, with frequencies given by a definite mathematical law, namely, that the logarithm of the frequency at any distance d from the centre of the distribution is less than the logarithm of the frequency at the centre by a quantity proportional to d^2. The distribution is therefore symmetrical, with the greatest frequency at the centre; although

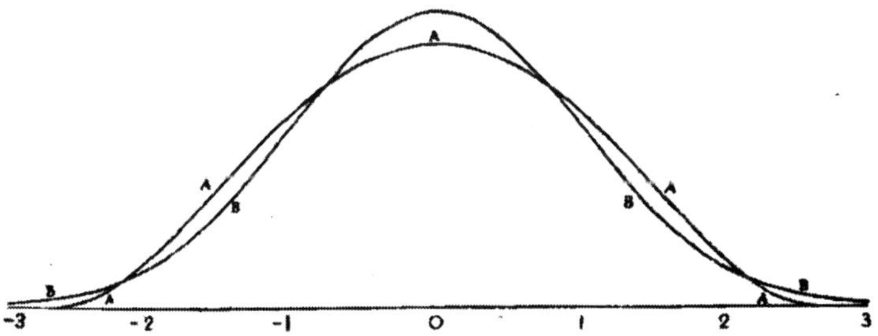

FIG. 6.—Showing a way in which a symmetrical frequency curve may depart from the normal distribution. A, flat-topped curve (γ_2 negative); B, normal curve ($\gamma_2 = 0$).

the variation is unlimited, the frequency falls off to exceedingly small values at any considerable distance from the centre, since a large negative logarithm corresponds to a very small number. Fig. 6 B represents a normal curve of distribution. The frequency in any infinitesimal range dx may be written as

$$df = \frac{1}{\sigma\sqrt{2\pi}} e^{-\frac{1}{2}\cdot\frac{(x-\mu)^2}{\sigma^2}} dx,$$

where $x-\mu$ is the distance of the observation, x, from the centre of the distribution, μ; and σ, called the **standard deviation**, measures in the same units the extent to which the individual values are scattered.

Geometrically σ is the distance, on either side of the centre, of the points at which the slope is steepest, or the points of inflexion of the curve (Fig. 4).

In practical applications we do not so often want to know the frequency at any distance from the centre as the total frequency beyond that distance; this is represented by the area of the tail of the curve cut off at any point. Tables of this total frequency, or probability integral, have been constructed from which, for any value of $(x-\mu)/\sigma$, we can find what fraction of the total population has a larger deviation; or, in other words, what is the probability that a value so distributed, chosen at random, shall exceed a given deviation. Tables I and II have been constructed to show the deviations corresponding to different values of this probability. The rapidity with which the probability falls off as the deviation increases is well shown in these tables. A deviation exceeding the standard deviation occurs about once in three trials. Twice the standard deviation is exceeded only about once in 22 trials, thrice the standard deviation only once in 370 trials, while Table II shows that to exceed the standard deviation sixfold would need nearly a thousand million trials. The value for which P = ·05, or 1 in 20, is 1·96 or nearly 2; it is convenient to take this point as a limit in judging whether a deviation is to be considered significant or not. Deviations exceeding twice the standard deviation are thus formally regarded as significant. Using this criterion we should be led to follow up a false indication only once in 22 trials, even if the statistics were the only guide available. Small effects will still escape notice if the data are insufficiently numerous to bring them out, but no lowering of the standard of significance would meet this difficulty.

Some little confusion is sometimes introduced by the fact that in some cases we wish to know the probability that the deviation, known to be positive, shall exceed an observed value, whereas in other cases the probability required is that a deviation, which is equally frequently positive and negative, shall exceed an observed value; the latter probability is always half the former. For example, Table I shows that the normal deviate falls outside the range $\pm 1{\cdot}598193$ in 11 per cent. of cases, and consequently that it exceeds $+1{\cdot}598193$ in 5·5 per cent. of cases.

The value of the deviation beyond which half the observations lie is called the **quartile** distance, and bears to the standard deviation the ratio ·67449. It was formerly a common practice to calculate the standard error and then, multiplying it by this factor, to obtain the **probable error.** The probable error is thus about two-thirds of the standard error, and as a test of significance a deviation of three times the probable error is effectively equivalent to one of twice the standard error. The common use of the probable error is its only recommendation; when any critical test is required the deviation must be expressed in terms of the standard error in using the tables of normal deviates (Tables I and II).

Further tables of the normal distribution are given in *Statistical Tables* IX and X, and in *Sheppard's Tables*, 1938.

13. Fitting the Normal Distribution

From a sample of n individuals of a normal population the mean and the standard deviation of the population may be **estimated** by using two easily calculated statistics. The best estimate of μ is $\bar{x}$ where

$$\bar{x} = \frac{1}{n} S(x),$$

while for the best estimate of σ, we calculate s from

$$s^2 = \frac{1}{n-1} S(x-\bar{x})^2;$$

these two statistics are calculated from the sums of the first two powers of the observations (*see* Appendix, p. 70), and are specially related to the normal distribution, in that they summarise the whole of the information which the sample provides as to the distribution from which it was drawn, provided the latter was normal. Fitting by sums of powers, and especially by the particular system of statistics known as **moments**, has also been widely applied to skew (asymmetrical) distributions, and others which are not normal; but such distributions have not generally the peculiar properties which make the first two powers especially appropriate, and where the distributions differ widely from the normal form the two statistics defined above may be of little or no use.

Ex. 2. *Fitting a normal distribution to a large sample.*—In calculating the statistics from a large sample it is not necessary to calculate individually the squares of the deviations from the mean of each measurement. The measurements are grouped together in equal intervals of the variate, and the whole of the calculation may be carried out rapidly as shown in Table 2, where the distribution of the stature of 1164 men is analysed.

The first column shows the central height in inches of each group, followed by the corresponding frequency. A central group (68·5″) is chosen as "working mean." To form the next column the frequencies are multiplied by 1, 2, 3, etc., according to their distance from the working mean; this process being repeated to form the fourth column, which is

TABLE 2.

Central Height (Inches).	Men (Frequency).	Frequency × Deviation.	Frequency × (Deviation)².	Women.
52·5	...	...	...	·5
53·5	...	...	...	·5
54·5	...	...	...	...
55·5	...	...	...	1
56·5	...	...	...	5
57·5	...	...	...	15
58·5	...	...	...	15·5
59·5	1	− 9	81	52
60·5	2·5	− 20	160	101
61·5	1·5	− 10·5	73·5	150
62·5	9·5	− 57	342	199
63·5	31	−155	775	223
64·5	56	−224	896	215
65·5	78·5	−235·5	706·5	169·5
66·5	127	−254	508	151·5
67·5	178·5	−178·5	178·5	81·5
68·5	189	−1143·5		40·5
69·5	137	137	137	19·5
70·5	137	274	548	10
71·5	93	279	837	5
72·5	52·5	210	840	...
73·5	39	195	975	1
74·5	17	102	612	...
75·5	6·5	45·5	318·5	...
76·6	3·5	28	224	...
77·5	1	9	81	...
78·5	2	20	200	...
79·5	1	11	121	...
	1164	1310·5 +167	8614	1456

			Estimated Variance.	S.D.
Mean	+·1435			
Correction for mean	167²÷1164	23·96		
Corrected sum of squares		8590·04	7·3861	2·7177
Sampling variance of mean			·006345	·0797
Sampling variance of variance			·09382	·3063
Adjustment for grouping			·0833	
Adjusted variance			7·3028	2·7024

summed from top to bottom in a single operation; in the third column, however, the upper portion, representing negative deviations, is summed separately and subtracted from the sum of the lower portion. The difference, in this case positive, shows that the whole sample of 1164 individuals has in all 167 inches more than if every individual were 68·5″ in height. This balance divided by 1164 gives the amount by which the mean of the sample exceeds 68·5″. The mean of the sample is therefore 68·6435″.

From the sum of the fourth column is subtracted a correction to give the value we should have obtained had the working mean been the true mean. This correction is the product of the total, 167″, and the mean 0·1435″ derived from it. The corrected sum of squares divided by 1163, one less than the sample number, provides the estimate of the variance, 7·3861 square inches, which is the basis of all subsequent calculations.

Corresponding to any estimate of a variance, we have, by taking the square root, the corresponding estimate of the standard deviation. Thus from the value 7·3861 square inches, we obtain at once the estimate 2·7177 inches for the standard deviation. This, however, represents the standard deviation of the population as grouped. The process of grouping may be represented as the addition to any true value of a grouping error, positive or negative, which takes all values from $-\frac{1}{2}$ to $\frac{1}{2}$ of a grouping unit with equal frequency. The effect of this on the population, and its average effect upon samples, is to add a constant quantity $\frac{1}{12}$ (=·0833) to the variance. Sheppard's adjustment for grouping consists in deducting this quantity from the estimate of variance of the population as grouped. This gives 7·3028 square inches for the adjusted variance, and 2·702 for the corresponding estimate of the standard deviation.

Any interval may be used as a unit of grouping; and the whole calculation is carried through in such units, the final results being transformed into other units if required, just as we might wish to transform the mean and standard deviation from inches to centimetres by multiplying by the appropriate factor. It is advantageous that the units of grouping should be exact multiples of the units of measurement; so that if the above sample had been measured to tenths of an inch, we might usefully have grouped them at intervals of 0·6″ or 0·7″.

Regarded as estimates of the mean and the standard deviation of a normal population of which the above is regarded as a sample, the values found are affected by errors of random sampling; that is, we should not expect a second sample to give us exactly the same values. The values for different (large) samples of the same size would, however, be distributed very accurately in normal distributions, so the accuracy of any one such estimate may be satisfactorily expressed by its standard error. These standard errors may be calculated from the variance of the grouped population, and in treating large samples we take our estimate of this variance as the basis of the calculation.

The formulæ for the variances of random sampling of estimates of the mean and of the variance of a normal population are (as given in Appendix, p. 70)

$$\frac{\sigma^2}{n}, \quad \frac{2\sigma^4}{n-1}.$$

Putting our value for k_2, 7·3861, in place of σ^2 in these formulæ, we find that our estimate of the mean has a sampling variance ·006345 square inches, or, taking the square root, a standard error ·0797 inches. From this value it is seen that our sample shows significant aberration (± twice standard error) from any population whose mean lay outside the limits 68·48″ to 68·80″. It is therefore probable, in the fiducial sense, that the mean of the population from which our sample was drawn lay between these limits. Similarly, our value for the variance of the population is seen to have a sampling variance ·09382, or a standard error ·3063; we have therefore equally good evidence that the variance of the grouped population from which our sample was drawn lay between 6·773 and 7·999 square inches. For the ungrouped population we should deduct ·083 from both limits.

It may be asked, Is nothing lost by grouping? Grouping in effect replaces the actual data by fictitious data placed arbitrarily at the central values of the groups; evidently a very coarse grouping might be very misleading. It has been shown that as regards obtaining estimates of the parameters of a normal population, the loss of information caused by grouping is less than 1 per cent., provided the group interval does not exceed one-quarter of the standard deviation; the grouping of the sample above in whole inches is thus somewhat too coarse; the loss in the estimation of the standard deviation is 2·28 per cent., or about 27 observations out of 1164; the loss in the estimation of the mean is half as great. With suitable group intervals, however, little is lost by grouping, and much labour is saved.

Another way of regarding the loss of information involved in grouping is to consider how near the estimates obtained for the mean and the standard deviation will be to the estimates obtained without grouping. From this point of view we may calculate a standard **error of grouping,** not to be confused with the standard error of random sampling which measures the deviation of the sample values from the population value. In grouping units, the standard error due to grouping of both the mean and the standard deviation is

$$\frac{1}{\sqrt{12n}},$$

or in this case ·0085″. For sufficiently fine grouping this should not exceed one-tenth of the standard error of random sampling.

In the analysis of a large sample the estimate of the variance often employed is

$$\frac{1}{n}\,S(x-\bar{x})^2,$$

which differs from the formula given previously (p. 46) in that we have divided by n instead of by $(n-1)$. In large samples the difference between these formulæ is small, and that using n may claim some theoretical advantage if we wish for an estimate to be used in conjunction with the estimate of the mean from the same sample, as in fitting a frequency curve to the data; in general it is best to use $(n-1)$. In small samples the difference is still small compared to the probable error, but becomes important if a variance is estimated by averaging estimates from a number of small samples. Thus if a series of experiments are carried out each with six parallels and we have reason to believe that the variation is in all cases due to the operation of analogous causes, we may take the average of such quantities as

$$\frac{1}{n-1}\,S(x-\bar{x})^2=\frac{1}{5}\,S(x-\bar{x})^2$$

to obtain an unbiased estimate of the variance, whereas we should underestimate it were we to divide by 6.

14. Test of Departure from Normality

It is sometimes necessary to test whether an observed sample does or does not depart significantly from normality. For this purpose the third, and sometimes the fourth powers, are used ; from each of these it is possible to calculate a quantity, g, the average value of which is zero for a normal distribution, and which is distributed normally for large samples—the standard error being calculable from the size of the sample. The quantity g_1, which is calculated from the third powers, is essentially a measure of asymmetry ; the parameter γ_1, of which it provides an estimate, may be equated to $\pm\sqrt{\beta_1}$ of Pearson's notation, though Pearson also used β_1 to designate a statistic which is not the equivalent of g_1^2 ; g_2, calculated from the fourth powers, is in like manner a measure of departure from normality, in this case of a symmetrical type, by which the apex and the two tails of the curve are increased at the expense of the intermediate portion, or when negative, the top and tails are depleted and the shoulders filled out, making a relatively flat-topped curve. (See Fig. 6, p. 43.)

Ex. 3. *Use of higher powers to test normality.*—Departures from normal form, unless very strongly marked, can only be detected in large samples ; conversely, they make little difference to statistical tests on other questions. We give an example (Table 3) of the calculation for 90 values of the yearly rainfall at Rothamsted ; the process of calculation is similar to that of finding the mean and standard deviation, but it is carried two stages further, in the summation of the 3rd and 4th powers. The formulæ by which the sums are reduced to the true mean and the statistics

TABLE 3

Test of Normality of Yearly Rainfall

Year's rain in inches.	Frequency.				
16	1	−12	144	−1728	20736
17	...	...	...	...	...
18	...	...	...	...	...
19	3	−27	243	−2187	19683
20	2	−16	128	−1024	8192
21	3	−21	147	−1029	7203
22	...	...	...	...	...
23	3	−15	75	−375	1875
24	2	−8	32	−128	512
25	12	−36	108	−324	972
26	4	−8	16	−32	64
27	7	−7	7	−7	7
28	4	...	...	...	...
29	8	8	8	8	8
30	9	18	36	72	144
31	6	18	54	162	486
32	7	28	112	448	1792
33	4	20	100	500	2500
34	4	24	144	864	5184
35	4	28	196	1372	9604
36	3	24	192	1536	12288
37	3	27	243	2187	19683
38	...	...	...	...	...
39	1	11	121	1331	14641
s	90	56	2106	1646	125574
Corrections to Mean			−34·84	−3931·2 +43·4	−4096·7 +4892·2 −40·5
S	90	...	2071·16	−2241·8	126329·0
k	...	·62̇	23·2715	−25·761	−162·487
Adjustment	...	...	−·0833		+·008
k'		·62̇	23·1882	−25·761	−162·479
g				−·231	−·302
Standard error				±·254	±·503

k and g are calculated, are gathered in an Appendix, p. 70. For the k statistics we obtain in terms of group intervals

$$k_1 = \cdot 62, \quad k_2 = 23\cdot 2715, \quad k_3 = -25\cdot 76, \quad k_4 = -162\cdot 49,$$

whence are calculated

$$g'_1 = k'_3/k'^{3/2}_2 = -\cdot 231, \quad g'_2 = k'_4/k'^2_2 = -\cdot 302.$$

For samples from a normal distribution the sampling variances of g_1 and g_2 are given exactly by the formulæ in the Appendix, and the numerical values of the standard error have been appended in Table 3. It will be seen that neither are significant, or even exceeds its standard error. A negative value of γ_1, which is suggested but not established by the data, would indicate an asymmetry of the distribution in the sense that moderately dry and very wet years are respectively less frequent than moderately wet and very dry years.

15. Discontinuous Distributions

Frequently a variable is not able to take all possible values, but is confined to a particular series of values, such as the whole numbers. This is obvious when the variable is a frequency, obtained by counting, such as the number of cells on a square of a hæmacytometer, or the number of colonies on a plate of culture medium. The normal distribution is the most important of the continuous distributions; but among discontinuous distributions the Poisson series is of the first importance. If a variate can take the values 0, 1, 2, . . ., x, . . ., and the relative frequencies with which the values occur are given by the series

$$e^{-m}\left(1, m, \frac{m^2}{2!}, \ldots, \frac{m^x}{x!}, \ldots\right)$$

(where $x!$ stands for "factorial x" $= x(x-1)(x-2)$ $\ldots 1$), then the number is distributed in the Poisson series. The total frequency is unity, since

$$e^m = 1+m+\frac{m^2}{2!}+\frac{m^3}{3!}+\cdots$$

Whereas the normal curve has two unknown parameters, μ and σ, the Poisson series has only one. This value may be estimated from a series of observations, by taking their mean, the mean being a statistic as appropriate to the Poisson series as it is to the normal curve. It may be shown theoretically that if the probability of an event is exceedingly small, but a sufficiently large number of independent cases are taken to obtain a number of occurrences, then this number will be distributed in the Poisson series. For example, the chance of a man being killed by horse-kick on any one day is exceedingly small, but if an army corps of men are exposed to this risk for a year, often one or more of them will be killed in this way. The following data (Bortkewitch's data) were obtained from the records of ten army corps for twenty years, supplying 200 such observations.

TABLE 4

Deaths.	Frequency observed.	Expected.
0	109	108·67
1	65	66·29
2	22	20·22
3	3	4·11
4	1	·63
5	...	·08
6	...	·01

The average, $\bar{x}$, is 0·61, and taking this as an estimate of m the numbers calculated agree excellently with those observed.

The importance of the Poisson series in biological research was first brought out in connexion with the accuracy of counting with a hæmacytometer. It was shown that when the technique of the counting process was effectively perfect, the number of cells on each square should be theoretically distributed in a Poisson series; it was further shown that this distribution was, in favourable circumstances, actually realised

TABLE 5

Number of Cells.	Frequency observed.	Frequency expected.
0	...	3·71
1	20	17·37
2	43	40·65
3	53	63·41
4	86	74·19
5	70	69·44
6	54	54·16
7	37	36·21
8	18	21·18
9	10	11·02
10	5	5·16
11	2	2·19
12	2	·86
13	...	·31
14	...	·10
15	...	·03
16	...	·01
Total .	400	400·00

in practice. Thus the preceding table (" Student's " data) shows the distribution of yeast cells in the 400 squares into which one square millimetre was divided.

The total number of cells counted is 1872, and the mean number is therefore 4·68. The expected frequencies calculated from this mean agree well with those observed. The methods of testing the agreement are explained in Chapter IV.

When a number is the sum of several components, each of which is independently distributed in a Poisson series, then the total number is also so distributed. Thus the total count of 1872 cells may be regarded as a sample of one individual from a series, for which m is not far from 1872. The variance of a Poisson series, like its mean is equal to m; and for such large values of m the distribution of numbers approximates closely to the normal form; we may therefore attach to the number counted, 1872, the standard error $\pm\sqrt{1872} = \pm 43{\cdot}26$, to represent the standard error of random sampling of such a count. The density of cells in the original suspension is therefore estimated with a standard error of 2·31 per cent. If, for instance, a parallel sample differed by 7 per cent., the technique of sampling would be suspect.

16. Small Samples of a Poisson Series

Exactly the same principles as govern the accuracy of a hæmacytometer count would also govern a count of bacterial or fungal colonies in estimating the numbers of those organisms by the dilution method, if it could be assumed that the technique of dilution afforded a perfectly random distribution of organisms, and that these could develop on the plate without mutual interference. Agreement of the observations with the Poisson distribution thus affords in the dilution method of counting a test of the suitability of the technique and medium similar to the test afforded of the technique of hæmacytometer counts. The great practical difference between these cases is that from the hæmacytometer we can obtain a record of a large number of squares with only a few organisms on each, whereas in a bacterial count we may have only 5 parallel plates, bearing perhaps 200 colonies apiece. From a single sample of 5 it would be impossible to demonstrate that the distribution followed the Poisson series; however, when a large number of such samples have been obtained under comparable conditions, it is possible to utilise the fact that for all Poisson series the variance is numerically equal to the mean.

For each set of parallel plates with $x_1, x_2, \ldots, x^n$ colonies respectively, after finding the mean $\bar{x}$, an index of dispersion may be calculated by the formula

$$\chi^2 = \frac{S(x-\bar{x})^2}{\bar{x}}.$$

It has been shown that for true samples of a Poisson series, χ^2 calculated in this way will be distributed in a known manner; Table III (p. 112) shows the principal values of χ^2 for this distribution; entering the table with n equal to one less than the number of parallel plates. For small samples the permissible range of variation of χ^2 is wide; thus for five plates with $n=4$, χ^2 will be less than 1·064 in 10 per cent. of cases, while the highest 10 per cent. will exceed 7·779; a single sample of 5 thus gives us little information; but if we have 50 or 100 such samples, we are in a position to verify with accuracy if the expected distribution is obtained.

Ex. 4. *Test of agreement with Poisson series of a number of small samples.*—From 100 counts of bacteria in sugar refinery products the following values were obtained (Table 6); there being 6 plates in each case, the values of χ^2 were taken from the χ^2 table for $n = 5$.

TABLE 6

χ^2.	Expected.	Observed.	Expected 43 per cent.
0			
	1	26	·43
·554			
	1	6	·43
·752			
	3	11	1·29
1·145			
	5	7	2·15
1·610			
	10	7	4·3
2·343			
	10	2	4·3
3·000			
	20	12	8·6
4·351			
	20	7	8·6
6·064			
	10	3	4·3
7·289			
	10	4	4·3
9·236			
	5	1	2·15
11·070			
	3	3	1·29
13·388			
	1	0	·43
15·086			
	1	11	·43
Total	100	100	43·00

It is evident that the observed series differs strongly from expectation; there is an enormous excess in the first class, and in the high values over 15; the relatively few values from 2 to 15 are not far from the expected proportions, as is shown in the last column by taking 43 per cent. of the expected values. It is possible then that even in this case nearly half of the samples were satisfactory, but about 10 per cent. were excessively variable, and in about 45 per cent. of the cases the variability was abnormally depressed.

It is often desirable to test if the variability is of the right magnitude when we have not accumulated a large number of counts, all with the same number of parallel plates, but where a certain number of counts are available with various numbers of parallels. In this case we cannot indeed verify the theoretical distribution with any exactitude, but can test whether or not the general level of variability conforms with expectation. The sum of a number of independent values of χ^2 is itself distributed in the manner shown in the Table of χ^2, provided we take for n the number $S(n)$, calculated by adding the several values of n for the separate experiments. Thus for six sets of 4 plates each the total value of χ^2 was found to be 13·85, the corresponding value of n is $6 \times 3 = 18$, and the χ^2 table shows that for $n = 18$ the value 13·85 is exceeded in between 70 and 80 per cent. of cases; it is therefore not an abnormal value to obtain. In another case the following values were obtained:

TABLE 7

Number of Plates in Set.	Number of Sets.	$S(n)$.	Total χ^2.
4	8	24	27·31
5	36	144	133·96
9	1	8	8·73
Total	...	176	170·00

We have therefore to test if $\chi^2 = 170$ is an unreasonably small or great value for $n = 176$. The χ^2 table has not been calculated beyond $n = 30$, but for higher values we make use of the fact that the distribution of χ becomes nearly normal. A good approximation is given by assuming that $(\sqrt{2\chi^2} - \sqrt{2n-1})$ is normally distributed about zero with unit standard deviation. If this quantity exceeds 2, or even 1·645 for the 5 per cent. level, the value of χ^2 significantly exceeds expectation. In the example before us

$$2\chi^2 = 340, \qquad \sqrt{2\chi^2} = 18{\cdot}44$$
$$2n-1 = 351, \qquad \sqrt{2n-1} = 18{\cdot}73$$
$$\text{Difference} = -{\cdot}29$$

The set of 45 counts thus shows variability between parallel plates, very close to that to be expected theoretically. The internal evidence thus suggests that the technique was satisfactory.

17. Presence and Absence of Organisms in Samples

When the conditions of sampling justify the use of the Poisson series, the number of samples containing 0, 1, 2, . . . organisms is, as we have seen, connected by a calculable relation with the mean number of organisms in the sample. With motile organisms, or in other cases which do not allow of discrete colony formation, the mean number of organisms in the sample may be inferred from the proportion of fertile cultures, provided a single organism is capable of developing. If m is the mean number of organisms in the sample, the proportion of samples containing none, that is the proportion of sterile samples, is e^{-m}, from which relation we can calculate, as in the following table, the mean number of organisms corresponding to 10 per cent., 20 per cent., etc., fertile samples.

TABLE 8

Percentage of fertile samples	10	20	30	40	50	60	70	80	90
Mean number of organisms	·1054	·2231	·3567	·5108	·6932	·9163	1·2040	1·6094	2·3026

In connexion with the use of the table above it is worth noting that for a given number of samples tested the frequency ratio of fertile to sterile is most accurately determined at 50 per cent. fertile, but for the minimum percentage error in the estimate of the number of organisms, nearly 80 per cent. fertile or 1·6 organism per sample is most accurate. At this point the standard error of sampling may be reduced to 10 per cent. by taking about 155 samples, whereas at 50 per cent., to obtain the same accuracy, 208 samples would be required. (See *Design of Experiments*, Section 68.)

The Poisson series also enables us to calculate what percentage of the fertile cultures obtained have been derived from a single organism, for the percentage of impure cultures, *i.e.* those derived from 2 or more organisms, can be calculated from the percentage of cultures which proved to be fertile. If e^{-m} are sterile, me^{-m} will be pure cultures, and the remainder impure. The following table gives representative values of the percentage of cultures which are fertile, and the percentage of fertile cultures which are impure :

TABLE 9

Mean number of organisms in sample	·1	·2	·3	·4	·5	·6	·7
Percentage fertile . . .	9·52	18·13	25·92	32·97	39·35	45·12	50·34
Percentage of fertile cultures impure . . .	4·92	9·67	14·25	18·67	22·92	27·02	30·95

If it is desired that the cultures should be pure with high probability, a sufficiently low concentration must be used to render at least nine-tenths of the samples sterile.

18. The Binomial Distribution

The binomial distribution is well known as the first example of a theoretical distribution to be established. It was found by Bernoulli, about the end of the seventeenth century, that if the probability of an event occurring were p and the probability of it not occurring were $q(=1-p)$, then if a random sample of n trial were taken, the frequencies with which the event occurred 0, 1, 2, . . ., n times were given by the expansion of the binomial

$$(q+p)^n.$$

This rule is a particular case of a more general theorem dealing with cases in which not only a simple alternative is considered, but in which the event may happen in s ways with probabilities $p_1, p_2, \ldots, p_s$; then it can be shown that the chance of a random sample of n giving a_1 of the first kind, a_2 of the second, . . ., a_s of the last is

$$\frac{n!}{a_1!a_2! \ldots a_s!} p_1^{a_1} p_2^{a_2} \ldots p_s^{a_s},$$

which is the general term in the multinomial expansion of

$$(p_1+p_2+ \ldots +p_s)^n.$$

Ex. 5. *Binomial distribution given by dice records.*—In throwing a true die the chance of scoring more than 4 is 1/3, and if 12 dice are thrown together the number of dice scoring 5 or 6 should be distributed with frequencies given by the terms in the expansion of

$$(\tfrac{2}{3}+\tfrac{1}{3})^{12}.$$

If, however, one or more of the dice were not true, but if all retained the same bias throughout the experiment, the frequencies should be given approximately by

$$(q+p)^{12},$$

where p is a fraction to be determined from the data. The following frequencies were observed (Weldon's data) in an experiment of 26,306 throws.

TABLE 10

Number of Dice with 5 or 6.	Observed Frequency.	Expected True Dice.	Expected Biased Dice.	Measure of Divergence $\frac{x^2}{m}$.	
				True Dice.	Biased Dice.
0	185	202·75	187·38	1·554	·030
1	1149	1216·50	1146·51	3·745	·005
2	3265	3345·37	3215·24	1·931	·770
3	5475	5575·61	5464·70	1·815	·019
4	6114	6272·56	6269·35	4·008	3·849
5	5194	5018·05	5114·65	6·169	1·231
6	3067	2927·20	3042·54	6·677	·197
7	1331	1254·51	1329·73	4·664	·001
8	403	392·04	423·76	·306	1·017
9	105	87·12	96·03	3·670	·838
10	14	13·07	14·69		
11	4	1·19	1·36	·952	·222
12	...	·05	·06		
	26306	26306·02	26306·00	35·491	8·179
				$n=10$	$n=9$

It is apparent that the observations are not compatible with the assumption that the dice were unbiased. With true dice we should expect more cases than have been observed of 0, 1, 2, 3, 4, and fewer cases than have been observed of 5, 6, . . ., 11 dice scoring more than four. The same conclusion is more clearly brought out in the fifth column, which shows the values of the measure of divergence

$$\frac{x^2}{m},$$

where m is the expected value and x the difference between the expected and observed values. The aggregate of these values is χ^2, which measures the deviation of the whole series from the expected series of frequencies, and the actual chance of χ^2 exceeding 35·49, the value for the hypothesis that the dice are true, is ·0001. (See Section 20.)

The total number of times in which a die showed 5 or 6 was 106,602, out of 315,672 trials, whereas the number expected with true dice is 105,224; from the former number, the value of p can be calculated, and proves to be ·337,698,6, and hence the expectations of the fourth column were obtained. These values are much more close to the observed series, and indeed fit them satisfactorily, showing that the conditions of the experiment were really such as to give a binomial series.

The variance of the binomial series is pqn. Thus with true dice and 315,672 trials the expected number of dice scoring more than 4 is 105,224 with variance 70149·3 and standard error 264·9; the observed number exceeds expectation by 1378, or 5·20 times its standard error; this is the most sensitive test of the bias, and it may be legitimately applied, since for such large samples the binomial distribution closely approaches the normal. From the table of the probability integral it appears that a normal deviation only exceeds 5·2 times its standard error once in 5 million times.

The reason why this last test gives so much higher odds than the test for goodness of fit, is that the latter is testing for discrepancies of any kind, such, for example, as copying errors would introduce. The actual discrepancy is almost wholly due to a single item, namely, the value of p, and when that point is tested separately its significance is more clearly brought out.

Ex. 6. *Comparison of sex ratio in human families with binomial distribution.*—Biological data are rarely so extensive as this experiment with dice ; Geissler's data on the sex ratio in German families will serve as an example. It is well known that male births are slightly more numerous than female births, so that if a family of 8 is regarded as a random sample of 8 from the general population, the number of boys in such families should be distributed in the binomial

$$(q+p)^8,$$

where p is the proportion of boys. If, however, families differ not only by chance, but by a tendency on the part of some parents to produce males or females, then the distribution of the number of boys should show an excess of unequally divided families, and a deficiency of equally or nearly equally divided families. The data in Table 11 show that there is evidently such an excess of very unequally divided families.

The observed series differs from expectation markedly in two respects : one is the excess of unequally divided families ; the other is the irregularity of the central values, showing an apparent bias in favour of even values. No biological reason is suggested for the latter discrepancy, which therefore detracts from the value of the data. The excess of the extreme types of family may be treated in more detail by comparing the observed with the expected variance. The expected variance, npq, is 1·998,28, while that calculated from the data is 2·067,45, showing an excess of ·06917, or 3·46 per cent. The sampling variance of this estimate of variance is (p. 77)

$$\frac{2\kappa_2^2}{N-1}+\frac{\kappa_4}{N}$$

where N is the number of families, and κ_2 and κ_4 are the second and fourth cumulants of the theoretical distribution, namely,

$$\kappa_2 = npq \qquad\qquad = 1{\cdot}99828$$
$$\kappa_4 = npq(1-6pq) = -{\cdot}99656.$$

The values given are calculated from the value of p as estimated from the frequency of boys in the sample. The standard error of the variance, which as the values show is nearly $\sqrt{7/N}$, is found to be ·01141. The excess of the observed variance over that appropriate to a binomial distribution is thus over six times its standard error.

TABLE 11

Number of Boys.	Number of Families Observed.	Expected.	Excess (x).	$\frac{x^2}{m}$.
0	215	165·22	+ 49·78	14·998
1	1485	1401·69	+ 83·31	4·952
2	5331	5202·65	+128·35	3·166
3	10649	11034·65	−385·65	13·478
4	14959	14627·60	+331·40	7·508
5	11929	12409·87	−480·87	18·633
6	6678	6580·24	+ 97·76	1·452
7	2092	1993·78	+ 98·22	4·839
8	342	264·30	+ 77·70	22·843
	53680	53680·00		91·869

One possible cause of the excessive variation lies in the occurrence of multiple births, for it is known that children of the same birth tend to be of the same sex. The multiple births are not separated in these data, but an idea of the magnitude of this effect may be obtained from other data for the German Empire. These show about 12 twin births per thousand, of which $\frac{5}{8}$ are of like sex and $\frac{3}{8}$ of unlike, so that one-quarter of the twin births, 3 per thousand, may be regarded as " identical " or necessarily alike in sex. Six children per thousand would therefore probably belong to such " identical " twin births, the additional effect of triplets, etc., being small. Now with a population of identical twins it is easy to see that the theoretical variance is doubled; consequently, to raise the variance by 3·46 per cent. we require that 3·46 per cent. of the children should be " identical " twins; this is more than five times the general average; and, although it is probable that the proportion of twins is higher in families of 8 than in the general population, we cannot reasonably ascribe more than a fraction of the excess variance to multiple births.

19. Small Samples of the Binomial Series

With small samples, such as ordinarily occur in experimental work, agreement with the binomial series cannot be tested with much precision from a single sample. It is, however, possible to verify that the variation is approximately what it should be, by calculating an index of dispersion similar to that used for the Poisson series.

Ex. 7. *The accuracy of estimates of infestation.*—The proportion of barley ears infested with gout-fly may be ascertained by examining 100 ears, and counting the infested specimens; if this is done repeatedly, the numbers obtained, if the material is homogeneous, should be distributed in the binomial

$$(q+p)^{100},$$

where p is the proportion infested, and q the proportion free from infestation. The following are the data from 10 such observations made on the same plot (J. G. H. Frew's data):

16, 18, 11, 18, 21, 10, 20, 18, 17, 21. Mean 17·0.

Is the variability of these numbers ascribable to random sampling; *i.e.* Is the material apparently homogeneous? Such data differ from those to which the Poisson series is appropriate, in that a fixed total of 100 is in each case divided into two classes, infested and not infested, so that in taking the variability of the infested series we are equally testing the variability of the series of numbers not infested. The modified form of χ^2, the index of dispersion, appropriate to the binomial is

$$\chi^2 = \frac{S(x-\bar{x})^2}{npq} = \frac{S(x-\bar{x})^2}{\bar{x}q},$$

differing from the form appropriate to the Poisson series in containing the divisor q, or in this case, ·83. The value of χ^2 is 9·21, which, as the χ^2 table shows, is a perfectly reasonable value for $n = 9$, one less than the number of values available.

Such a test of the single sample is, of course, far from conclusive, since χ^2 may vary within wide limits. If, however, a number of such small samples are available, though drawn from plots of very different infestation, we can test, as with the Poisson series, if the general trend of variability accords with the binomial distribution. Thus from 20 such plots the total χ^2 is 193·64, while S(n) is 180. Testing as before (p. 61), we find

$$\sqrt{387\cdot28} = 19\cdot68$$
$$\sqrt{359} = 18\cdot95$$
$$\text{Difference} \quad +\cdot73.$$

The difference being less than one, we conclude that the variance shows no sign of departure from that of the binomial distribution. The difference between the method appropriate for this case, in which the samples are small (10), but each value is derived from a considerable number (100) of observations, and that appropriate for the sex distribution in families of 8, where we had many families, each of only 8 observations, lies in the omission of the term

$$\kappa_4 = npq(1-6pq)$$

in calculating the standard error of the variance. When n is 100 this term is very small compared to $2n^2p^2q^2$, and in general the χ^2 method is highly accurate if the number in all the observational categories is as high as 10.

Appendix on Technical Notation and Formulæ

A. *Statistics derived from sums of powers.*

If we have n observations of a variate x, it is easy to calculate for the sample the sums of the simpler powers of the values observed; these we may write

$$s_1 = \text{S}(x) \qquad s_2 = \text{S}(x^2)$$
$$s_3 = \text{S}(x^3) \qquad s_4 = \text{S}(x^4)$$

and so on.

It is convenient arithmetically to calculate from

these the sums of powers of deviations from the mean defined by the equations

$$S_2 = s_2 - \frac{1}{n} s_1^2$$

$$S_3 = s_3 - \frac{3}{n} s_2 s_1 + \frac{2}{n^2} s_1^3$$

$$S_4 = s_4 - \frac{4}{n} s_3 s_1 + \frac{6}{n^2} s_2 s_1^2 - \frac{3}{n^3} s_1^4.$$

Many statistics in frequent use are derived from these values.

(i) Moments about the arbitrary origin, $x = 0$; these are derived simply by dividing the corresponding sum by the number in the sample; in general if p stand for 1, 2, 3, 4, . . ., they are defined by the formula

$$m'_p = \frac{1}{n} s_p$$

Clearly m'_1 is the arithmetic mean, usually written $\bar{x}$.

(ii) In order to obtain values independent of the arbitrary origin, and more closely related to the intrinsic characteristics of the population sampled, values called "moments about the mean" are widely used, which are found by dividing the sums of powers about the mean by the sample number; thus if $p = 2, 3, 4, \ldots$

$$m_p = \frac{1}{n} S_p;$$

these are the moments which would have been obtained if, as would usually be inconvenient arithmetically, the arithmetic mean had been chosen as origin.

(iii) A more recent system which has been shown to have great theoretical advantages is to replace the mean and the moments about the mean by the single series of k-statistics

$$k_1 = \frac{1}{n} s_1$$

$$k_2 = \frac{1}{n-1} S_2$$

$$k_3 = \frac{n}{(n-1)(n-2)} S_3$$

$$k_4 = \frac{n}{(n-1)(n-2)(n-3)} \left\{ (n+1)S_4 - 3\frac{n-1}{n} S_2^2 \right\}.$$

It is easy to verify the following relations :

$$m'_1 = k_1$$

$$m_2 = \frac{n-1}{n} k_2$$

$$m_3 = \frac{(n-1)(n-2)}{n^2} k_3$$

$$m_4 = \frac{n-1}{n^2(n+1)} \left\{ (n-2)(n-3)k_4 + 3(n-1)^2 k_2^2 \right\},$$

by which the moment statistics, when they are wanted, may be obtained from the k-statistics.

(iv) It is of historical interest to note that a series of statistics, termed half-invariants, were defined by Thiele, which are related to the moment statistics m' and m in exactly the same way as the cumulants (see B below) are related to the moments μ' and μ of the population. Thus if h_1, h_2, h_3, . . . stand for the half-invariants, we have

$$h_1 = m'_1 \qquad h_2 = m_2 \qquad h_3 = m_3$$
$$h_4 = m_4 - 3m_2^2 \qquad h_5 = m_5 - 10m_3m_2$$

and so on. Thiele used the same term "half-invariants" also to designate the population parameters of which these statistics may be regarded as estimates, just as the single term "moments" has been used in both senses by Pearson and his followers, so that the cumulants have been frequently referred to as half-invariants or semi-invariants of the population, and even the k-statistics have been mistakenly called semi-invariants of the sample. The half-invariants as originally defined by Thiele are not now of importance, and are only mentioned here to clear up the confusion of terminology.

B. *Moments and cumulants of theoretical distributions.*

Either of the systems of statistics derived from sums of powers may be regarded as estimates of corresponding parameters of theoretical distributions, to which they would usually tend if the sample were increased indefinitely. These true, or population, values are designated by Greek letters; thus m'_4 is an estimate of μ'_4, the fourth moment of the population about an arbitrary origin, m_4 is an estimate of μ_4, the fourth moment of the population about its mean, and k_4 is an estimate of κ_4, the fourth cumulant of the population. The relations between these population values are simpler than those between m and k, thus

$$\mu'_1 = \kappa_1 \qquad \mu_2 = \kappa_2 \qquad \mu_3 = \kappa_3$$
$$\mu_4 = \kappa_4 + 3\kappa_2^2 \qquad \mu_5 = \kappa_5 + 10\kappa_3\kappa_2$$

and so on. The general rule for the formation of the coefficients may be seen from the facts that three is the number of ways of dividing four objects into two sets of two each, while ten is the number of ways of dividing five objects into sets of two and three respectively.

In respect of the relationship between the estimates

and the corresponding parameters, the only elementary point to be noted is that whereas the mean value of any m' from samples of n is equal to the corresponding μ' and the mean value of any k equal to the corresponding κ, this property is not enjoyed by the series of moments about the mean m_2, m_3, m_4, . . ., for

$$\bar{m}_2 = \frac{n-1}{n}\mu_2$$

$$\bar{m}_3 = \frac{(n-1)(n-2)}{n^2}\mu_3$$

$$\bar{m}_4 = \frac{n-1}{n^3}\left\{(n^2-3n+3)\mu_4 + 3(2n-3)\mu_2^2\right\}$$

a series of formulæ which sufficiently exhibits the practical inconvenience of using the moments about the mean, and which is typical of the much heavier algebra to which the use of these statistics leads, in comparison with the k-statistics.

The half-invariants, h, of Thiele suffer from the same drawback; for, though they may be regarded as estimates of the cumulants κ, their mean values from the aggregate of finite samples are not equal to the corresponding values κ. In fact,

$$\bar{h}_2 = \frac{n-1}{n}\kappa_2$$

$$\bar{h}_3 = \frac{(n-1)(n-2)}{n^2}\kappa_3$$

$$h_4 = \frac{n-1}{n^3}\left\{(n^2-6n+6)\kappa_4 - 6n\kappa_2^2\right\},$$

showing that the higher members of this series suffer from the same degree of troublesome complexity as do the moments about the mean.

The table below gives the first four cumulants of the three distributions considered in this chapter in terms of the parameters of the distribution :

	Symbol.	Normal.	Poisson.	Binomial.
Mean . .	κ_1	μ	m	np
Variance . .	κ_2	σ^2	m	npq
Third cumulant .	κ_3	0	m	$-npq(p-q)$
Fourth cumulant .	κ_4	0	m	$npq(1-6pq)$

C. *Sampling variance of statistics derived from samples of* N.

Sampling variances are needed primarily for tests of significance. The principal use so far developed for sums of powers higher than the second is in testing normality. The two simplest measures of departure from normality are those dependent from the statistics of the 3rd and 4th degree, defined as

$$g_1 = k_3/k_2^{3/2} \qquad g_2 = k_4/k_2^2.$$

It should be noted that these do not exactly correspond to the statistics γ_1 and γ_2 defined in the first three editions. These Greek symbols are best used not for statistics, but for the parameters of which g_1 and g_2 are estimates. The sampling variances are shown below.

Variance of	General Form.	Normal.
k_1	$\frac{\kappa_2}{N}$	$\frac{\sigma^2}{N}$
k_2	$\frac{\kappa_4}{N}+\frac{2\kappa_2^2}{N-1}$	$\frac{2\sigma^4}{N-1}$
g_1	...	$\frac{6N(N-1)}{(N-2)(N+1)(N+3)}$
g_2	...	$\frac{24N(N-1)^2}{(N-3)(N-2)(N+3)(N+5)}$

D. *Adjustments for grouping.*

When the sums of powers are calculated from grouped data, it is desirable for some purposes to introduce an adjustment designed to annul the average effect of the grouping process. These adjustments were worked out for the moment notation by Sheppard, and affect the sums of even powers about the mean. Using unit grouping interval, the adjusted values of the second and fourth *k*-statistics, represented by k'_2 and k'_4, may be obtained from the formulæ

$$k'_2 = k_2 - \tfrac{1}{12} \qquad k'_4 = k_4 + \tfrac{1}{120}.$$

These adjustments should be used for purposes of estimation, but not usually for tests of significance. Thus k'_2 will be a better estimate of the variance than k_2, but the sampling variance, or standard error, both of the mean and of the variance, should be calculated from the unadjusted value, k_2.

TABLE I

TABLE OF x

The deviation in the normal distribution in terms of the standard deviation.

	·01.	·02.	·03.	·04.	·05.	·06.	·07.	·08.	·09.	·10.
·00	2·575829	2·326348	2·170090	2·053749	1·959964	1·880794	1·811911	1·750686	1·695398	1·644854
·10	1·598193	1·554774	1·514102	1·475791	1·439521	1·405072	1·372204	1·340755	1·310579	1·281552
·20	1·253565	1·226528	1·200359	1·174987	1·150349	1·126391	1·103063	1·080319	1·058122	1·036433
·30	1·015222	·994458	·974114	·954165	·934589	·915365	·896473	·877896	·859617	·841621
·40	·823894	·806421	·789192	·772193	·755415	·738847	·722479	·706303	·690309	·674490
·50	·658838	·643345	·628006	.612813	·597760	·582841	·568051	·553385	·538836	·524401
·60	·510073	·495850	·481727	·467699	·453762	·439913	·426148	·412463	·398855	·385320
·70	·371856	·358459	·345125	·331853	·318639	·305481	·292375	·279319	·266311	·253347
·80	·240426	·227545	·214702	·201893	·189118	·176374	·163658	·150969	·138304	·125661
·90	·113039	·100434	·087845	·075270	·062707	·050154	·037608	·025069	·012533	0

The value of P for each entry is found by adding the column heading to the value in the left-hand margin. The corresponding value of x is the deviation such that the probability of an observation falling outside the range from $-x$ to $+x$ is P. For example, P = ·03 for x = 2·170090; so that 3 per cent. of normally distributed values will have positive or negative deviations exceeding the standard deviation in the ratio 2·170090 at least.

TABLE II

VALUES OF x FOR SMALL VALUES OF P

P . .	·001	·000,1	·000,01	·000,001	·000,000,1	·000,000,01	·000,000,001
x . .	3·29053	3·89059	4·41717	4·89164	5·32672	5·73073	6·10941

IV

TESTS OF GOODNESS OF FIT, INDEPENDENCE AND HOMOGENEITY; WITH TABLE OF χ^2

20. The χ^2 Distribution

In the last chapter some use has been made of the χ^2 distribution as a means of testing the agreement between observation and hypothesis; in the present chapter we shall deal more generally with the very wide class of problems which may be solved by means of the same distribution.

The element common to these tests is the comparison of the numbers actually observed to fall into any number of classes with the numbers which upon some hypothesis are expected. If m is the number expected, and $m+x$ the number observed, in any class, we calculate

$$\chi^2 = S\left(\frac{x^2}{m}\right),$$

the summation extending over all the classes. This formula gives the value of χ^2, and it is clear that the more closely the observed numbers agree with those expected the smaller will χ^2 be; in order to utilise the table it is necessary to know also the value of n with which the table is to be entered. The rule for finding n is that n is equal to the number of degrees of freedom in which the observed series may differ from the hypothetical; in other words, it is equal to the number of classes the frequencies in which may be filled up arbitrarily, without altering the expectations. Several examples will be given to illustrate this rule.

For any value of n, which must be a whole number, the form of distribution of χ^2 was established by Pearson in 1900; it is therefore possible to calculate in what proportion of cases any value of χ^2 will be exceeded. This proportion is represented by P, which is therefore the probability that χ^2 shall exceed any specified value. To every value of χ^2 there thus corresponds a certain value of P; as χ^2 is increased from 0 to infinity, P diminishes from 1 to 0. Equally, to any value of P in this range there corresponds a certain value of χ^2. Algebraically the relation between these two quantities is a complex one, so that it is necessary to have a table of corresponding values, if the χ^2 test is to be available for practical use.

An important table of this sort was prepared by Elderton, and is known as Elderton's Table of Goodness of Fit. Elderton gives the values of P to six decimal places corresponding to each integral value of χ^2 from 1 to 30, and thence by tens to 70. In place of n, the quantity n' ($= n+1$) was used, since it was then believed that this could be equated to the number of frequency classes. Values of n' from 3 to 30 were given, these corresponding to values of n from 2 to 29. A table for $n' = 2$, or $n = 1$, was subsequently supplied by Yule. Owing to copyright restrictions we have not reprinted Elderton's table, but have given a new table (Table III, p. 112) in a form which experience has shown to be more convenient. Instead of giving the values of P corresponding to an arbitrary series of values of χ^2, we have given the values of χ^2 corresponding to specially selected values of P. We have thus been able in a compact form to cover those parts of the distributions which have hitherto not been available, namely, the values of χ^2 less than unity, which frequently occur for small values of n, and the values exceeding 30, which for larger values of n become of importance.

It is of interest to note that the measure of dispersion, Q, introduced by the German economist Lexis, is, if accurately calculated, equivalent to χ^2/n of our notation. In the many references in English to the method of Lexis, it has not, I believe, been noted that the discovery of the distribution of χ^2 in reality completed the method of Lexis. If it were desired to use Lexis' notation, our table could be transformed into a table of Q merely by dividing each entry by n.

In preparing this table we have borne in mind that in practice we do not want to know the exact value of P for any observed χ^2, but, in the first place, whether or not the observed value is open to suspicion. If P is between ·1 and ·9 there is certainly no reason to suspect the hypothesis tested. If it is below ·02 it is strongly indicated that the hypothesis fails to account for the whole of the facts. We shall not often be astray if we draw a conventional line at ·05, and consider that higher values of χ^2 indicate a real discrepancy.

To compare values of χ^2, or of P, by means of a "probable error" is merely to substitute an inexact (normal) distribution for the exact distribution given by the χ^2 table.

The term Goodness of Fit has caused some to fall into the fallacy of believing that the higher the value of P the more satisfactorily is the hypothesis verified. Values over ·999 have sometimes been reported which, if the hypothesis were true, would only occur once in a thousand trials. Generally such cases are demonstrably due to the use of inaccurate formulæ, but occasionally small values of χ^2 beyond the expected range do occur, as in Ex. 4 with the colony numbers obtained in the plating method of bacterial counting. In these cases the hypothesis considered is as definitely disproved as if P had been ·001.

When a large number of values of χ^2 are available for testing, it may be possible to reveal discrepancies which are too small to show up in a single value; we may then compare the observed distribution of χ^2 with that expected. This may be done immediately by simply distributing the observed values of χ^2 among the classes bounded by values given in the χ^2 table, as in Ex. 4, p. 58. The expected frequencies in these classes are easily written down, and, if necessary, the χ^2 test may be used to test the agreement of the observed with the expected frequencies.

It is useful to remember that the sum of any number of quantities, χ^2, is distributed in the χ^2 distribution, with n equal to the sum of the values of n corresponding to the values of χ^2 used. Such a test is sensitive, and will often bring to light discrepancies which are hidden or appear obscurely in the separate values.

The table we give has values of n up to 30; beyond this point it will be found sufficient to assume that $\sqrt{2\chi^2}$ is distributed normally with unit standard deviation about a mean $\sqrt{2n-1}$. The values of P obtained by applying this rule to the values of χ^2 given for $n = 30$, may be worked out as an exercise. The errors are small for $n = 30$, and become progressively smaller for higher values of n.

Ex. 8. *Comparison with expectation of Mendelian class frequencies.*—In a cross involving two Mendelian factors we expect by interbreeding the hybrid (F_1) generation to obtain four classes in the ratio 9 : 3 : 3 : 1; the hypothesis in this case is that the two factors segregate independently, and that the four classes of offspring are equally viable. Are the following observations on *Primula* (de Winton and Bateson) in accordance with this hypothesis?

TABLE 12

	Flat Leaves.		Crimped Leaves.		Total.
	Normal Eye.	Primrose Queen Eye.	Lee's Eye.	Primrose Queen Eye.	
Observed ($m+x$)	328	122	77	33	560
Expected (m) .	315	105	105	35	560
x^2/m . .	·537	2·752	7·467	·114	10·870

The expected values are calculated from the observed total, so that the four classes must agree in their sum, and if three classes are filled in arbitrarily the fourth is therefore determinate; hence $n = 3$; $\chi^2 = 10·87$, the chance of exceeding which value is between ·01 and ·02; if we take P = ·05 as the limit of significant deviation, we shall say that in this case the deviations from expectation are clearly significant.

Let us consider a second hypothesis in relation to the same data, differing from the first in that we suppose that the plants with crimped leaves are to some extent less viable than those with flat leaves. Such a hypothesis could of course be tested by means of additional data; we are here concerned only with the question whether or no it accords with the values before us. The hypothesis tells us nothing of what degree of relative viability to expect; we therefore take the totals of flat and crimped leaves observed, and divide each class in the ratio 3 : 1.

TABLE 13

	Flat Leaves.		Crimped Leaves.		χ^2.
	Normal Eye.	Primrose Queen Eye.	Lee's Eye.	Primrose Queen Eye.	
Observed .	328	122	77	33	...
Expected .	337·5	112·5	82·5	27·5	...
x^2/m . .	·267	·802	·367	1·100	2·536

The value of n is now 2, since only two entries can be made arbitrarily; the value of χ^2, however, is so much reduced that P exceeds ·2, and the departure from expectation is no longer significant. The significant part of the original discrepancy lay in the proportion of flat to crimped leaves.

It was formerly believed that, in entering the χ^2 table, n was always to be equated to one less than the number of frequency classes; this view led to many discrepancies, and has since been disproved with the establishment of the rule stated above. On the old view, any complication of the hypothesis such as that which in the instance above admitted differential viability, was bound to give an apparent improvement in the agreement between observation and hypothesis. When the change in n is allowed for, this bias disappears, and if the value of P, rightly calculated, is many fold increased, as in this instance, the increase may safely be ascribed to an improvement in the hypothesis, and not to a mere increase in the number of parameters which may be adjusted to suit the observations.

Ex. 9. *Comparison with expectation of the Poisson series and Binomial series.*—In Table 5, p. 56, we give the observed and expected frequencies in the case of a Poisson series. In applying the χ^2 test to such a series it is desirable that the number expected should in no group be less than 5, since the calculated distribution of χ^2 is not very closely realised for very small classes. We therefore pool the numbers for 0 and 1 cells, and also those for 10 and more, and obtain the following comparison :

TABLE 14

	0 and 1	2	3	4	5	6	7	8	9	10 and more	Total
Observed	20	43	53	86	70	54	37	18	10	9	400
Expected	21·08	40·65	63·41	74·19	69·44	54·16	36·21	21·18	11·02	8·66	400
x^2/m	·055	·136	1·709	1·880	·005	·000	·017	·477	·093	·013	4·385

Using 10 frequency classes we have $\chi^2 = 4{\cdot}385$; in ascertaining the value of n we have to remember that the expected frequencies have been calculated, not only from the total number of values observed (400), but also from the observed mean ; there remain, therefore, 8 degrees of freedom, and $n = 8$. For this value the χ^2 table shows that P is between ·8 and ·9, showing a close, but not an unreasonably close, agreement with expectation.

Similarly, in Table 10, p. 64, we have given the value of χ^2 based upon 11 classes for the two hypotheses of " true dice " and " biased dice " ; with " true dice " the expected values are calculated from the total number of observations alone, and $n = 10$, but in allowing for bias we have brought also the means into agreement so that n is reduced to 9. In the first case χ^2 is far outside the range of the table showing a highly significant departure from expectation; in the second it appears that P lies between ·5 and ·7, so that the value of χ^2 is within the expected range.

21. Tests of Independence, Contingency Tables

A special and important class of cases where the agreement between expectation and observation may be tested comprises the tests of **independence**. If the same group of individuals is classified in two (or more) different ways, as persons may be classified as inoculated and not inoculated, and also as attacked and not attacked by a disease, then we may require to know if the two classifications are independent.

In the simplest case, when each classification comprises only two classes, we have a 2×2 table, or, as it is often called, a fourfold table.

Ex. 10. The following table is taken from Greenwood and Yule's data for Typhoid:

TABLE 15
OBSERVED

	Attacked.	Not Attacked.	Total.
Inoculated . .	56	6,759	6,815
Not inoculated .	272	11,396	11,668
Total .	328	18,155	18,483

TABLE 16
EXPECTED

	Attacked.	Not Attacked.	Total.
Inoculated .	120·94	6,694·06	6,815
Not Inoculated .	207·06	11,460·94	11,668
Total .	328	18,155	18,483

In testing independence we must compare the observed values with values calculated so that the four frequencies are *in proportion*; since we wish to test independence only, and not any hypothesis as to the total numbers attacked, or inoculated, the "expected" values are calculated from the marginal totals observed, so that the numbers expected agree with the numbers observed in the margins; only one value need be calculated, *e.g.*

$$\frac{328 \times 6815}{18483} = 120\cdot94;$$

the others are written down at once by subtraction from the margins. It is thus obvious that the observed values can differ from those expected in only 1 degree of freedom, so that in testing independence in a fourfold table, $n = 1$. Since $\chi^2 = 56\cdot234$ the observations are clearly opposed to the hypothesis of independence. Without calculating the expected values, χ^2 may, for fourfold tables, be directly calculated by the formula

$$\chi^2 = \frac{(ad-bc)^2(a+b+c+d)}{(a+b)(c+d)(a+c)(b+d)},$$

where a, b, c, and d are the four observed numbers.

When only one of the classifications is of two classes, the calculation of χ^2 may be simplified to some extent, if it is not desired to calculate the expected numbers. If a, a' represent any pair of observed frequencies, and n, n' the corresponding totals, we may, following Pearson, calculate from each pair

$$\frac{1}{a+a'}(an'-a'n)^2,$$

and the sum of these quantities divided by nn' will be χ^2.

An alternative formula, which besides being quicker, has the advantage of agreeing more closely with the general method used in the Analysis of Variance, has been developed by Brandt and Snedecor. From each pair of frequencies the fraction,

$$p = a/(a+a'),$$

is calculated, and from the totals

$$\bar{p} = n/(n+n');$$

then

$$\chi^2 = \frac{1}{\bar{p}\bar{q}}\left\{S(ap) - n\bar{p}\right\},$$

where $\bar{q} = 1 - \bar{p}$. It is a further advantage of this method of calculation that it shows the actual fractions observed in each class; where there is any great difference between the two rows it is usually convenient to use the smaller series of fractions.

Ex. 11. *Test of independence in a* $2 \times n'$ *classification.*—From the pigmentation survey of Scottish children (Tocher's data) the following are the numbers of boys and girls from the same district (No. 1) whose hair colour falls into each of five classes:

TABLE 17

HAIR COLOUR

	Fair.	Red.	Medium.	Dark.	Jet Black.	Total.
Boys . .	592	119	849	504	36	2100
Girls . .	544	97	677	451	14	1783
Total .	1136	216	1526	955	50	3883
Sex Ratio	·52113	·55093	·55636	·52775	·72000	·54082

The sex ratio, proportion of boys, is given under the total for each hair colour; multiplying each by the number of boys, and deducting the corresponding product for the total, there remains 2·603, which on dividing by $\bar{p}\bar{q}$ gives $\chi^2 = 10{\cdot}48$.

In this table 4 values could be filled in arbitrarily without conflicting with the marginal totals, so that $n = 4$. The value of P is between ·02 and ·05, so that sex difference in the classification by hair colours is probably significant as judged by this district alone. It is to be noticed that, with this method, the ratios must be calculated with somewhat high precision. Using five decimal places, the value of χ^2 given is not quite correct in the second decimal, and to avoid doubts as to the precision of calculation two more places would have been desirable. It is evident from the ratios that the principal discrepancy is due to the excess of boys in the "Jet Black" class.

Ex. 12. *Test of independence in a* 4×4 *classification.*—As an example of a more complex contingency table we may take the results of a serie of back-crosses in mice, involving the two factors Black-Brown, Self-Piebald (Wachter's data):

TABLE 18

	Black Self.	Black Piebald.	Brown Self.	Brown Piebald.	Total.
Coupling—					
F_1 Males .	88 (85·37)	82 (75·24)	75 (70·93)	60 (73·46)	305
F_1 Females	38 (34·43)	34 (30·34)	30 (28·60)	21 (29·63)	123
Repulsion—					
F_1 Males .	115 (117·00)	93 (103·11)	80 (97·21)	130 (100·68)	418
F_1 Females	96 (100·20)	88 (88·31)	95 (83·26)	79 (86·23)	358
Total .	337	297	280	290	1204

The back-crosses were made in four ways, according as the male or female parents were heterozygous (F_1) in the two factors, and according to whether the two dominant genes were received both from one (Coupling) or one from each parent (Repulsion).

The simple Mendelian ratios may be disturbed by differential viability, by linkage, or by linked lethals. Linkage is not suspected in these data, and if the only disturbance were due to differential viability of the four genotypes, these should always appear in the same proportion; to test if the data show significant departures we may apply the χ^2 test to the whole 4×4 table. The values expected on the hypothesis that the proportions are independent of the matings used, or that the four series are homogeneous, are given above in brackets. The contributions to χ^2 made by each cell are given below (Table 19).

TABLE 19

·081	·607	·234	2·466	3·388
·370	·442	·069	2·514	3·395
·034	·991	3·047	8·539	12·611
·176	·001	1·655	·606	2·438
·661	2·041	5·005	14·125	21·832

The value of χ^2 is therefore 21·832; the value of n is 9, for we could fill up a block of three rows and three columns and still adjust the remaining entries to check with the margins. In general for a contingency table of r rows and c columns $n = (r-1)(c-1)$. For $n = 9$, the value of χ^2 shows that P is less than ·01, and therefore the departures from proportionality are not fortuitous; it is apparent that the discrepancy is due to the exceptional number of Brown Piebalds in the F_1 males Repulsion series.

It should be noted that the methods employed in this chapter are not designed to measure the *degree* of association between one classification and another, but solely to test whether the observed departures from independence are or are not of a magnitude ascribable to chance. The same degree of association may be significant for a large sample but insignificant for a small one; if it is insignificant we have no reason on the data present to suspect any degree of association at all, and it is useless to attempt to measure it. If, on the other hand, it is significant the value of χ^2 indicates the fact, but does not measure the degree of association. Provided the deviation is clearly significant, it is of no practical importance whether P is ·01 or ·000,001, and it is for this reason that we have not tabulated the value of χ^2 beyond ·01. To measure the degree of association it is necessary to have some hypothesis as to the nature of the departure from independence to be measured. With Mendelian frequencies, for example, the recombination percentage may be used to measure the degree of association of two factors, and the significance of evidence for linkage may be tested by comparing the difference between the recombination percentage and 50 per cent. (the value for unlinked factors), with its standard error. Such a comparison, if accurately carried out, must agree absolutely with the conclusion drawn from the χ^2 test. To take a second example, the values in a four-fold table may be sometimes regarded as due to the partition of a normally correlated pair of variates, according as the values are above or below arbitrarily chosen dividing-lines; as if a group of stature measurements of fathers and sons were divided between those above and those below 68 inches. In this case the departure from independence may be properly measured by the correlation in stature between father and son; this quantity can be estimated from the observed frequencies, and a comparison between the value obtained and its standard error, if accurately carried out, will agree with the χ^2 test as to the significance of the association; the significance will become more and more pronounced as the sample is increased in size, but the correlation obtained will tend to a fixed value. The χ^2 test does not attempt to measure the degree of association, but as a test of significance it is independent of all additional hypctheses as to the nature of the association.

Tests of **homogeneity** are mathematically identical with tests of independence; the last example may equally be regarded in either light; in Chapter III the tests of agreement with the Binomial series were essentially tests of homogeneity; the ten samples of 100 ears of barley (Ex. 7, p. 68) might have been represented as a 2×10 table. The χ^2 index of dispersion would then be equivalent to the χ^2 obtained from the contingency table. The method of this chapter is more general, and is applicable to cases in which the successive samples are not all of the same size.

Ex. 13. *Homogeneity of different families in respect of ratio black : red.*—The following data show in 33 families of *Gammarus* (Huxley's data) the numbers with black and red eyes respectively:

TABLE 20

Black	79	120	24	117	62	79	66	45	61	64	208	154	31	158	21	105	28
Red	14	31	6	29	17	20	12	11	14	13	52	45	4	45	4	28	7
Total	93	151	30	146	79	99	78	56	75	77	260	199	35	203	25	133	35
Black	58	81	25	95	47	67	30	70	139	179	129	44	24	19	45	91	2565
Red	19	27	8	29	16	21	11	28	57	62	44	17	9	8	23	41	772
Total	77	108	33	124	63	88	41	98	196	241	173	61	33	27	68	132	3337

The totals 2565 black and 772 red are distinctly not in the ratio 3 : 1; the discrepancy is ascribed to linkage. The question before us is whether or not all the families indicate the same ratio between black and red, or whether the discrepancy is due to a few families only. For the whole table $\chi^2 = 35{\cdot}620$, $n = 32$. This is beyond the range of the table, so we apply the method explained on p. 81 :

$$\sqrt{2\chi^2} = 8{\cdot}44;$$
$$\sqrt{2n-1} = 7{\cdot}94;$$
$$\text{Difference} = +{\cdot}50 \pm 1.$$

The series is therefore not significantly heterogeneous; effectively all the families agree and confirm each other in indicating the black-red ratio observed in the total.

Exactly the same procedure would be adopted if the black and red numbers represented two samples distributed according to some character or characters each into 33 classes. The question "Are these samples of the same population?" is in effect identical with the question "Is the proportion of black to red the same in each family?" To recognise this identity is important, since it has been very widely disregarded.

21·01. Yates' Correction for Continuity

The distribution of χ^2, tabulated as in Table III, is a continuous distribution. The distribution of frequencies must, however, always be discontinuous. Consequently, the use of χ^2 in the comparison of observed with expected frequencies can only be of approximate accuracy, the continuous distribution being in fact the limit towards which the true discontinuous distribution tends as the sample is made ever larger. It was in order to avoid the irregularities produced by small numbers that we have stipulated above that in no group shall the expected number be less than five. This safeguard generally ensures that the number of possible sets of observations shall be large, each occurring with only a small frequency, so giving to χ^2 a distribution closely simulating the continuous distribution of the table.

A case of special interest arises, however, when there is only 1 degree of freedom, and when the value of χ^2 can, consequently, be calculated from the number observed in a single class. If the number in this class is small, *e.g.* 3, the probability of this number may be by no means negligible compared with the sum of the probabilities of the more extreme deviations represented by 2, 1, or 0 occurrences in the class. If we want to know whether the observed number, 3, is so small as to indicate a significant departure from expectation, we require to know whether the sum of the probabilities of 3, 2, 1 or 0 together is less than a standard value, such as ·05; or, in other words, whether the total probability of obtaining our observed deviation, or any deviation more extreme, is so small that we should be unwilling to ascribe the deviation observed to mere chance.

Our actual problem, therefore, when stated exactly, concerns a limited number of finite probabilities, which in simple cases it may be convenient to calculate directly. The Table of χ^2, on the other hand, gives the area of the tail of a continuous curve. Inasmuch, however, as this curve supplies a close approximation to the actual distribution, the area between the values of χ^2 corresponding to observed frequencies of $3\frac{1}{2}$ and $2\frac{1}{2}$ will be a good approximation to the actual probability of observing 3; and the area of the tail beyond the value of χ^2 corresponding to $3\frac{1}{2}$ will be a good approximation to the sum of the probabilities of observing 3 or less. Thus our actual problem will best be resolved by entering the table of χ^2, not with the value calculated from the actual frequencies, but with the value it would have if our observed frequencies had been less extreme than they really are each by half a unit. This useful adjustment is due to F. Yates.

Ex. 13·1. *Frequency of criminality among the twin brothers or sisters of criminals.*—Among 13 criminals who were monozygotic twins Lange reports that 10 had twin brothers or sisters who had also been convicted, while in 3 cases the twin brother had, apparently, not taken to crime. Among 17 criminals who were dizygotic twins (of like sex), 2 had convicted twin brothers or sisters, while those of the other 15 were not known to be criminals. It is argued that the environmental circumstances are as much alike for dizygotic twins of like sex as for monozygotic twins, and that if the latter are more alike in their social reactions these reactions must be largely conditioned by genetic factors. Do Lange's data show that criminality is significantly more frequent among the monozygotic twins of criminals than among the dizygotic twins of criminals?

Our data consist of the four-fold table :—

TABLE 20·1

	Convicted.	Not Convicted.	Total.
Monozygotic . .	10	3	13
Dizygotic . .	2	15	17
Total . .	12	18	30

The difference $(ad-bc)$ is 144 and

$$\chi^2 = \frac{144^2 . 30}{12 . 18 . 13 . 17} = 13.032$$

a very significant value, equivalent to a normal deviate 3·61 times its standard error. The probability of exceeding such a deviation in the right direction is about 1 in 6500.

Using Yates' adjustment we should rewrite the table with the larger frequencies 10 and 15 reduced by a half, and the smaller frequencies 2 and 3 increased by half.

The difference between the cross products $ad-bc$ is now reduced to 129, which, it may be noted, is just 15, or half the total number of observations, less than its previous value, 144. In other respects the calculation is unchanged. The new value of χ^2 is 10·458, still a very significant value for 1 degree of freedom, but now corresponding to a normal deviation of 3·234 times its standard error, or to odds of 1 in 1638. The exact odds in this case are 1 in 2150, as will be shown in the next section. The adjustment has slightly over-corrected the exaggeration of significance due to using a table of a continuous distribution.

21·02. The Exact Treatment of 2×2 Tables

The treatment of frequencies by means of χ^2 is an approximation, which is useful for the comparative simplicity of the calculations. The exact treatment is somewhat more laborious, though necessary in cases of doubt, and valuable as displaying the true nature of the inferences which the method of χ^2 is designed to draw.

If p is the probability of any event, the probability that it will occur a times in $(a+b)$ independent trials is the term of the binomial expansion,

$$\frac{(a+b)!}{a!\,b!}p^a q^b,$$

where $q = 1-p$. The probability that in a sample of $(c+d)$ trials it will occur c times is

$$\frac{(c+d)!}{c!\,d!}p^c q^d.$$

So that the probability of the observed frequencies a, b, c, and d in a 2×2 table is the product

$$\frac{(a+b)!\,(c+d)!}{a!\,b!\,c!\,d!}p^{a+c}q^{b+d},$$

and this in general must be unknown if p is unknown. The unknown factor involving p and q will, however, be the same for all tables having the same marginal frequencies $a+c$, $b+d$, $a+b$, $c+d$, so that among possible sets of observations having the same marginal frequencies, the probabilities are in proportion to

$$\frac{1}{a!\,b!\,c!\,d!},$$

whatever may be the value of p, or, in other words for all populations in which the four frequencies are in proportion.

Now the sum of the quantities $1/a!\ b!\ c!\ d!$ for all samples having the same margins is found to be

$$\frac{n!}{(a+b)!\ (c+d)!\ (a+c)!\ (b+d)!}$$

where $n = a+b+c+d$; so that, given the marginal frequencies, the probability of any observed set of entries is

$$\frac{(a+b)!\ (c+d)!\ (a+c)!\ (b+d)!}{n!} \cdot \frac{1}{a!\ b!\ c!\ d!}.$$

In the case considered in Ex. 13·1, we have therefore

$$\frac{18!\ 12!\ 17!\ 13!}{30!}\left\{\frac{1}{2!\ 3!\ 10!\ 15!},\ \frac{1}{2!\ 11!\ 16!},\ \frac{1}{1!\ 12!\ 17!}\right\}$$

for the probabilities of the set of frequencies observed, and the two possible more extreme sets of frequencies which might have been observed. Without any assumption or approximation, therefore, the table observed may be judged significantly to contradict the hypothesis of proportionality if

$$\frac{18!\ 13!}{30!}(2992+102+1)$$

is a small quantity. This amounts to 619/1330665, or about 1 in 2150, showing that if the hypothesis of proportionality were true, observations of the kind recorded would be highly exceptional.

21·03. Exact Tests based on the χ^2 Distribution

In its primary purpose of the comparison of a series of observed frequencies with those expected on the hypothesis to be tested, the χ^2 test is an approximate one, though validly applicable in an immense range of important cases. For other tests where the observations are measurements, instead of frequencies, it provides exact tests of significance. Of these the two most important are :—

(i) its use to test whether a sample from a normal distribution confirms or contradicts the variance which this distribution is expected on theoretical grounds to have, and

(ii) its use in combining the indications drawn from a number of independent tests of significance.

Ex. 14. *Agreement with expectation of normal variance.*—If x_1, x_2, . . ., are a sample of a normal population, the standard deviation of which population is σ, then

$$\frac{1}{\sigma^2} S(x-\bar{x})^2$$

is distributed in random samples as is χ^2, taking n one less than the number in the sample. J. W. Bispham gives three series of experimental values of the partial correlation coefficient, each based on thirty observations of the values of three variates, which he assumes should be distributed so that $1/\sigma^2=29$, but which properly should have $1/\sigma^2=28$. The values of $S(x-\bar{x})^2$ for the three samples of 1000, 200, 100 respectively are, as judged from the grouped data,

$$35{\cdot}0279, \quad 7{\cdot}4573, \quad 3{\cdot}6146,$$

whence the values of χ^2 on the two theories are those given in Table 21.

TABLE 21

	Exp. 1.	2.	3.	Total.	$\sqrt{2\chi^2}$.	Difference.
29 $S(x-\bar{x})^2$ . .	1015·81	216·26	104·82	1336·89	51·71	+·79
28 $S(x-\bar{x})^2$ . .	980·78	208·80	101·21	1290·79	50·81	−·11
Expectation (n) .	999	199	99	1297	50·92	

It will be seen that the true formula for the variance gives slightly the better agreement. That the difference is not significant may be seen from the last two columns. About 6000 observations would be needed to discriminate experimentally, with any certainty, between the two formulæ.

21·1. The Combination of Probabilities from Tests of Significance

When a number of quite independent tests of significance have been made, it sometimes happens that although few or none can be claimed individually as significant, yet the aggregate gives an impression that the probabilities are on the whole lower than would often have been obtained by chance. It is sometimes desired, taking account only of these probabilities, and not of the detailed composition of the data from which they are derived, which may be of very different kinds, to obtain a single test of the significance of the aggregate, based on the product of the probabilities individually observed.

The circumstance that the sum of a number of values of χ^2 is itself distributed in the χ^2 distribution with the appropriate number of degrees of freedom, may be made the basis of such a test. For in the particular case when $n = 2$, the natural logarithm of the probability is equal to $-\frac{1}{2}\chi^2$. If therefore we take the natural logarithm of a probability, change its sign and double it, we have the equivalent value of χ^2 for 2 degrees of freedom. Any number of such values may be added together, to give a composite test, using the Table of χ^2 to examine the significance of the result.

Ex. 14·1. *Significance of the product of a number of independent probabilities.*—Three tests of significance have yielded the probabilities ·145, ·263, ·087; test whether the aggregate of these three tests should be regarded as significant. We have

P	$-\log_e P$	Degrees of Freedom.
·145	1·9310	2
·263	1·3356	2
·087	2·4419	2
	5·7085	6

$$\chi^2 = 11{\cdot}4170$$

For 6 degrees of freedom we have found a value 11·417 for χ^2. The 5 per cent. value is 12·592 while the 10 per cent. value is 10·645. The probability of the aggregate of the three tests occurring by chance therefore exceeds ·05, and is not far from ·075.

In applying this method it will be noticed that we require to know from the individual tests not only whether they are or are not individually significant, but also, to two or three figure accuracy, what are the actual probabilities indicated. For this purpose it is convenient and sufficiently accurate for most purposes to interpolate in the table given (Table III), using the logarithms of the values of P shown. Either natural or common logarithms may equally be employed. We may exemplify the process by applying it to find the probability of χ^2 exceeding 11·417, when $n = 6$.

Our value of χ^2 exceeds the 10 per cent. point by ·772, while the 5 per cent. point exceeds the 10 per cent. point by 1·947; the fraction

$$\frac{\cdot 772}{1\cdot 947} = \cdot 397.$$

The difference between the common logarithm of 5 and of 10 is ·3010, which multiplied by ·397 gives ·119; the negative logarithm of the required probability is thus found to be 1·119, and the probability to be ·076. For comparison, the value calculated by exact methods is ·07631.

22. Partition of χ^2 into its Components

Just as values of χ^2 may be aggregated together to make a more comprehensive test, so in some cases it is possible to separate the contributions to χ^2 made by the individual degrees of freedom, and so to test the separate components of a discrepancy.

Ex. 15. *Partition of observed discrepancies from Mendelian expectation.*—The table on p. 102 (de Winton and Bateson's data) gives the distribution of sixteen families of Primula in the eight classes obtained from a back-cross with the triple recessive.

The theoretical expectation is that the eight classes should appear in equal numbers, corresponding to the hypothesis that in each factor the allelomorphs occur with equal frequency, and that the three factors are unlinked. This expectation is fairly realised in the totals of the sixteen families, but the individual families are somewhat irregular. The values of χ^2 obtained by comparing each family with expectation are given in the lowest line. These values each correspond to 7 degrees of freedom, and it appears that in 6 cases out of 16, P is less than ·1, and of these

TABLE 22

Type.	Family Number.																Total.
	54.	55.	58.	59.	107.	110.	119.	121.	122.	127.	129.	131.	132.	133.	135.	178.	
Ch G W	5	18	17	2	12	17	9	10	24	9	3	16	20	9	11	10	192
Ch G w	10	13	11	12	20	16	10	7	23	3	6	24	18	2	13	12	200
Ch g W	4	10	17	3	14	10	6	8	19	5	5	23	18	10	7	12	171
Ch g w	9	17	11	11	13	13	9	8	9	6	3	12	18	1	9	12	161
ch G W	13	22	20	10	5	5	16	2	30	3	8	21	19	4	9	12	199
ch G w	14	16	18	9	12	6	14	3	16	5	7	13	14	4	13	10	174
ch g W	10	11	12	6	7	3	18	2	11	5	4	14	23	4	6	13	149
ch g w	7	12	16	6	10	8	10	4	23	5	4	22	23	7	8	16	181
Total	72	119	122	59	93	78	92	44	155	41	40	145	153	41	76	97	1427
χ^2	9·78	7·86	5·48	13·00	12·55	19·23	10·09	12·36	18·06	4·86	4·80	9·21	3·18	14·22	5·05	2·05	151·78

2 are less than ·02. This confirms the impression of irregularity, and the total value of χ^2 (not to be confused with χ^2 derived from the totals), which corresponds to 112 degrees of freedom, is 151·78.

Now
$$\sqrt{223} = 14·93;$$
$$\sqrt{303·56} = 17·42;$$
$$\text{Difference} = +2·49;$$

so that, judged by the total χ^2, the general evidence for departures from expectation in individual families is clear.

Each family is free to differ from expectation in seven independent ways. To carry the analysis further, we must separate the contribution to χ^2 of each of these 7 degrees of freedom. Mathematically the subdivision may be carried out in more than one way, but the only way which appears to be of biological interest is that which separates the parts due to inequality of the allelomorphs of the three factors, and the three possible linkage connexions. If we separate the frequencies into positive and negative values according to the following seven ways:—

TABLE 23

	Ch.	G.	W.	G W.	Ch W.	Ch G.	Ch G W.
Ch G W .	+	+	+	+	+	+	+
Ch G w .	+	+	−	−	−	+	−
Ch g W .	+	−	+	−	+	−	−
Ch g w .	+	−	−	+	−	−	+
ch G W .	−	+	+	+	−	−	−
ch G w .	−	+	−	−	+	−	+
ch g W .	−	−	+	−	−	+	+
ch g w .	−	−	−	+	+	+	−

then it will be seen that all seven subdivisions are wholly independent, since any two of them agree in four signs and disagree in four. The first 3 degrees of freedom represent the inequalities in the allelomorphs of the three factors **Ch, G,** and **W**; the next are the degrees of freedom involved in an inquiry into the linkage of the three pairs of factors, while the 7th degree of freedom has no simple biological meaning but is necessary to complete the analysis. If we take in the first family, for example, the difference between the numbers of the **W** and **w** plants, namely 8, then the contribution of this degree of freedom to χ^2 is found by squaring the difference and dividing by the number in the family, *e.g.* $8^2 \div 72 = \cdot 889$. In this way the contribution of each of the 112 degrees of freedom in the sixteen families is found separately, as shown in the following table :—

TABLE 24

Family.	Ch.	G.	W.	G W.	Ch W.	Ch G.	Ch GW.	Total.
54	3·556	2·000	·889	·222	2·000	·889	·222	9·778
55	·076	3·034	·076	3·034	·412	1·017	·210	7·859
58	·820	·820	·820	·295	1·607	·820	·295	5·477
59	·153	·831	4·898	·017	6·119	·831	·153	13·002
107	6·720	·269	3·108	1·817	·097	·269	·269	12·549
110	14·821	1·282	·821	·821	·205	1·282	0	19·232
119	6·261	·391	·391	·174	2·130	·043	·696	10·086
121	11·000	0	0	·364	·818	·091	·091	12·364
122	·161	6·200	1·090	1·865	·523	·316	7·903	18·058
127	·610	·024	·220	·610	1·195	·220	1·976	4·855
129	·900	1·600	0	·400	·100	·900	·900	4·800
131	·172	·062	·062	·062	·062	·338	8·448	9·206
132	·163	·791	·320	·320	·059	1·471	·059	3·183
133	·220	·220	4·122	·024	8·805	·220	·610	14·221
135	·211	3·368	1·316	·053	·053	0	·053	5·054
178	·258	·835	·093	·093	·010	·258	·505	2·052
Total	46·102	21·727	18·226	10·171	24·195	8·965	22·390	151·776

Looking at the total values of χ^2 for each column, since n is 16 for these, we see that all except the first have values of P between ·05 and ·95, while the contribution of the 1st degree of freedom is very clearly significant. It appears then that the greater part, if not the whole, of the discrepancy is ascribable to the behaviour of the Sinensis-Stellata factor, **Ch**, and its behaviour strongly suggests close linkage with a recessive lethal gene of one of the familiar types. In four families, 107-121, the only high contribution is in the first column. If these four families are excluded $\chi^2 = 97{\cdot}545$, and this exceeds the expectation for $n = 84$ by only just over the standard error; the total discrepancy cannot therefore be regarded as significant.

There does, however, appear to be an excess of very large entries, and it is noticeable of the seven largest, that six appear in pairs belonging to the same family. The distribution of the remaining 12 families according to the value of P is as follows :—

TABLE 25

P . .	1·0	·9	·8	·7	·5	·3	·2	·1	·05	·02	·01	0	Total
Families	1	1	0	4	1	2	0	1	1	1	0		12

from which it would appear that there is some slight evidence of an excess of families with high values of χ^2. This effect, like other non-significant effects, is only worth further discussion in connexion with some plausible hypothesis capable of explaining it.

The general procedure to follow in analysing χ^2 into its components will be developed in Section 55.

Ex. 15·1. *Complex test on homogeneity in data with hierarchical subdivisions.*—Table 25·1 shows the total number of offspring and the number of recom-

TABLE 25·1

TOTAL PLANTS (T) AND RECOMBINATIONS (c) IN 22 PROGENIES AND IN THE AGGREGATES OF PROGENIES IN WHICH THEY ARE GROUPED.

Descendants of									
Single Plants.		Fraternities.		Parents F_3.		Grandparents F_2.		Total.	
T	c	T	c	T	c	T	c	T	c
34	3	77	11						
43	8			171	21				
94	10	94	10						
73	3								
20	2	130	8			427	42		
16	2								
21	1			256	21				
31	6								
51	4	126	13						
29	2								
15	1							922	105
64	9	119	22	119	22	119	22		
55	13								
55	7	89	12	89	12				
34	5								
37	3	37	3	37	3				
45	7					376	41		
28	0	108	9						
35	2			250	26				
68	8								
44	5	142	17						
30	4								

binations found in 22 progenies of the garden pea, grown by Rasmusson. Each progeny was derived from a single plant, tested by back-crossing. Unequal numbers of these plants belonged, as shown by the table, to 9 different fraternities, for each of which the total number of offspring and the total recom-

TABLE 25·2

VALUES OF $\frac{c^2}{T}$ FOR ALL GROUPS AND SUBGROUPS

Individual Plants.	Fraternities.	Parents F_2.	Grandparents F_1.	Total.
0·26471	1·57143			
1·48837		2·57895		
1·06383	1·06383			
0·12329				
0·20000			4·13115	
0·25000	0·49231			
0·04762				
1·16129		1·72266		
0·31373				
0·13793	1·34127			
0·06667				11·95770
1·26562				
3·07273	4·06723	4·06723	4·06723	
0·89091				
0·73529	1·61798	1·61798		
0·24324	0·24324	0·24324		
1·08889			4·47074	
0·00000	0·75000			
0·11429				
0·94118		2·70400		
0·56818	2·03521			
0·53333				
14·57110	13·18250	12·93406	12·66912	11·95770
1·38860	0·24844	0·26494	0·71142	Differences.
13·760	2·462	2·625	7·050	χ^2
13	3	3	2	n

binations are shown in the table. In three cases, moreover, 2 fraternities had been derived by different matings of the same parent plants, which had been bred with a view to this linkage test, so that the 9 fraternities were the offspring of 6 F_3 parents, which in turn were derived from 3 F_2 grandparents. In all, the final generation yielded 922 plants, of which 105 were of the types recognised as recombinations. It is required to test whether heterogeneity in the fraction of recombinations obtained occurs at any of the four stages represented by the groups and subgroups of progenies.

The method of Brandt and Snedecor is of great value when adapted to the analysis of data of this kind. If in any progeny, or group of progenies, we have c recombinations out of T plants, we may at once calculate c^2/T for each group in the record. These ratios appear in Table 25·2 arranged to show the affiliations of the different groups and subgroups. Whenever the proportion of recombinations observed is different for different subgroups of the same group, the values for these subgroups will together exceed the value for the corresponding group; thus the five totals shown in Table 25·2 form a diminishing series, the successive differences between the terms of which afford measures of the heterogeneity observable.

If such a process were applied to completely homogeneous material, it would only be necessary to divide each of these differences by the same quantity, pq, where p is the proportion of recombinations and q of old combinations, to obtain values distributed in χ^2 distributions. The numbers of degrees of freedom appropriate to each are the differences between the numbers of entries in the successive columns.

It is apparent from the values at the foot of the table that the only apparent heterogeneity in the linkage values occurs among the F_2 plants, or at the earliest stage at which segregation might appear. Here the value of χ^2 is 7·050 for 2 degrees of freedom, a value which lies between the 5 per cent. and the 2 per cent. points. It is probable, therefore, that segregations affecting linkage occurred at this stage, and, in consequence, the values we have obtained for later stages must be revised with this heterogeneity in view.

TABLE 25·3

DIFFERENCES AMONG SISTER PLANTS AND SUBGROUPS, WITH DEGREES OF FREEDOM CORRESPONDING

Sister Plants.	Half-sister Progenies.	F_3 Plants.	F_2 Plants.
·18165 (1)	·05631 (1)		
...		·17046 (1)	
·12860 (3)	·11092 (1)		
·33835 (3)			
·27112 (1)	...	...	·71142 (2)
·00822 (1)	...		
...	...	·09448 (2)	
·45318 (2)	·08121 (1)		
·00748 (2)			

A generally applicable procedure would be to recalculate the divisor, pq, for each of the three F_2 plants. In this case, however, it is evident that the first and third of these differ but little, having recombination fractions 9·836 per cent. and 10·904 per cent. respectively, while both show closer linkage than is shown by the descendants of the second plant, which gave 18·487 per cent. We shall, therefore, in recalculating χ^2 use the same fraction, 83/803, for the descendants of the first and third F_2 plants, and the fraction 22/119 for the descendants of the second plant.

When different factors are to be applied in different parts of the table a convenient first step is to take the differences between the total value for the subgroups, and the value for the group to which they belong, in each available case, as is shown in Table 25·3. In this table the whole set of 21 degrees of freedom has been partitioned among 13 entries. The values of χ^2 to which these parts correspond depend on the values of pq, by which they are divided. In the case of the 2 degrees of freedom among the F_2 plants we must use $p = 105/922$, obtaining as before $\chi^2 = 7·0498$ for 2 degrees of freedom. For the descendants of the first and third F_2 plants we divide by ·0926786, and for the descendants of the second plant by ·1506956, so obtaining the values of χ^2 shown in Table 25·4.

TABLE 25·4

χ^2 FOR 13 RELEVANT SUBDIVISIONS

Sister Plants.	Half-sister Progenies.	F_3 Plants.	F_2 Plants.
1·9600 (1)	·6076 (1)		
...		1·8393 (1)	
1·3876 (3)	1·1968 (1)		
3·6508 (3)			
1·7991 (1)	...	...	7·0498 (2)
·0887 (7)	...		
...	...	1·0194 (2)	
4·8898 (2)	·8763 (1)		
·0807 (2)			
13·8567	2·6807	2·8587	7·0498
13	3	3	2

The totals for the different subdivision stages do not differ greatly from those shown in Table 25·2, but afford a better test for heterogeneity in these later stages, once it is suspected that the F_2 plants were not homogeneous. It will be observed, in fact, that the value of χ^2 for the 3 degrees of freedom representing differences between the pairs of half-sister progenies from the same F_3 plants, and that for differences among the F_3 plants, are slightly raised, through using a smaller divisor for the descendants of the first and third F_2 plants, since in these columns there is no compensation due to using a larger divisor for the descendants of the second plant.

The absence of significant values in the first three columns of Table 25·4 shows that no further modifications of the divisors are necessary, since there is no further evidence of heterogeneity.

[TABLE

TABLE III—

n.	P=·99.	·98.	·95.	·90.	·80.	·70.
1	·000157	·000628	·00393	·0158	·0642	·148
2	·0201	·0404	·103	·211	·446	·713
3	·115	·185	·352	·584	1·005	1·424
4	·297	·429	·711	1·064	1·649	2·195
5	·554	·752	1·145	1·610	2·343	3·000
6	·872	1·134	1·635	2·204	3·070	3·828
7	1·239	1·564	2·167	2·833	3·822	4·671
8	1·646	2·032	2·733	3·490	4·594	5·527
9	2·088	2·532	3·325	4·168	5·380	6·393
10	2·558	3·059	3·940	4·865	6·179	7·267
11	3·053	3·609	4·575	5·578	6·989	8·148
12	3·571	4·178	5·226	6·304	7·807	9·034
13	4·107	4·765	5·892	7·042	8·634	9·926
14	4·660	5·368	6·571	7·790	9·467	10·821
15	5·229	5·985	7·261	8·547	10·307	11·721
16	5·812	6·614	7·962	9·312	11·152	12·624
17	6·408	7·255	8·672	10·085	12·002	13·531
18	7·015	7·906	9·390	10·865	12·857	14·440
19	7·633	8·567	10·117	11·651	13·716	15·352
20	8·260	9·237	10·851	12·443	14·578	16·266
21	8·897	9·915	11·591	13·240	15·445	17·182
22	9·542	10·600	12·338	14·041	16·314	18·101
23	10·196	11·293	13·091	14·848	17·187	19·021
24	10·856	11·992	13·848	15·659	18·062	19·943
25	11·524	12·697	14·611	16·473	18·940	20·867
26	12·198	13·409	15·379	17·292	19·820	21·792
27	12·879	14·125	16·151	18·114	20·703	22·719
28	13·565	14·847	16·928	18·939	21·588	23·647
29	14·256	15·574	17·708	19·768	22·475	24·577
30	14·953	16·306	18·493	20·599	23·364	25·508

For larger values of *n*, the expression $\sqrt{2\chi^2} - \sqrt{2n-1}$

TABLE OF χ^2

·50.	·30.	·20.	·10.	·05.	·02.	·01.
·455	1·074	1·642	2·706	3·841	5·412	6·635
1·386	2·408	3·219	4·605	5·991	7·824	9·210
2·366	3·665	4·642	6·251	7·815	9·837	11·345
3·357	4·878	5·989	7·779	9·488	11·668	13·277
4·351	6·064	7·289	9·236	11·070	13·388	15·086
5·348	7·231	8·558	10·645	12·592	15·033	16·812
6·346	8·383	9·803	12·017	14·067	16·622	18·475
7·344	9·524	11·030	13·362	15·507	18·168	20·090
8·343	10·656	12·242	14·684	16·919	19·679	21·666
9·342	11·781	13·442	15·987	18·307	21·161	23·209
10·341	12·899	14·631	17·275	19·675	22·618	24·725
11·340	14·011	15·812	18·549	21·026	24·054	26·217
12·340	15·119	16·985	19·812	22·362	25·472	27·688
13·339	16·222	18·151	21·064	23·685	26·873	29·141
14·339	17·322	19·311	22·307	24·996	28·259	30·578
15·338	18·418	20·465	23·542	26·296	29·633	32·000
16·338	19·511	21·615	24·769	27·587	30·995	33·409
17·338	20·601	22·760	25·989	28·869	32·346	34·805
18·338	21·689	23·900	27·204	30·144	33·687	36·191
19·337	22·775	25·038	28·412	31·410	35·020	37·566
20·337	23·858	26·171	29·615	32·671	36·343	38·932
21·337	24·939	27·301	30·813	33·924	37·659	40·289
22·337	26·018	28·429	32·007	35·172	38·968	41·638
23·337	27·096	29·553	33·196	36·415	40·270	42·980
24·337	28·172	30·675	34·382	37·652	41·566	44·314
25·336	29·246	31·795	35·563	38·885	42·856	45·642
26·336	30·319	32·912	36·741	40·113	44·140	46·963
27·336	31·391	34·027	37·916	41·337	45·419	48·278
28·336	32·461	35·139	39·087	42·557	46·693	49·588
29·336	33·530	36·250	40·256	43·773	47·962	50·892

may be used as a normal deviate with unit variance.

V

TESTS OF SIGNIFICANCE OF *MEANS*, DIFFERENCES OF MEANS, AND REGRESSION COEFFICIENTS

23. The Standard Error of the Mean

THE fundamental proposition upon which the statistical treatment of mean values is based is that—If a quantity be normally distributed with variance σ^2, then the mean of a random sample of n such quantities is normally distributed with variance σ^2/n.

The utility of this proposition is somewhat increased by the fact that even if the original distribution were not exactly normal, that of the mean usually tends to normality, as the size of the sample is increased; the method is therefore applied widely and legitimately to cases in which we have not sufficient evidence to assert that the original distribution was normal, but in which we have reason to think that it does not belong to the exceptional class of distributions for which the distribution of the mean does not tend to normality.

If, therefore, we know the variance of a population, we can calculate the variance of the mean of a random sample of any size, and so test whether or not it differs significantly from any fixed value. If the difference is many times greater than the standard error, it is certainly significant, and it is a convenient convention to take twice the standard error as the limit of significance; this is roughly equivalent to the corresponding limit P = ·05, already used for the χ^2 distribution. The deviations in the normal distribution corresponding to a number of values of P are given in the lowest line of the Table of t at the end of this chapter (p. 174). More detailed information has been given in Table I.

Ex. 16. *Significance of mean of a large sample.*—We may consider from this point of view Weldon's die-casting experiment (Ex. 5, p. 63). The variable quantity is the number of dice scoring "5" or "6" in a throw of 12 dice. In the experiment this number varies from zero to eleven, with an observed mean of 4·0524; the expected mean, on the hypothesis that the dice were true, is 4, so that the deviation observed is ·0524. If now we estimate the variance of the whole sample of 26,306 values as explained in Ex. 2, without using Sheppard's correction (for the data are not grouped, and even with grouped data, since the mean is affected by grouping errors, its variance should be estimated without this adjustment), we find

$$\sigma^2 = 2{\cdot}69826,$$

whence $$\sigma^2/n = {\cdot}0001026,$$

and $$\sigma/\sqrt{n} = {\cdot}01013,$$

The standard error of the mean is therefore about ·01, and the observed deviation is nearly 5·2 times as great; thus by a slightly different path we arrive at the same conclusion as that of p. 65. The difference between the two methods is that our treatment of the mean does not depend upon the hypothesis that the distribution is of the binomial form, but on the other hand we do assume the correctness of the value of σ derived from the observations. This assumption breaks down for small samples, and the principal purpose of this chapter is to show how accurate allowance can be made in these tests of significance for the errors in our estimates of the standard deviation.

To return to the cruder theory, we may often, as in the example above, wish to compare the observed mean with the value appropriate to a hypothesis which we wish to test; but equally or more often we wish to compare two experimental values and to test their agreement. In such cases we require the variance of the difference between two quantities whose variances are known; to find this we make use of the proposition that the variance of the difference of two *independent* variates is equal to the sum of their variances. Thus, if the standard deviations are σ_1, σ_2, the variances are σ_1^2 and σ_2^2; consequently the variance of the difference is $\sigma_1^2+\sigma_2^2$, and the standard error of the difference is $\sqrt{\sigma_1^2+\sigma_2^2}$.

Ex. 17. *Standard error of difference of means from large samples.*—In Table 2 is given the distribution in stature of a group of men, and also of a group of women; the means are 68·64 and 63·87 inches, giving a difference of 4·77 inches. The variance obtained for the men was 7·3861 square inches. Dividing this by 1164, we find the variance of the mean is ·006345. Similarly, the variance for the women is 6·7832, which divided by 1456 gives the variance of the mean of the women as ·004659. To find the variance of the difference between the means, we must add together these two contributions, and find in all ·011004; the standard error of the difference between the means is therefore ·1049 inches. The sex difference in stature may therefore be expressed as

$$4{\cdot}77 \pm {\cdot}105 \text{ inches.}$$

It is manifest that this difference is significant, the value found being over 45 times its standard error. In this case we can not only assert a significant difference, but place its value with some confidence at between 4½ and 5 inches. It should be noted that we have treated the two samples as *independent*, as though they had been given by different authorities; as a matter of fact, in many cases brothers and sisters appeared in the two groups; since brothers and sisters tend to be alike in stature, we have overestimated the probable error of our estimate of the sex difference. Whenever possible, advantage should be taken of such facts in designing experiments. In the common phrase, sisters provide a better "control" for their brothers than do unrelated women. (See *Design of Experiments*, Chap. III.) The sex difference could therefore be more accurately estimated from the comparison of each brother with his own sister. In the following example (Pearson and Lee's data), taken from a correlation table of stature of brothers and sisters, the material is nearly of this form; it differs from it in that in some instances the same individual has been compared with more than one sister, or brother.

Ex. 18. *Standard error of mean of differences.*—The following table gives the distribution of the excess in stature of a brother over his sister in 1401 pairs.

TABLE 26

Stature difference in inches	−5	−4	−3	−2	−1	0	1	2	3	4	5
Frequency	·25	1·5	1·25	4·5	11·25	27·5	71·75	122·75	171·75	209·75	220·5

Stature difference in inches	6	7	8	9	10	11	12	13	14	15	16	Total
Frequency	205·5	148·75	95·75	57	26	11·25	8·5	2·75	1		·75	1401

Treating this distribution as before, we obtain: mean = 4·895, estimate of variance = 6·5480, variance of mean = ·004674, standard error of mean = ·0684; showing that we may estimate the mean sex difference as $4\frac{3}{4}$ to 5 inches.

In the examples given above, which are typical of the use of the standard error applied to mean values, we have assumed that the variance of the population is determined with exactitude. It was pointed out by "Student" in 1908, with small samples, such as are of necessity usual in field and laboratory experiments, where the variance of the population can only be roughly estimated from the sample, that the errors of estimation are calculable, and that accurate allowance can be made for them.

If x (for example the mean of a sample) is a value normally distributed about zero, and σ is its true standard error, then the probability that x/σ exceeds any specified value may be obtained from the appropriate table of the normal distribution; but if we do not know σ, but in its place have s, an estimate of the value of σ, the distribution required will be that of x/s, and this is not normal. The true value has been divided by a factor, s/σ, which introduces an error. We have seen in the last chapter that the distribution in random samples of s^2/σ^2 is that of χ^2/n, when n is equal to the number of degrees of freedom, in the group (or groups) of which s^2 is the mean square deviation. Consequently, the distribution of s/σ is calculable, and although σ is unknown, we can use in its place the fiducial distribution of σ given s to find the probability of x exceeding a given multiple of s. Hence the true distribution of x/s is all that is required. The only modification required in these cases depends solely on the number n, representing the number of degrees of freedom available for the estimation of σ. The necessary distributions were given by " Student " in 1908 ; fuller tables have since been given by the same author, and at the end of this chapter (p. 174) we give the distributions in a similar form to that used for our Table of χ^2.

24. The Significance of the Mean of a Unique Sample

If $x_1, x_2, \ldots x_{n'}$ is a sample of n' values of a variate x, and if this sample constitutes the whole of the information available on the point in question, then we may test whether the mean of x differs significantly from zero by calculating the statistics

$$\bar{x} = \frac{1}{n'} S(x),$$

$$\frac{s^2}{n'} = \frac{1}{n'(n'-1)} S(x-\bar{x})^2,$$

$$t = \bar{x} \div \sqrt{\frac{s^2}{n'}},$$

$$n = n'-1.$$

Arithmetically, the calculations depend on the simple fact that the sum of squares of deviations from the mean may be obtained from the sum of squares of deviations from zero by deducting the product of the total and the mean. Thus,

$$S(x^2) = S(x-\bar{x})^2 + \bar{x}S(x).$$

This is a sub-division of the sum of squares of x into two portions, the first of which represents variation within the sample, while the second is due only to the deviation of the observed mean from zero. The first part has $n-1$ degrees of freedom, and the second part only 1. The more complex cases treated in later chapters are greatly simplified by setting out these two sub-divisions, of the sum of squares and of the degrees of freedom, in parallel columns and comparing the mean squares in each class. Thus in this case we have

	Degrees of Freedom.	Sum of Squares.	Mean Square.
Deviation . .	1	$\bar{x}S(x)$	t^2s^2
Within sample .	$n-1$	$S(x-\bar{x})^2$	s^2
Total . .	n	$S(x^2)$	

The mean squares are obtained in each class by dividing the sum of squares by the corresponding degrees of freedom. The observed ratio of the mean squares is, in this case, t^2. This useful form of arrangement is of much wider application than the algebraical expressions by which the calculations can be expressed, and is known as the Analysis of Variance.

The distribution of t for random samples of a normal population distributed about zero as mean is given in the Table of t for each value of n. The successive columns show, for each value of n, the values of t for which P, the probability of falling outside the range $\pm t$, takes the values ·9, . . ., ·01, at the head of the columns. Thus the last column shows that, when $n = 10$, just 1 per cent. of such random samples will give values of t exceeding $+3·169$, or less than $-3·169$. If it is proposed to consider the chance of exceeding the given values of t, in a positive (or negative) direction only, then the values of P should be halved. It will be seen from the table that for any degree of certainty we require higher values of t, the smaller the value of n. The bottom line of the table, corresponding to infinite values of n, gives the values of a normally distributed variate, in terms of its standard deviation, for the same values of P.

Ex. 19. *Significance of mean of a small sample.*— The following figures (Cushny and Peebles' data), which I quote from "Student's" paper, show the result of an experiment with ten patients on the effect of two supposedly soporific drugs, A and B, in producing sleep.

TABLE 27

ADDITIONAL HOURS OF SLEEP GAINED BY THE USE OF TWO TESTED DRUGS.

Patient.	A.	B.	Difference (B—A).
1	+0·7	+1·9	+1·2
2	−1·6	+0·8	+2·4
3	−0·2	+1·1	+1·3
4	−1·2	+0·1	+1·3
5	−0·1	−0·1	0·0
6	+3·4	+4·4	+1·0
7	+3·7	+5·5	+1·8
8	+0·8	+1·6	+0·8
9	0·0	+4·6	+4·6
10	+2·0	+3·4	+1·4
Mean ($\bar{x}$)	+·75	+2·33	+1·58

The last column gives a controlled comparison of the efficacy of the two drugs as soporifics, for the same patients were used to test each; from the series of differences we find

$$\bar{x} = +1{\cdot}58,$$

$$\frac{s^2}{10} = {\cdot}1513.$$

$$s/\sqrt{10} = {\cdot}3890,$$

$$t = 4{\cdot}06.$$

For $n = 9$, only one value in a hundred will exceed 3·250 by chance, so that the difference between the results is clearly significant. By the methods of the previous chapters we should, in this case, have been led to the same conclusion with almost equal certainty; for if the two drugs had been equally effective, positive and negative signs would occur in the last column with equal frequency. Of the 9 values other than zero, however, all are positive, and it appears from the binomial distribution,

$$(\tfrac{1}{2}+\tfrac{1}{2})^9,$$

that all will be of the same sign, by chance, only twice in 512 trials. The method of the present chapter differs from that in taking account of the actual values and not merely of their signs, and is consequently the more sensitive method when the actual values are available.

24·1. Comparison of Two Means

In experimental work it is even more frequently necessary to test whether two samples differ significantly in their means, or whether they may be regarded as belonging to the same population. In the latter case any difference in treatment which they may have received will have shown no significant effect.

If $x_1, x_2, \ldots, x_{n_1+1}$ and $x'_1, x'_2, \ldots, x'_{n_2+1}$ be two samples, the significance of the difference between their means may be tested by calculating the following statistics:

$$\bar{x} = \frac{1}{n_1+1} S(x), \quad \bar{x}' = \frac{1}{n_2+1} S(x'),$$

$$s^2 = \frac{1}{n_1+n_2} \left\{ S(x-\bar{x})^2 + S(x'-\bar{x}')^2 \right\}$$

$$t = \frac{\bar{x}-\bar{x}'}{s} \sqrt{\frac{(n_1+1)(n_2+1)}{n_1+n_2+2}},$$

$$n = n_1+n_2.$$

The means are calculated as usual; the standard deviation is estimated by pooling the sums of squares from the two samples and dividing by the total number of the degrees of freedom contributed by them; if σ were the true standard deviation, the variance of the first mean would be $\sigma^2/(n_1+1)$, of the second mean $\sigma^2/(n_2+1)$, and therefore that of the difference would be $\sigma^2\{1/(n_1+1)+1/(n_2+1)\}$; t is therefore found by dividing $\bar{x}-\bar{x}'$ by its standard error as estimated, and the error of the estimation is allowed for by entering the table with n equal to the number of degrees of freedom available for estimating s; that is $n=n_1+n_2$. It is thus possible to extend "Student's" treatment of the error of a mean to the comparison of the means of two samples.

The method of building the corresponding analysis of variance for this case should be studied. If we put down the analyses for the two samples separately and add their items, we have

	Degrees of Freedom.	Sum of Squares.
Deviations .	2	$\bar{x}S(x)+\bar{x}'S(x')$
Within samples .	n_1+n_2	$S(x-\bar{x})^2+S(x'-\bar{x}')^2$
Total .	n_1+n_2+2	$S(x^2)+S(x'^2)$

But if we had treated all the observations as a single sample with mean m, we should have

	Degrees of Freedom.	Sum of Squares.
Deviations .	1	$mS(x)+mS(x')$
Within samples .	n_1+n_2+1	$S(x-m)^2+S(x'-m)^2$
Total .	n_1+n_2+2	$S(x^2)+S(x'^2)$

These are two different analyses of the same total, and since all comparisons within the separate samples are also comparisons within the grand sample made by throwing them together, we may subtract one from the other, obtaining

	Degrees of Freedom.	Sum of Squares.
Difference .	1	$\bar{x}S(x)+\bar{x}'S(x')-mS(x)-mS(x')$
Within samples .	n_1+n_2	$S(x-\bar{x})^2+S(x'-\bar{x}')^2$
Total .	n_1+n_2+1	$S(x^2)+S(x'^2)-mS(x)-mS(x')$

Each item is now easily calculated. The student will do well to verify that t^2 obtained from the procedure first set out is in fact the ratio of the mean squares obtained from the analysis of variance.

It may be noted in connexion with this method, and with later developments, which also involve a pooled estimate of the variance, that a difference in variance between the populations from which the samples are drawn will tend sometimes to enhance the value of t obtained. The test, therefore, is decisive, if the value of t is significant, in showing that the samples could not have been drawn from the same population; but it might conceivably be claimed that the difference indicated lay in the variances and not in the means. The theoretical possibility, that a significant value of t should be produced by a difference between the variances only, seems to be unimportant in the application of the method to experimental data; as a supplementary test, however, the significance of the difference between the variances may always be tested directly by the method of Section 41.

It has been repeatedly stated, perhaps through a

misreading of the last paragraph, that our method involves the " assumption " that the two variances are equal. This is an incorrect form of statement; the equality of the variances is a necessary part of the hypothesis to be tested, namely that the two samples are drawn from the same normal population. The validity of the t-test, as a test of this hypothesis, is therefore absolute, and requires no assumption whatever. It would, of course, be legitimate to make a different test of significance appropriate to the question: Might these samples have been drawn from different normal populations having the same mean? This problem has, in fact, been solved, but in relation to the real situations arising in biological research, the question it answers appears to be somewhat academic. Numerical tables of this test were first calculated by P. V. Sukhatmé, and are of use, when there is reason to suspect unequal variances, in removing any doubt from the interpretation of the test of significance. (*Statistical Tables*, V1 and V2.)

Ex. 20 *Significance of difference of means of small samples.*—Let us suppose that the figures of Table 27 had been obtained using different patients for the two drugs; the experiment would have been less well controlled, and we should expect to obtain less certain results from the same number of observations, for it is *a priori* probable, and the above figures suggest, that personal variations in response to the drugs will be to some extent similar.

Taking, then, the figures to represent two different sets of patients, we have

$$\begin{aligned} \bar{x}-\bar{x}' &= +1{\cdot}58, \\ s^2\left(\tfrac{1}{10}+\tfrac{1}{10}\right) &= {\cdot}7210, \\ t &= +1{\cdot}861, \\ n &= 18. \end{aligned}$$

The value of P is, therefore, between ·1 and ·05, and cannot be regarded as significant. This example shows clearly the value of design in small scale experiments, and that the efficacy of such design is capable of statistical measurement.

The use of "Student's" distribution enables us to appreciate the value of observing a sufficient number of parallel cases; their value lies, not only in the fact that the standard error of a mean decreases inversely as the square root of the number of parallels, but in the fact that the accuracy of our estimate of the standard error increases simultaneously. The need for duplicate experiments is sufficiently widely realised; it is not so widely understood that in some cases, when it is desired to place a high degree of confidence (say P = ·01) on the results, triplicate experiments will enable us to detect differences as small as one-seventh of those which, with a duplicate experiment, would justify the same degree of confidence.

The confidence to be placed in a result depends not only on the magnitude of the mean value obtained, but equally on the agreement between parallel experiments. Thus, if in an agricultural experiment a first trial shows an apparent advantage of 8 bushels to the acre, and a duplicate experiment shows an advantage of 9 bushels, we have $n = 1$, $t = 17$, and the results would justify some confidence that a real effect had been observed; but if the second experiment had shown an apparent advantage of 18 bushels, although the mean is now higher, we should place not more but less confidence in the conclusion that the treatment was beneficial, for t has fallen to 2·6, a value which for $n = 1$ is often exceeded by chance. The apparent paradox may be explained by pointing out that the difference of 10 bushels between the experiments indicates the existence of uncontrolled circumstances so influential that in both cases the apparent benefit may be due to chance, whereas in the former case the relatively close agreement of the results suggests that the uncontrolled factors were not so very influential. Much of the advantage of further replication lies in the fact that when few tests are made, and these only duplicated, our estimate of the importance of the uncontrolled factors is extremely hazardous.

In cases in which each observation of one series corresponds in some respects to a particular observation of the second series, it is always legitimate to take the differences and test them, as in Ex. 19, as a single sample; but it is not always desirable to do so. A more precise comparison is obtainable by this method only if the corresponding values of the two series are positively correlated, and only if they are correlated to a sufficient extent to counterbalance the loss of precision due to basing our estimate of variance upon fewer degrees of freedom. An example will make this plain.

Ex. 21. *Significance of change in bacterial numbers.* — The following table shows the mean number of bacterial colonies per plate obtained by

TABLE 28

Method.	4 P.M.	8 P.M.	Difference.
A	29·75	39·20	+9·45
B	27·50	40·60	+13·10
C	30·25	36·20	+5·95
D	27·80	42·40	+14·60
Mean	28·825	39·60	+10·775

four slightly different methods from soil samples taken at 4 P.M. and 8 P.M. respectively (H. G. Thornton's data).

From the series of differences we have $\bar{x} = +10{\cdot}775$, $\frac{1}{4}s^2 = 3{\cdot}756$, $t = 5{\cdot}560$, $n = 3$, whence the table shows that P is between ·01 and ·02. If, on the contrary, we use the method of Ex. 20, and treat the two separate series, we find $\bar{x}-\bar{x}' = +10{\cdot}775$, $\frac{1}{2}s^2 = 2{\cdot}188$, $t = 7{\cdot}285$, $n = 6$; this is not only a larger value of n but a larger value of t, which is now far beyond the range of the table, showing that P is extremely small. In this case the differential effects of the different methods are either negligible, or have acted quite differently in the two series, so that precision was lost in comparing each value with its counterpart in the other series. In cases like this it sometimes occurs that one method shows no significant difference, while the other brings it out; if either method indicates a definitely significant difference, its testimony cannot be ignored, even if the other method fails to show the effect. When no correspondence exists between the members of one series and those of the other, the second method only is available.

25. Regression Coefficients

The methods of this chapter are applicable not only to mean values, in the restricted sense of the word, but to the very wide class of statistics known as regression coefficients. The idea of regression used usually to be introduced in connexion with the theory correlation, but it is in reality a more general, and a simpler idea; moreover, the regression coefficients are of interest and scientific importance in many classes of data where the correlation coefficient, if used at all, is an artificial concept of no real utility. The following qualitative discussion is intended to familiarise the student with the concept of regression, and to prepare the way for the accurate treatment of numerical examples.

It is a commonplace that the height of a child depends on his age, although, knowing his age, we cannot accurately calculate his height. At each age the heights are scattered over a considerable range in a frequency distribution characteristic of that age; any feature of this distribution, such as the mean, will be a continuous function of age. The function which represents the mean height at any age is termed the regression function of height on age; it is represented graphically by a regression curve, or regression line. In relation to such a regression line *age* is termed the **independent** variate, and *height* the **dependent** variate.

The two variates bear very different relations to the regression line. If errors occur in the heights, this will not influence the regression of height on age, provided that at all ages positive and negative errors are equally frequent, so that they balance in the averages. On the contrary, errors in age will in general alter the regression of height on age, so that from a record with ages subject to error, or classified in broad age groups, we should not obtain the true physical relationship between mean height and age A second difference should also be noted: the regression function does not depend on the frequency distribution of the independent variate, so that a true regression line may be obtained even when the age groups are arbitrarily selected, as when an investigation deals with children of "school age." On the other hand, a selection of the dependent variate may change the regression line altogether.

It is clear from these two instances that the regression of height on age is quite different from the regression of age on height; and that one may have a definite physical meaning in cases in which the other has only the conventional meaning given to it by mathematical definition. In certain cases both regressions are of equal standing; thus, if we express in terms of the height of the father the average adult height of sons of fathers of a given height, observation shows that each additional inch of the fathers' height corresponds to about half an inch in the mean height of the sons. Equally, if we take the mean height of the fathers of sons of a given height, we find that each additional inch of the sons' height corresponds to half an inch in the mean height of the fathers. No selection has been exercised in the heights either of fathers or of sons; each variate is distributed normally, and the aggregate of pairs of values forms a normal correlation surface. Both regression lines are straight, and it is consequently possible to express the facts of regression in the simple rules stated above.

When the regression line with which we are concerned is straight, or, in other words, when the regression function is linear, the specification of regression is much simplified, for in addition to the general means we have only to state the ratio which the increment of the mean of the dependent variate bears to the corresponding increment of the independent variate. Such ratios are termed regression coefficients. The regression function takes the form

$$Y = a + b(x - \bar{x}),$$

where b is the regression coefficient of y on x, and Y is the predicted value of y for each value of x. The physical dimensions of the regression coefficient depend on those of the variates; thus, over an age range in which growth is uniform we might express the regression of height on age in inches per annum, in fact as an average growth rate, while the regression of father's height on son's height is half an inch per inch, or simply $\frac{1}{2}$. Regression coefficients may, of course, be positive or negative.

Curved regression lines are of common occurrence; in such cases we may have to use such a regression function as

$$Y = a+bx+cx^2+dx^3,$$

in which all four coefficients of the regression function may, by an extended use of the term, be called regression coefficients. More elaborate functions of x may be used, but their practical employment offers difficulties in cases where we lack theoretical guidance in choosing the form of the regression function, and at present the simple power series (or polynomial in x) is alone in frequent use. By far the most important case in statistical practice is the straight regression line.

26. Sampling Errors of Regression Coefficients

The linear regression formula contains two parameters which are to be estimated from the data. If we use the form

$$Y = a+b(x-\bar{x})$$

then the value chosen for a will be simply the mean, $\bar{y}$, of the observed values of the dependent variate. This ensures that the sum of the residuals $y-Y$ shall be zero, for the sum of the values of $b(x-\bar{x})$ must be zero, whatever may be the value of b.

The value given to b, our estimate of the regression coefficient of y on x, is obtained from the sum of the products of x and y. Just as with a single variate we estimate the variance from the sum of squares, first by deducting $n\bar{x}^2$, so as to obtain the sum of the squares of deviations from the mean, in accordance with the formula,

$$S\{(x-\bar{x})^2\} = S(x^2)-n\bar{x}^2,$$

and then dividing by $(n-1)$ to obtain an estimate of the variance; so with any two variates x and y, we may obtain the sum of the products of deviations from the means by deducting $n\bar{x}\bar{y}$; for

$$S\{(x-\bar{x})(y-\bar{y})\} = S(xy)-n\bar{x}\bar{y}.$$

The mean product of two variates, thus measured from their means, is termed their **covariance**, and, just as in the case of the variance of a single variate, we estimate its value by dividing the sum of products by $n-1$. The sum of products from which the covariance is estimated may evidently be written equally in the forms

$$S\{y(x-\bar{x})\}, \qquad S\{x(y-\bar{y})\}.$$

Our estimate of b is simply the ratio of the covariance of the two variates, to the variance of the independent variate; or, since we may ignore the factor $(n-1)$ which appears in both terms of the ratio, our method of estimation may be expressed by the formula

$$b=\frac{S\{y(x-\bar{x})\}}{S\{(x-\bar{x})^2\}}.$$

We thus have estimates calculable from the observations, of the two parameters, needed to specify the straight line. The true regression formula, which we should obtain from an infinity of observations, may be represented by

$$Y = \alpha + \beta(x - \bar{x})$$

and the differences $a-\alpha$, $b-\beta$, are the errors of random sampling of our statistics.

To ascertain the magnitude of the sampling errors to which they are subject consider a population of samples having the same values for x. The variations from sample to sample in our statistics will be due only to the fact that for a given value of x the values of y in the population sampled are not all equal. If σ^2 represent the variance of y for a given value of x, then clearly the error of a is merely the mean of n' independent errors each having a variance σ^2, so that the variance of a is σ^2/n'. The second statistic b is also a linear function of the values, y, and its sampling variance may be obtained by an extension of the same reasoning. In this case each deviation of y from the true regression formula is multiplied by $x-\bar{x}$; the variance of the product is therefore $\sigma^2(x-\bar{x})^2$, and that of the sum of the products, which is the numerator of the expression for b, must be

$$\sigma^2 S(x-\bar{x})^2.$$

To find b we divide this numerator by $S\{(x-\bar{x})^2\}$ so that the variance of b is found by dividing the variance of the numerator by $S^2\{(x-\bar{x})^2\}$ which gives us the expression

$$\frac{\sigma^2}{S(x-\bar{x})^2}$$

for the sampling variance of the statistic b.

It will be noticed that the value stated for the sampling variance of a is not merely the sampling variance of our estimate of the mean of y, but of our estimate of the mean of y for a given value of x, this value being chosen at, or near to, the mean of our sample, and supposed invariable from sample to sample. The distinction, which at first sight appears somewhat subtle, is worth bearing in mind. From a set of measurements of school children we may make estimates of the mean stature at age ten, and of the mean stature of the school, and these estimates will be equal if the mean age of the school children is exactly ten. Nevertheless, the former will usually be the more accurate estimate, for it eliminates the variation in mean school age, which will doubtless contribute somewhat to the variation in mean school stature.

In order to test the significance of the difference between b, and any hypothetical value, β, to which it is to be compared, we must estimate the value of σ^2; the best estimate for the purpose is

$$s^2 = \frac{1}{n'-2} S(y-Y)^2,$$

found by summing the squares of the deviations of y from its calculated value Y, and dividing by $(n'-2)$. The reason the divisor is $(n'-2)$ is that from the n' values of y two statistics have already been calculated which enter into the formula for Y, consequently the group of differences, $y-Y$, represent in reality only $n'-2$ degrees of freedom.

When n' is small, the estimate of s^2 obtained above is somewhat uncertain, and in comparing the difference $b-\beta$ with its standard error, in order to test its significance we shall have to use " Student's " method, with $n = n'-2$. When n' is large the t-distribution tends to normality. The value of t with which the table must be entered is found by dividing $(b-\beta)$ by its standard error as estimated, and is therefore,

$$t=\frac{(b-\beta)\sqrt{S(x-\bar{x})^2}}{s}.$$

Similarly, to test the significance of the difference between a and any hypothetical value α, the table is entered with

$$t=\frac{(a-\alpha)\sqrt{n'}}{s}, \quad n=n'-2;$$

this test for the significance of a will be more sensitive than that ignoring the regression, if the variation in y is to any considerable extent expressible in terms of that of x, for the value of s obtained from the regression line will then be smaller than that obtained from the original group of observations. On the other hand, 1 degree of freedom is always lost, so that if b is small, no greater precision is obtained.

In general, when the mean value of the dependent variate is estimated for values other than the mean of the independent variate, we need, as was shown by Working and Hotelling, to know the sampling variance of the estimate

$$Y=a+b(x-\bar{x}).$$

Since the sampling errors of a and b are independent, this is given by

$$V(a)+(x-\bar{x})^2V(b),$$

where $V(a)$ and $V(b)$ stand for the sampling variances of our estimates a and b.

We have, therefore,

$$V(Y)=\sigma^2\left(\frac{1}{n'}+\frac{(x-\bar{x})^2}{S(x-\bar{x})^2}\right)$$

where σ^2 is the true variance of y for given x. For values of x near the mean, that is, where $(x-\bar{x})$ is small, this variance will not greatly exceed that at the mean of the observed sample, but for values more remote from the centre of our experience the precision of the estimate is naturally lower, and the second component of error, due to the estimation of b, becomes predominant.

Ex. 22. *Effect of nitrogenous fertilisers in maintaining yield.*—The yields of dressed grain in bushels per acre shown in Table 29 were obtained from two plots on Broadbalk wheat field during thirty years; the only difference in manurial treatment was that " 9 *a* " received nitrate of soda, while " 7 *b* " received an equivalent quantity of nitrogen as sulphate of ammonia. In the course of the experiment plot " 9 *a* " appears to be gaining in yield on plot " 7 *b*." Is this apparent gain significant?

A great part of the variation in yield from year to year is evidently similar in the two plots; in consequence, the series of differences will give the clearer result. In one respect these data are especially simple, for the thirty values of the independent variate form a series with equal intervals between the successive values, with only one value of the dependent variate corresponding to each. In such cases the work is simplified by using the formula

$$S(x-\bar{x})^2 = \tfrac{1}{12}n'(n'^2-1),$$

where n' is the number of terms, or 30 in this case.

To evaluate b it is necessary to calculate the sum of products

$$S\{y(x-\bar{x})\};$$

which bears the same relation to the covariance of two

variates as does the sum of squares to the variance of a single variate; this may be done in several ways.

TABLE 29

Harvest Year.	9 *a*.	7 *b*.	9 *a*—7 *b*.	
1855	29·62	33·00	−3·38	
1856	32·38	36·91	−4·53	
1857	43·75	44·84	−1·09	
1858	37·56	38·94	−1·38	
1859	30·00	34·66	−4·66	
1860	32·62	27·72	+4·90	$S(x-\bar{x})^2 = \frac{n'(n'^2-1)}{12} = 2247{\cdot}5$
1861	33·75	34·94	−1·19	
1862	43·44	35·88	+7·56	
1863	55·56	53·66	+1·90	$b = {\cdot}26679$
1864	51·06	45·78	+5·28	
1865	44·06	40·22	+3·84	$S(y-\bar{y})^2 = 1020{\cdot}56$
1866	32·50	29·91	+2·59	$b^2S(x-\bar{x})^2 = 159{\cdot}97$
1867	29·13	22·16	+6·97	
1868	47·81	39·19	+8·62	$S(y-Y)^2 = 860{\cdot}59$
1869	39·00	28·25	+10·75	
1870	45·50	41·37	+4·13	$s^2 = 30{\cdot}74$
1871	34·44	22·31	+12·13	
1872	40·69	29·06	+11·63	$s^2/S(x-\bar{x})^2 = {\cdot}013675$
1873	35·81	22·75	+13·06	
1874	38·19	39·56	−1·37	$= ({\cdot}11694)^2$
1875	30·50	26·63	+3·87	
1876	33·31	25·50	+7·81	$t = 2{\cdot}2814$
1877	40·12	19·12	+21·00	
1878	37·19	32·19	+5·00	$n = 28$
1879	21·94	17·25	+4·69	
1880	34·06	34·31	−·25	
1881	35·44	26·13	+9·31	
1882	31·81	34·75	−2·94	
1883	43·38	36·31	+7·07	
1884	40·44	37·75	+2·69	
Mean	37·50	33·03	+4·47	

We may multiply the successive values of y by −29, −27, . . . +27, +29, add, and divide by 2. This is the direct method suggested by the formula. The same result is obtained by multiplying 1, 2, . . ., 30 and subtracting $15\frac{1}{2}\left(=\frac{n'+1}{2}\right)$ times the sum of values of y; the latter method may be conveniently carried out by successive addition. Starting from the bottom of the column, the successive sums 2·69, 9·76, 6·82, . . . are written down, each being found by adding a new value of y to the total already accumulated; the sum of the new column, less $15\frac{1}{2}$ times the sum of the previous column, will be the value required. In this case we find the value 599·615, and dividing by 2247·5, the value of b is found to be ·26679. The yield of plot "9 *a*" thus appears to have gained on that of "7 *b*" at a rate somewhat over a quarter of a bushel per acre per annum.

To estimate the standard error of b, we require the value of the sum of squares of the deviations, or residuals, from the regression formula,

$$S(y-Y)^2;$$

knowing the value of b, it is easy to calculate the thirty values of Y from the formula

$$Y=\bar{y}+(x-\bar{x})b;$$

for the first value, $x-\bar{x}=-14{\cdot}5$, and the remaining values of Y may be found in succession by adding b each time. By subtracting each value of Y from the corresponding y, squaring, and adding, the required quantity may be calculated directly. This method is laborious, and it is preferable in practice to utilise the algebraical fact that

$$\begin{aligned} S(y-Y)^2 &= S(y-\bar{y})^2-b^2S(x-\bar{x})^2 \\ &= S(y^2)-n'\bar{y}^2-b^2S(x-\bar{x})^2. \end{aligned}$$

The work then consists in squaring the values of y and adding, then subtracting the two quantities, which can be directly calculated from the mean value of y and the value of b. In using this shortened method it should be noted that small errors in $\bar{y}$ and b may introduce considerable errors in the result, so that it is necessary to be sure that these are calculated accurately to as many significant figures as are needed in the quantities to be subtracted. Errors of arithmetic which would have little effect in the first method may altogether vitiate the results if the second method is used. The subsequent work in calculating the standard error of b may best be followed in the scheme given beside the table of data; the estimated standard error is ·1169, so that in testing the hypothesis that $\beta = 0$, that is that plot "9 *a*" has not been gaining on plot "7 *b*," we divide b by this quantity and find $t = 2{\cdot}2814$. Since s was found from 28 degrees of freedom $n = 28$, and the result of t shows that P is between ·02 and ·05.

The result must be judged significant, though barely so; in view of the data we cannot ignore the possibility that on this field, and in conjunction with the other manures used, nitrate of soda has conserved the fertility better than sulphate of ammonia; the data do not, however, demonstrate this point beyond possibility of doubt.

The standard error of $\bar{y}$, calculated from these data, is 1·012, so that there can be no doubt that the difference in mean yields is significant; if we had tested the significance of the mean, without regard to the order of the values, that is calculating s^2 by dividing 1020·56 by 29, the standard error would have been 1·083. The value of b was therefore high enough to have reduced the standard error. This suggests the possibility that if we had fitted a more complex regression line to the data the probable errors would be further reduced to an extent which would put the significance of b beyond doubt. We shall deal later with the fitting of curved regression lines to this type of data.

26·1. The Comparison of Regression Coefficients

Just as the method of comparison of means is applicable when the samples are of different sizes, if we obtain an estimate of the error by combining the sums of squares derived from the two different samples, so we may compare regression coefficients when the series of values of the independent variate are not identical; or if they are identical we can ignore the fact in comparing the regression coefficients.

Ex. 23. *Comparison of relative growth rate of two cultures of an alga.*—Table 30 shows the logarithm (to the base 10) of the volumes occupied by algal cells on successive days, in parallel cultures, each taken over a period during which the relative growth rate was approximately constant. In culture A nine values are available, and in culture B eight (Dr M. Bristol-Roach's data).

The method of finding $Sy(x-\bar{x})$ by summation is shown in the second pair of columns: the original values are added up from the bottom, giving successive totals from 6·087 to 43·426; the final value should, of course, tally with the total below the original values. From the sum of the column of totals is subtracted the sum of the original values multiplied by 5 for A and by $4\frac{1}{2}$ for B. The differences are $Sy(x-\bar{x})$; these must be divided by the respective values of $S(x-\bar{x})^2$, namely, 60 and 42, to give the values of b, measuring the relative growth rates of the two cultures. To test if the difference is significant we calculate in the two cases $S(y^2)$, and subtract successively the product of the mean with the total, and the product of b with $Sy(x-\bar{x})$; this process leaves the two values of $S(y-Y)^2$, which are added as shown in the table, and

TABLE 30

	Log Values.		Summation Values.			
	A.	B	A.	B.		
	3·592	3·538	43·426	38·358	$S(y-Y)^2$, A	·05089
	3·823	3·828	39·834	34·820	,, B	·07563
	4·174	4·349	36·011	30·992		
	4·534	4·833	31·837	26·643	ns^2	·12652
	4·956	4·911	27·303	21·810	s^2	·009732
	5·163	5·297	22·347	16·899	$s^2/60$	·0001622
	5·495	5·566	17·184	11·602	$s^2/42$	·0002317
	5·602	6·036	11·689	6·036		
	6·087	...	6·087	...		·0003939
Total	43·426	38·358	235·718	187·160	Standard error	·01985
Mean	4·8251	4·7947	217·130	172·611	$b'-b$	·0366
			$Sy(x-\bar{x})$ 18·588	14·549	t	1·844
			b ·3098	·3464	n	13

the sum divided by n, to give s^2. The value of n is found by adding the 7 degrees of freedom from series A to the 6 degrees from series B, and is therefore 13. Estimates of the variance of the two regression coefficients are obtained by dividing s^2 by 60 and 42, and that of the variance of their difference is the sum of these. Taking the square root we find the standard error to be ·01985, and $t = {}^{-}1{\cdot}844$. The difference between the regression coefficients, though relatively large, cannot be regarded as significant. There is not sufficient evidence to assert that culture B was growing more rapidly than culture A.

26·2. The Ratio of Means and Regression Coefficients

Ex. 23·1. When pairs of observations are available, such as those shown in Table 27 (page 121), showing as these do a decidedly significant difference between the means, we have gained some idea of the magnitude of the true difference between the means, which we may expect to lie between limits given by the observed value plus or minus an appropriate multiple of its standard error. This multiple specifies the level of significance chosen and, in a sense, the probability that the true difference should lie between the limits assigned. Thus this probability is 95 per cent. if we choose as the appropriate multiplier the 5 per cent. value of t for the number of degrees of freedom available, or 2·262 for the 9 degrees of freedom in that example.

It may well be that the difference between the average effects of two treatments is of less intrinsic interest than the ratio of their effects. This will be so if the effect of each drug is proportional to the quantity used, but in other cases also the ratio of the effects may be constant, so that at any dosage the ratio of the effects provides an estimate of the potency ratio; while the difference between the average effects of a chosen dose will depend greatly on the experimental material used, on the conditions of the experiment, and on the actual amount of the dose. It is useful, therefore, to be able to assign similar limits for a presumed constant ratio between the effects in place of those for a presumed constant difference.

Now, if x and y are the observed effects of treatments A and B in any particular case, and α stands for the potency of A relative to that of B (in the simplest case, the weight of B equivalent to unit weight of A), then we may consider the quantity

$$z = x - \alpha y$$

as an observed value, variations of which from case to case may be estimated from the experimental data. The arithmetic required is nearly the same as that of Example 20, namely the means and sums of squares of the variates x and y, with the addition of their sum of products.

Thus for x we have

$S(x^2)$	34·43
$\bar{x}S(x)$	5·625
$S(x-\bar{x})^2$	28·805 ;

for y

$S(y^2)$	90·37
$\bar{y}S(y)$	54·289
$S(y-\bar{y})^2$	36·081 ;

and, for the product,

$S(xy)$	43·11
$\bar{x}S(y) = \bar{y}S(x)$	17·475
$S(x-\bar{x})(y-\bar{y})$	25·635.

Then, leaving α still undetermined, it is clear that

$$S(z) = 7{\cdot}5 - 23{\cdot}3\alpha$$

and

$$S(z-\bar{z})^2 = 28{\cdot}805 - 2\alpha(25{\cdot}635) + \alpha^2(36{\cdot}081).$$

Moreover, the data will show a significant deviation from the value of α adopted if

$$\frac{9}{10} S^2(z) > t^2 S(z-\bar{z})^2.$$

Taking, for the 5 per cent. point,

$$t = 2{\cdot}262, \qquad t^2 = 5{\cdot}116644,$$

then the equation for α becomes

$$303{\cdot}9874\alpha^2 - 26{\cdot}1098(2\alpha) - 96{\cdot}7599 = 0,$$

which is satisfied by the values

$$\alpha = +{\cdot}6566 \text{ and } -{\cdot}4848.$$

It is thus clear that no estimate of the relative potency of drug A compared with drug B exceeding ·6566, or rather less than two-thirds, is compatible with the data presented. The fact that the other value is negative shows that these data do not establish any positive soporific effect at all for drug A at the significance level used. It might, in fact, have exerted an antisoporific effect nearly one-half as potent as the soporific effect of drug B before the observed difference in efficacy between the two drugs would be significantly exceeded.

A method very similar in principle may be used to find limits for the value of the independent variate at which the regression function attains a given value, or the value at which two regression lines intersect.

If α_1 and α_2 are the true means and β_1, β_2 the true coefficients of regression of two dependent variates, then the point of intersection is the value of the unknown, X, satisfying the condition

$$\alpha_1 + (X - \bar{x}_1)\beta_1 = \alpha_2 + (X - \bar{x}_2)\beta_2.$$

Now the sampling variance of

$$a_1 + (X - \bar{x}_1)b_1 - a_2 - (X - \bar{x}_2)b_2$$

is

$$s^2\left\{\frac{1}{N_1} + \frac{1}{N_2} + \frac{(X - \bar{x}_1)^2}{S_1} + \frac{(X - \bar{x}_2)^2}{S_2}\right\},$$

where S_1 and S_2 are the sums of squares of deviations of the independent variate for the two samples, and s^2 is the mean square deviation of the dependent variates from the fitted regression lines. Hence if we equate

$$\{a_1-a_2-b_1\bar{x}_1+b_2\bar{x}_2+X(b_1-b_2)\}^2$$

to

$$s^2t^2\left\{\frac{1}{N_1}+\frac{1}{N_2}+\frac{\bar{x}_1^2}{S_1}+\frac{\bar{x}_2^2}{S_2}-2X\left(\frac{\bar{x}_1}{S_1}+\frac{\bar{x}_2}{S_2}\right)+X^2\left(\frac{1}{S_1}+\frac{1}{S_2}\right)\right\},$$

we shall have a quadratic equation for X of which the roots are the limiting values possible at the level of significance represented by the value t.

Ex. 23·2. *The age at which girls become taller than boys.*—Karn (1934) gives values derived from measurements of 4007 school children in the borough of Croydon.

	Number N	Mean age $\bar{x}$ (years)	Mean Height a (inches)	Regression b (ins./yr.)	$S(x-\bar{x})^2$ (yr.)^2
Boys	1946	12·2016	56·004	1·60	337·894
Girls	2061	12·1300	56·550	2·45	382·835

The mean square deviation from the fitted regression lines, s^2, is

$$8{\cdot}17915,$$

based on 3991 degrees of freedom. For limits at the 5 per cent. point we may therefore take

$$t = 1{\cdot}96$$

and

$$s^2t^2 = 31{\cdot}421.$$

From the remaining data we have, taking x as the excess of the age over 12 years,

$a_2-a_1-b_2\bar{x}_2+b_1\bar{x}_1$	$\cdot 55016$
$(b_2-b_1)X$	$\cdot 85X$
$\frac{1}{N_1}+\frac{1}{N_2}+\frac{\bar{x}_1^2}{S_1}+\frac{\bar{x}_2^2}{S_2}$	$\cdot 001163582$
$-\left(\frac{\bar{x}_1}{S_1}+\frac{\bar{x}_2}{S_2}\right)2X$	$-\cdot 000936405(2X)$
$\left(\frac{1}{S_1}+\frac{1}{S_2}\right)X^2$	$\cdot 00557160(X^2)$.

The quadratic equation for X is therefore

$$(\cdot 547435)X^2+(\cdot 497064)2X+\cdot 266122=0,$$

of which the roots are

$$-1\cdot 490, \quad -\cdot 326$$

corresponding with ages

10·510 and 11·674 years.

The estimate derived from the means and regressions given is 11·353 years, much nearer to the upper than to the lower limit. The children were nearly all measured in their 11th and 12th years, and the precision of the comparison falls considerably at the lower ages, with the consequence that the lower limit differs widely from the direct estimate. With this number of children a much higher accuracy would have been obtained had they been measured a year earlier, or over a wider age-range.

27. The Fitting of Curved Regression Lines

But slight use has been made of the theory of the fitting of curved regression lines, save in the limited but most important case when the variability of the dependent variate is the same for all values of the independent variate, and is normal for each such value. When this is the case a technique has been fully worked out for fitting by successive stages any line of the form

$$Y = a+bx+cx^2+dx^3+ \dots;$$

we shall give details of the case where the successive values of x are at equal intervals. The more general case, when varying numbers of observations occur at different values of x, is best treated by the method of Section 29·2; when the intervals also are unequal, the general method of Section 29 is available, using the powers of x as independent variates.

As it stands the form given would be inconvenient in practice, in that the fitting could not be carried through in successive stages. What is required is to obtain successively the mean of y, an equation linear in x, an equation quadratic in x, and so on, each equation being obtained from the last by adding a new term; this being calculated by carrying a single process of computation through a new stage. In order to do this we take

$$Y = A+B\xi_1+C\xi_2+D\xi_3+ \dots,$$

where ξ_1, ξ_2, ξ_3 shall be functions of x of the 1st, 2nd, and 3rd degrees, out of which the regression formula may be built.

These functions of x may be regarded as the coefficients of the corresponding observations in certain comparisons, or components of variation among them. Thus ξ_1 is always chosen to be $x-\bar{x}$; *e.g.* if there were 7 observations the values of ξ_1 would be -3, -2, -1, 0, 1, 2, 3; so that the comparison corresponding with the 1st degree in x is

(i) $$-3y_1-2y_2-y_3+0y_4+y_5+2y_6+3y_7.$$

Again, ξ_2 might be taken as the coefficients in the comparison

(ii) $$5y_1+0y_2-3y_3-4y_4-3y_5+0y_6+5y_7.$$

Here the coefficients are expressible as a quadratic in x, namely

$$(x-\bar{x})^2-4=\xi_1^2-4=\xi_2,$$

and it is to be noticed that the sum of the coefficients, and the sum of their products with those of ξ_1, are both zero.

For the 3rd, 4th and 5th degrees we may use in turn

(iii) $-y_1+y_2+y_3-y_5-y_6+y_7$ $\xi_1(\xi_1^2-7)/6$

(iv) $3y_1-7y_2+y_3+6y_4+y_5-7y_6+3y_7$ $(7\xi_1^4-67\xi_1^2+72)/12$

(v) $-y_1+4y_2-5y_3+5y_5-4y_6+y_7$; $(21\xi_1^5-245\xi_1^3+524\xi_1)/60$.

Note that the sum of the coefficients is zero in each case, so that each expression is properly a comparison among the values of y; moreover, the sum of the products of corresponding coefficients in any two expressions is zero, so that the comparisons made are properly independent.

In fitting a curve, the expressions in y are evaluated, each divided by the sum of the squares of its coefficients, and are then used as multipliers of the corresponding functions of x in the fitted curve. Thus the sums of squares of the five expressions above are 28, 84, 6,

154, 84. Consequently, the successive terms of the fitted curve are :—

$$(-3y_1-2y_2-y_3+y_5+2y_6+3y_7)\xi_1/28$$
$$(5y_1-3y_3-4y_4-3y_5+5y_7)(\xi_1^2-4)/84$$
$$(-y_1+y_2+y_3-y_5-y_6+y_7)(\xi_1^3-7\xi_1)/36$$
$$(3y_1-7y_2+y_3+6y_4+y_5-7y_6+3y_7)(7\xi_1^4-67\xi_1^2+72)/1848$$
$$(-y_1+4y_2-5y_3+5y_5-4y_6+y_7)(21\xi_1^5-245\xi_1^3+524\xi_1)/5040$$

The first of these expressions gives the best fitting straight line. By using the first two terms we have the best fitting parabola, the 3rd terms adjust it to the best fitting cubic, and so on.

Based on these orthogonal polynomials, independent comparisons convenient for fitting series to the 5th degree are given so far as $n = 75$ in *Statistical Tables*. The general formulæ are given in editions 3 to 6 of this book, but for higher degrees and longer series it is best to use the arithmetical approach illustrated in the following sections.

The components are also expressible in terms of the successive differences of the series y_n. Thus those given above might be written

(i) $\Delta(3y_1+5y_2+6y_3+6y_4+5y_5+3y_6)$
(ii) $\Delta^2(5y_1+10y_2+12y_3+10y_4+5y_5)$
(iii) $\Delta^3(y_1+2y_2+2y_3+y_4)$
(iv) $\Delta^4(3y_1+5y_2+3y_3)$
(v) $\Delta^5(y_1+y_2)$

where Δy_1 stands for y_2-y_1, and so on. In place of the sum of the squares of the coefficients of the explicit formulæ, we should then use the square of the sum of the coefficients of the differences of the appropriate degree, divided by

$$\frac{n(n^2-1)\ \ldots\ (n^2-r^2)}{(2.6)(6.10)\ \ldots\ \{(4r-2)(4r+2)\}}$$

for the term of degree r. This device of using differences sometimes saves an immense amount of labour, since the differences are often smaller numbers than those from which they are derived, and fewer of them are to be used. The sign of the coefficients also is always positive. Coefficients of such expansions in differences may be found for any degree by starting with unity, and multiplying successively by

$$\frac{(r+1)(n-r-1)}{1(n-1)}, \frac{(r+2)(n-r-2)}{2(n-2)}, \ldots$$

a method which may be simply illustrated by constructing in this way the formula given above for $n = 7$, $r = 4$; thence by differencing four times construct the actual coefficients of the fourth component.

Although, for arithmetical purposes, it is convenient to leave these expressions indeterminate in respect of constant factors, so that on removing any common factor, or clearing fractions, the expression may be used in its simplest form, algebraically, it is convenient to introduce the convention that in the polynomials the coefficient of the leading term is unity. Thus ξ_3 above is taken to be $\xi_1^3 - 7\xi_1$, with values 6 times the coefficients of the expression used. With this convention, the sum of the squares of the coefficients is found to be

$$\frac{n(n^2-1)\ldots(n^2-r^2)}{12.15\ldots(16-4/r^2)} = \frac{(n+r)!}{(n-r-1)!} \cdot \frac{r!^4}{(2r)!(2r+1)!}$$

so that the process of fitting may now be represented by the equations

$$A = \bar{y} = \frac{1}{n'} S(y),$$

$$B = \frac{12}{n'(n'^2-1)} S(y\xi_1),$$

$$C = \frac{180}{n'(n'^2-1)(n'^2-4)} S(y\xi_2),$$

where, in general, the coefficient of the term of the rth degree is

$$\frac{(2r)!(2r+1)!}{(r!)^4 n'(n'^2-1)\ .\ .\ .\ (n'^2-r^2)} S(y\xi_r).$$

As each term is fitted the regression line approaches more nearly to the observed values, and the sum of the squares of the deviations

$$S(y-Y)^2$$

is diminished. It is desirable to be able to calculate this quantity, without evaluating the actual values of Y at each point of the series; this can be done by subtracting from $S(y^2)$ the successive quantities

$$n'A^2, \quad \frac{n'(n'^2-1)}{12} B^2, \quad \frac{n'(n'^2-1)(n'^2-4)}{180} C^2,$$

or more simply

$$AS(y), \ BS(y\xi_1), \ CS(y\xi_2),$$

and so on. These quantities represent the reduction which the sum of the squares of the residuals suffers each time the regression curve is fitted to a higher degree; and enable its value to be calculated at any stage by a mere extension of the process already used in the preceding examples. To obtain an estimate, s^2, of the residual variance, we divide by n, the number of degrees of freedom left after fitting, which is found from n' by subtracting from it the number of constants in the regression formula. Thus, if a straight line has been fitted, $n = n'-2$; while if a curve of the 5th degree has been fitted, $n = n'-6$.

28. The Arithmetical Procedure of Fitting

The main arithmetical labour of fitting curved regression lines to data of this type may be reduced to a repetition of the process of summation illustrated in

Ex. 23. We shall assume that the values of y are written down in a column in order of increasing values of x, and that at each stage the summation is commenced at the top of the column (not at the bottom, as in that example). The sums of the successive columns will be denoted by $S_1, S_2, \ldots$ When these values have been obtained, each is divided by an appropriate divisor, which depends only on n', giving us a new series of quantities $a, b, c, \ldots$ according to the following equations

$$a = \frac{1}{n'} S_1 = \frac{1}{n'} S(y) = \bar{y},$$

$$b = \frac{1.2}{n'(n'+1)} S_2,$$

$$c = \frac{1.2.3}{n'(n'+1)(n'+2)} S_3,$$

and so on.

From these a third series of quantities $a', b', c' \ldots$ are obtained by equations independent of n', of which we give below the first six, which are enough to carry the process of fitting up to the 5th degree:

$$\begin{aligned} a' &= a, \\ b' &= a-b, \\ c' &= a-3b+2c, \\ d' &= a-6b+10c-5d, \\ e' &= a-10b+30c-35d+14e, \\ f' &= a-15b+70c-140d+126e-42f. \end{aligned}$$

The rule for the formation of the coefficients is to multiply successively by

$$\frac{r(r+1)}{1.2}, \quad \frac{(r-1)(r+2)}{2.3}, \quad \frac{(r-2)(r+3)}{3.4},$$

and so on till the series terminates.

These new quantities are proportional to the required coefficients of the regression equation, and need only be divided by a second group of divisors to give the actual values. The equations are

$$A = a', \qquad B = \frac{6}{n'-1} b',$$

$$C = \frac{30}{(n'-1)(n'-2)} c', \qquad D = \frac{140}{(n'-1)(n'-2)(n'-3)} d',$$

$$E = \frac{630}{(n'-1)(n'-2)\dots(n'-4)} e', \quad F = \frac{2772}{(n'-1)\dots(n'-5)} f',$$

the numerical part of the factor being

$$\frac{(2r+1)!}{(r!)^2}$$

for the term of degree r.

If an equation of degree r has been fitted, the estimate of the standard errors of the coefficients are all based upon the same value of s^2, *i.e.*

$$s^2 = \frac{1}{n'-r-1} \left\{ S(y^2) - n'A^2 - \frac{n'(n'^2-1)}{12} B^2 - \dots \right\},$$

from which the estimated standard error of any coefficient, such as that of ξ_p, is obtained by dividing by

$$S(\xi_p^2) = \frac{(p!)^4}{(2p)!(2p+1)!} n'(n'^2-1) \dots (n'^2-p^2)$$

and taking out the square root. The number of degrees of freedom upon which the estimate is based is $(n'-r-1)$, and this must be equated to n in using the Table of t.

A suitable example for using this method may be obtained by fitting the values of Ex. 22 (p. 136) with a curve of the 2nd or 3rd degree.

28·1. The Calculation of the Polynomial Values

The methods of the preceding sections provide an analysis of a series into the components which can be represented by polynomial terms of any required degree, and the remainder which cannot be so represented. For much work of this kind it is desirable to carry out this analysis without the labour of calculating the polynomial values, Y, at each point of the series. Sometimes, however, it is desirable to have these values, either to construct a graph, to examine the deviations in regions of special interest, or because doing so provides a completely satisfactory check upon the results calculated.

The very tedious procedure of calculating the individual values of ξ, and from them, and the calculated coefficients, forming the individual values of the polynomial, may be avoided by building up the whole series, by a continuous process, from its differences. The process is obvious when a straight line is fitted. For the terminal value, and the constant difference between successive values, we take

$$Y_1 = a' + 3b',$$

$$\Delta Y_1 = -\frac{6}{n'-1} b',$$

and build up all the other values of Y by continuous addition of the constant difference. The method is, however, applicable to polynomials of high order, and in such cases appears to save more than three-quarters of the labour of calculation. For curves of the 2nd degree the equations are:

$$Y_1 = a' + 3b' + 5c',$$

$$\Delta Y_1 = -\frac{6}{n'-1}(b' + 5c'),$$

$$\Delta^2 Y_1 = \frac{60}{(n'-1)(n'-2)} c'.$$

Starting with the terminal value ΔY_1, the series of first differences is built up by successive addition of the constant second difference $\Delta^2 Y_1$; then starting from Y_1, and adding successively the first differences, the series of values of Y is built up in turn.

The formulæ for any degree are constructed using the factors, with alternate positive and negative signs,

$$1, \quad \frac{-2.3}{n'-1}, \quad \frac{3.4.5}{(n'-1)(n'-2)}, \quad \frac{-4.5.6.7}{(n'-1)(n'-2)(n'-3)}, \ldots$$

together with expressions in a', b', c', . . . with the same coefficients, as given in Table 30·2, whatever the degree of the curve.

The arithmetical procedure, which consists almost entirely of successive addition, may be illustrated on the series of Ex. 22. Table 30·1 shows on the left the

TABLE 30·1

Observed Values.	1st Sum.	2nd Sum.	3rd Sum.	Polynomial Values.	1st Difference.	2nd Difference.	3rd Difference.
...	...	...	...	...	...	...	
−0·25	117·88	960·77	4440·58	5·86	·739	−·1280	
+9·31	127·19	1087·96	5528·54	4·99	·871	−·1320	
−2·94	124·25	1212·21	6740·75	3·98	1·008	−·1361	
+7·07	131·32	1343·53	8084·28	2·84	1·148	−·1402	
+2·69	134·01	1477·54	9561·82	1·544	1·2919	−·14423	·004061
134·01	1477·54	9561·82	39167·21	134·00			
4·467000	3·177505	1·927786	0·957165				
4·467000	1·289495	−1·209431	−·105995				

last five lines of the summations needed to fit a curve of the 3rd degree, and on the right the first five lines of the summations by which the polynomial values are built up.

Below the first four columns are shown the values of *a*, . . ., *d* derived directly from the totals, and of

$a', \ldots, d'$ derived from them. If we want the values of Y to two decimal places, it will be as well to calculate Y_1 to three places, and each difference to one more place than the last, discarding one place for the subsequent differences of each series. With this in view six decimal places will be sufficient for $a, \ldots, d$. Any further degree of accuracy required may be obtained merely by retaining additional digits. The sum of the column of polynomial values, which must tally with that of those observed, provides an excellent check of the latter parts of the procedure, but not of the correctness of the initial summations.

TABLE 30·2

COEFFICIENTS OF $a', b', c', \ldots$ IN THE TERMINAL VALUES OF Y AND ITS DIFFERENCES

1	3	5	7	9	11	13	15	17	19	21
	1	5	14	30	55	91	140	204	285	385
		1	7	27	77	182	378	714	1254	2079
			1	9	44	156	450	1122	2508	5148
				1	11	65	275	935	2717	7007
					1	13	90	442	1729	5733
						1	15	119	665	2940
							1	17	152	952
								1	19	189
									1	21
										1

The coefficients used in this method in the expression for $Y_1, \Delta Y_1, \Delta^2 Y_1, \ldots$ in terms of $a', b', c', \ldots$ are given in Table 30·2 up to the 10th degree.

29. Regression with several Independent Variates

It frequently happens that the data enable us to express the average value of the dependent variate y, in terms of a number of different independent variates $x_1, x_2, \ldots x_p$. For example, the rainfall at any point within a district may be recorded at a number of stations for which the longitude, latitude, and altitude are all known. If all of these three variates influence the rainfall, it may be required to ascertain the average effect of each separately. In speaking of longitude, latitude, and altitude as independent variates, all that is implied is that it is in terms of them that the average rainfall is to be expressed; it is not implied that these variates vary independently, in the sense that they are uncorrelated. On the contrary, it may well happen that the more southerly stations lie on the whole more to the west than do the more northerly stations, so that for the stations available longitude measured to the west may be negatively correlated with latitude measured to the north. If, then, rainfall increased to the west but was independent of latitude, we should obtain, merely by comparing the rainfall recorded at different latitudes, a fictitious regression indicating that rain decreased towards the north. What we require is an equation, taking account of all three variates at each station, and agreeing as nearly as possible with the values recorded; this is called a **partial** regression equation, and its coefficients are known as partial regression coefficients.

To simplify the algebra we shall suppose that y, x_1, x_2, x_3, are all measured from their mean values, and that we are seeking a formula of the form

$$Y = b_1x_1+b_2x_2+b_3x_3.$$

If S stands for summation over all the sets of observations we construct the three equations

$$\begin{aligned} b_1S(x_1^2)+b_2S(x_1x_2)+b_3S(x_1x_3) &= S(x_1y), \\ b_1S(x_1x_2)+b_2S(x_2^2)+b_3S(x_2x_3) &= S(x_2y), \\ b_1S(x_1x_3)+b_2S(x_2x_3)+b_3S(x_3^2) &= S(x_3y), \end{aligned}$$

of which the nine coefficients are obtained from the data either by direct multiplication and addition, or, if the data are numerous, by constructing correlation tables for each of the six pairs of variates. The three simultaneous equations for b_1, b_2, and b_3 are solved in the ordinary way; first b_3 is eliminated from the first and third, and from the second and third equations, leaving two equations for b_1 and b_2; eliminating b_2 from these, b_1 is found, and thence by substitution, b_2 and b_3.

It frequently happens that, for the same set of values of the independent variates, it is desired to examine the regressions for more than one set of values of the dependent variate; as, for example, if for the same set of rainfall stations we had data for several different months or years. In such cases it is preferable to avoid solving the simultaneous equations afresh on each occasion, but to obtain a simpler formula which may be applied to each new case.

This may be done by solving once and for all the three sets, each consisting of three simultaneous equations:

$$\begin{aligned} b_1S(x_1^2)+b_2S(x_1x_2)+b_3S(x_1x_3) &= 1, \quad 0, \quad 0, \\ b_1S(x_1x_2)+b_2S(x_2^2)+b_3S(x_2x_3) &= 0, \quad 1, \quad 0, \\ b_1S(x_1x_3)+b_2S(x_2x_3)+b_3S(x_3^2) &= 0, \quad 0, \quad 1; \end{aligned}$$

the three solutions of these three sets of equations may be written

$$\begin{aligned} b_1 &= c_{11}, \; c_{12}, \; c_{13}, \\ b_2 &= c_{12}, \; c_{22}, \; c_{23}, \\ b_3 &= c_{13}, \; c_{23}, \; c_{33}. \end{aligned}$$

Once the six values of c are known, then the partial regression coefficients may be obtained in any particular case merely by calculating $S(x_1y)$, $S(x_2y)$, $S(x_3y)$ and substituting in the formulæ,

$$b_1 = c_{11}S(x_1y)+c_{12}S(x_2y)+c_{13}S(x_3y),$$
$$b_2 = c_{12}S(x_1y)+c_{22}S(x_2y)+c_{23}S(x_3y),$$
$$b_3 = c_{13}S(x_1y)+c_{23}S(x_2y)+c_{33}S(x_3y).$$

The c-values, which are known as the covariance matrix, also serve to determine the precision of the regression co-efficients, so that this indirect method of obtaining them is generally to be recommended.

The method of partial regression is of very wide application. It is worth noting that the different independent variates may be related in any way; for example, if we desired to express the rainfall as a linear function of the latitude and longitude, and as a quadratic function of the altitude, the square of the altitude would be introduced as a fourth independent variate, without in any way disturbing the process outlined above, save in such points as that $S(x_3x_4) = S(x_3^3)$ would be calculated directly from the distribution of altitude.

The analysis of sequences, exhibited in Section 27 and 28 by means of orthogonal polynomials, could therefore alternatively have been carried out by the multiple regression method. In the case specially treated, in which we have a simple sequence of observations of a dependent variate, one for each of a series of equally spaced values of the independent variate, as in annual returns of economic and sociological data, the use of orthogonal polynomials presents manifest advantages. When, however, the number of observations is variable, or the intervals are not equally spaced, the method of orthogonal polynomials, which can be generalised to cover such cases, is artificial, and less direct than the treatment of the data by multiple regression. The equations of multiple regression are moreover equally applicable to regression equations involving not merely powers, but other functions such as logarithms, exponentials or trigonometric functions of the independent variate.

In estimating the sampling errors of partial regression coefficients we require to know how nearly our calculated value, Y, has reproduced the observed values of y; as in previous cases, the sum of the squares of $(y-Y)$ may be calculated by differences, for, with three variates,

$$S(y-Y)^2 = S(y^2) - b_1S(x_1y) - b_2S(x_2y) - b_3S(x_3y).$$

If we had n' sets of observations, and p independent variates, we should therefore first calculate

$$s^2 = \frac{1}{n'-p-1} S(y-Y)^2,$$

and to test if b_1 differed significantly from any hypothetical value, β_1, we should calculate

$$t = \frac{b_1-\beta_1}{s\sqrt{c_{11}}},$$

entering the Table of t with $n = n'-p-1$.

In the practical use of a number of variates it is convenient to use cards, on each of which is entered the values of the several variates which may be required. By sorting these cards in suitable grouping units with respect to any two variates the corresponding correlation table may be constructed with little risk of error, and thence the necessary sums of squares and products obtained.

Ex. 24. *Dependence of rainfall on position and altitude.*—The situations of 57 rainfall stations in

Hertfordshire have a mean longitude 12′·4 W., a mean latitude 51° 48′·5 N., and a mean altitude 302 feet. Taking as units two minutes of longitude, one minute of latitude, and twenty feet of altitude, the following values of the sums of squares and products of deviations from the mean were obtained :

$$S(x_1^2) = 1934{\cdot}1, \qquad S(x_2x_3) = +119{\cdot}6,$$
$$S(x_2^2) = 2889{\cdot}5, \qquad S(x_3x_1) = +924{\cdot}1,$$
$$S(x_3^2) = 1750{\cdot}8, \qquad S(x_1x_2) = -772{\cdot}2.$$

To find the multipliers suitable for any particular set of weather data from these stations, first solve the equations

$$\begin{aligned} 1934{\cdot}1\ c_{11} - 772{\cdot}2\ c_{12} + 924{\cdot}1\ c_{13} &= 1 \\ -772{\cdot}2\ c_{11} + 2889{\cdot}5\ c_{12} + 119{\cdot}6\ c_{13} &= 0 \\ +924{\cdot}1\ c_{11} + 119{\cdot}6\ c_{12} + 1750{\cdot}8\ c_{13} &= 0; \end{aligned}$$

using the last equation to eliminate c_{13} from the first two, we have

$$\begin{aligned} 2532{\cdot}3\ c_{11} - 1462{\cdot}5\ c_{12} &= 1{\cdot}7508 \\ -1462{\cdot}5\ c_{11} + 5044{\cdot}6\ c_{12} &= 0; \end{aligned}$$

from these eliminate c_{12}, obtaining

$$10{,}635{\cdot}5\ c_{11} = 8{\cdot}8321;$$

whence

$$c_{11} = {\cdot}00083044, \quad c_{12} = {\cdot}00024075, \quad c_{13} = -{\cdot}00045477,$$

the last two being obtained successively by substitution.

Since the corresponding equations for c_{12}, c_{22}, c_{23} differ only in changes in the right-hand member, we can at once write down

$$-1462{\cdot}5\ c_{12} + 5044{\cdot}6\ c_{22} = 1{\cdot}7508;$$

whence, substituting for c_{12} the value already obtained,

$$c_{22} = {\cdot}00041686, \quad c_{23} = -{\cdot}00015555;$$

finally, to obtain c_{33} we have only to substitute in the equation

$$924 \cdot 1\ c_{13} + 119 \cdot 6\ c_{23} + 1750 \cdot 8\ c_{33} = 1,$$

giving

$$c_{33} = \cdot 00082183.$$

It is usually worth while, to facilitate the detection of small errors by checking, to retain, as above, one more decimal place than the data warrant.

The partial regression of any particular weather data on these three variates can now be found with little labour. In January 1922 the mean rainfall recorded at these stations was 3·87 inches, and the sums of products of deviations with those of the three independent variates were (taking 0·1 inch as the unit for rain)

$$S(x_1 y) = +1137 \cdot 4, \quad S(x_2 y) = -592 \cdot 9, \quad S(x_3 y) = +891 \cdot 8;$$

multiplying these first by c_{11}, c_{12}, c_{13} and adding, we have for the partial regression on longitude

$$b_1 = \cdot 39624;$$

similarly, using the multipliers c_{12}, c_{22}, c_{23} we obtain for the partial regression on latitude

$$b_2 = -\cdot 11204;$$

and finally, by using c_{13}, c_{23}, c_{33},

$$b_3 = \cdot 30788$$

gives the partial regression on altitude.

Remembering now the units employed, it appears that in the month in question rainfall increased by ·0198 of an inch for each minute of longitude westwards, it decreased by ·0112 of an inch for each minute of latitude northwards, and increased by ·00154 of an inch for each foot of altitude.

Let us calculate to what extent the regression on altitude is affected by sampling errors. For the 57 recorded deviations of the rainfall from its mean value, in the units previously used

$$S(y^2) = 1786 \cdot 6\,;$$

whence, knowing the values of b_1, b_2, and b_3 we obtain by subtraction

$$S(y-Y)^2 = 994 \cdot 9.$$

To find s^2, we must divide this by the number of degrees of freedom remaining after fitting a formula involving three variates—that is, by 53—so that

$$s^2 = 18 \cdot 772\,;$$

multiplying this by c_{33} and taking the square root,

$$s\sqrt{c_{33}} = \cdot 12421.$$

Since n is as high as 53 we shall not be far wrong in taking the regression of rainfall on altitude to be in working units ·308, with a standard error ·124; or in inches of rain per 100 feet as ·154, with a standard error ·062.

The importance of the procedure developed in Ex. 24 lies in the generality of its applications, and in the fact that the same process is used to give in succession (*a*) the best regression equation of a given form, and (*b*) the materials for studying the residual variation, and the precision of the coefficients of our equation.

We have illustrated and used the fact that the sampling variance of any coefficient, such as b_1, is given by multiplying the estimated residual variance, s^2, by the factor c_{11} derived wholly from the independent variates. In many applications the calculation of the multipliers c is of further value owing to the fact that the sampling covariance of any two coefficients, such as b_1 and b_2, is given by multiplying the same estimated variance by c_{12}. We may, therefore, without repeating the primary calculations, review the results from a variety of different points of view. Although it would be of little interest in the meteorological problem, it will in other cases be frequently important to compare the magnitude of two different coefficients, *e.g.* to ask if b_1 is significantly greater than b_2. We need to compare the difference b_1-b_2 with its estimated standard error, and this will be the square root of

$$s^2(c_{11}-2c_{12}+c_{22}),$$

since the variance of the differences of any two quantities must be the sum of their variances, less twice their covariance, as is apparent from the algebraic identity

$$(x-y)^2 = x^2-2xy+y^2.$$

By the use of the c multipliers, we are thus able to test the significance of the sum or difference, or indeed any linear function, of two or more regression coefficients, by calculating its standard error, and recognising the ratio it bears to its standard error as t, having degrees of freedom appropriate to the estimation of the residual variance.

29·1. The Omission of an Independent Variate

It may happen that after a regression equation has been worked out, it appears that one of the independent variates used is of little interest, and that it would have been preferable to have omitted it, and to have calculated the regression on the others. This could be done by solving anew the set of equations involving only the squares and products of the remaining variates, but this labour may be avoided. The omission of a single variate will always increase the number of residual degrees of freedom by unity, and correspondingly will increase the sum of squares of deviations from the regression formula by a quantity corresponding to this 1 degree of freedom. If x_3 stands for the variate to be omitted, we may recall that the variance of the corresponding coefficient b_3 was given by the expression $\sigma^2 c_{33}$. The variance of $b_3/\sqrt{c_{33}}$ will therefore be σ^2, and

$$b_3^2/c_{33}$$

must be the increment added to the sum of squares by the omission of the variate x_3.

Equally, if, in the regression formula, we had wished to replace b_3, not by zero, but by a theoretical value β_3, the increment would have been

$$(b_3-\beta_3)^2/c_{33}.$$

We may also wish to adjust the coefficients of the remaining variates, which have been already calculated, to what they would have been if any particular variate, such as x_3, had been omitted. This is easily done by subtracting from b_1 the quantity

$$\frac{c_{13}}{c_{33}} b_3,$$

and applying a similar adjustment of the other coefficients.

I owe to Professor H. Shultz of Chicago a more comprehensive application of this method than was given in the fifth edition. This is to recalculate the c-matrix from formulæ of the form

$$c'_{12} = c_{12} - \frac{c_{13}\, c_{23}}{c_{33}}.$$

The values c' supply the c-matrix which would have been obtained had variate (3) been omitted. These give the variances and covariances of the adjusted coefficients, and also the means of making the further adjustments needed should it be desired to omit a second variate, or indeed more, in succession.

Thus, if the regression of a dependent variate be worked out on a considerable group of six or more variates, which are regarded as possibly influential, it is always possible, with very little labour, if any one of them is found to be really unimportant, to obtain from our formula the result which would have been obtained had this one been omitted from the original calculations. More laboriously a succession of unwanted variates may be discarded in turn.

29·2. Polynomial Fitting when the Frequencies are Unequal

The advantages of the arithmetical procedure of Sections 28 and 28·1 may still be obtained when it is desired to fit a polynomial regression curve of any specified degree to a set of observations of the dependent variate, the frequencies of which at different values of the independent variate are unequal. Here we shall not be concerned to obtain a sequence of polynomials of different degrees, but only to obtain a single formula, the coefficients of which will not require separate tests of significance. We shall illustrate the process in detail for fitting a cubic curve to the times taken to run 100 yards by 988 boys at various ages from 9·25 to 19·25 years (H. Gray's data).

The addition process is applied separately to the frequencies and to the *totals* of sprinting time. Table 30·3 shows the frequencies in 21 half-year classes. To fit a cubic, these are summed seven times (numbered from 0 to 6), though the last summation need not be written out. Much labour is saved by choosing a "working zero," which we have placed

TABLE 30·3

ABBREVIATED SUMMATION PROCESS FOR FREQUENCIES

Age.	Frequency.	Summation.						
		0.	1.	2.	3.	4.	5.	6.
9·25	6	6	6	6	6	6	6	
9·75	8	14	20	26	32	38	44	
10·25	10	24	44	70	102	140	184	
10·75	28	52	96	166	268	408	592	
11·25	29	81	177	343	611	1019	1611	
11·75	46	127	304	647	1258	2277	3888	
12·25	40	167	471	1118	2376	4653	8541	
12·75	53	220	691	1809	4185	8838	17379	
13·25	54	274	965	2774	6959	15797	33176	
13·75	66	340	1305	4079	11038	26835	60011	
14·25	87	648						
14·75	71	561	2296					
15·25	98	490	1735	4975				
15·75	84	392	1245	3240	7398			
16·25	85	308	853	1995	4158	7961		
16·75	67	223	545	1142	2163	3803	6309	
17·25	65	156	322	597	1021	1640	2506	
17·75	44	91	166	275	424	619	866	
18·25	25	47	75	109	149	195	247	
18·75	16	22	28	34	40	46	52	
19·25	6	6	6	6	6	6	6	
	S	988	991	9054	−3640	34796	−53702	129109

at 14·25 years. Only the frequencies for age groups younger than this are summed forward. The frequencies for the older age groups are summed backward. The first backward summation (number 0) includes the working zero; the others each stop one step short of the summation before. For the columns of even number the forward and backward totals are added, while for those of odd number the forward is subtracted from the backward total. The resulting sums are represented by $S_0, S_1, \ldots S_6$.

TABLE 30·4

SUMMATION OF TOTAL TIMES

Age	Total Times.	0.	1.	2.	3.
9·25	101·4	101·4	101·4	101·4	
9·75	127·2	228·6	330·0	431·4	
10·25	167·0	395·6	725·6	1157·0	
10·75	445·2	840·8	1566·4	2723·4	
11·25	475·6	1316·4	2882·8	5606·2	
11·75	713·0	2029·4	4912·2	10518·4	
12·25	612·0	2641·4	7553·6	18072·0	
12·75	800·3	3441·7	10995·3	29067·3	
13·25	810·0	4251·7	15247·0	44314·3	
13·75	943·8	5195·5	20442·5	64756·8	
14·25	1209·3	8354·9			
14·75	958·5	7145·6	28656·9		
15·25	1303·4	6187·1	21511·3	61169·6	
15·75	1075·2	4883·7	15324·2	39658·3	
16·25	1088·0	3808·5	10440·5	24334·1	
16·75	830·8	2720·5	6632·0	13893·6	
17·25	780·0	1889·7	3911·5	7261·6	
17·75	541·2	1109·7	2021·8	3350·1	
18·25	297·5	568·5	912·1	1328·3	
18·75	198·4	271·0	343·6	416·2	
19·25	72·6	72·6	72·6	72·6	
		13550·4	8214·4	125926·4	—86433·4

A similar process with only four summations (0 to 3) is then applied to the total sprinting times, as in Table 30·4, using the same working zero.

In the previous sections, where our regression function is built up of polynomials of specially chosen simplicity, the coefficients were obtained by the solution of simple equations. In this, as in the last section, the equations are simultaneous. Four will be needed for the coefficients of a cubic, and we take the four sums obtained above from the total times as the right-hand members of them. The coefficients of the unknowns on the left-hand sides are obtained from the totals $S_0 \ldots S_6$, derived from the frequencies, according to the following scheme :

S_0	S_1	S_2	S_3
S_1	$2S_2+S_1$	$3S_3+2S_2$	$4S_4+3S_3$
S_2	$3S_3+2S_2$	$6S_4+6S_3+S_2$	$10S_5+12S_4+3S_3$
S_3	$4S_4+3S_3$	$10S_5+12S_4+3S_3$	$20S_6+30S_5+12S_4+S_3$

This table is not changed, but if necessary extended, when curves are fitted of degrees other than three. It is a good intelligence test to write down the next two or three rows and columns from those given for a cubic curve. We are brought therefore to the equations

Equation	Right-hand Values.	Check Column.
$988A + 991B + 9054C - 3640D =$	13550·4	20943·4
$991A + 19099B + 7188C + 128264D =$	8214·4	163756·4
$9054A + 7188B + 195990C - 130388D =$	125926·4	207770·4
$-3640A + 128264B - 130388C + 1385032D =$	−86433·4	1292834·6

where the unknowns A, B, C and D are the polynomial value at the working zero, and its first three advancing differences. The process of solution is shown in full below. Since the coefficients on the left form a symmetrical matrix, duplicate values may be omitted. The work in this example is also arranged to exhibit the use of a check column, which is merely the sum of the numbers in the same row, irrespective of which side of the equation they belong to. The numbers in this column are treated just as are those in the adjacent column at each stage of the solution of the equations, and afford a check for each row of figures as it is completed. The arithmetical details are given in Table 30·5 as arranged for machine calculation.

TABLE 30·5

STEPS IN THE DIRECT SOLUTION OF FOUR EQUATIONS

Coefficients of Unknowns.				Right-hand Side.	Check Column.
988	991	9054	−3640	13550·4	20943·4
	19099	7188	128264	8214·4	163756·4
		195990	−130388	125926·4	207770·4
			1385032	−86433·4	1292834·6
1·355162	1·839448	12·06547		18·45312	33·71320
	10·00107	26·67970		22·46350	60·98372
		254·4514		163·1422	456·3388
1·992473	1·461470			27·27035	30·72429
	18·32980			13·63284	33·42411
34·385737					

When the number of equations has been reduced to one, the value of A is calculated ; B is then found by substitution in the second equation, and a new value for A from the first of the pair of equations at the penultimate stage. In the same way C, B and A are calculated from the trio of equations, and D, C, B and A from the original equations by substitution for each unknown always in its appropriate equation. Such a

TABLE 30·6

SOLUTIONS CHECKED BY EACH EQUATION

A.	B.	C.	D.
13·95742			
42	−·3690990		
42	90	·01802630	
42	83	49	·01015438

TABLE 30·7

Development of Polynomial Values from the Solutions of the Equations

Observed Mean Times.	Fitted Polynomial Values.	Differences.		
		1st.	2nd.	3rd.
16·9	16·40			
		+·009		
15·9	16·41		−·0835	
		−·074		
16·7	16·34		−·0734	
		−·148		
15·9	16·19		−·0632	
		−·211		
16·4	15·98		−·0530	
		−·264		
15·5	15·72		−·0429	
		−·307		
15·3	15·41		−·0327	
		−·340		
15·1	15·07		−·0226	
		−·362		
15·0	14·71		−·0124	
		−·375		
14·3	14·33		−·0023	
		−·377		
13·9	13·957		+·0079	
		−·3691		
13·5	13·59		·01803	
		−·351		·010154
13·3	13·24		·0282	
		−·323		
12·8	12·91		·0383	
		−·285		
12·8	12·63		·0485	
		−·236		
12·4	12·39		·0586	
		−·178		
12·0	12·21		·0688	
		−·109		
12·3	12·11		·0790	
		−·030		
11·9	12·08		·0891	
		+·059		
12·4	12·14		·0993	
		·159		
12·1	12·29			

complete system of checking obviates all arithmetical errors, and from the extent of the variations observed in the solutions gives an idea of the extent to which the limited accuracy of the process of solution can affect the results.

To obtain the fitted polynomial values to 2 decimal places, we may retain 3, 4, 5 and 6 places in A, B, C, D and build up the polynomial by successive addition as in Table 30·7. It will be understood that in forming the second differences on a machine, 6 places are visible at each stage, although only 4 need be written down, using the nearest integer in the 4th place. For the rest, the table explains itself.

The sum of the squares of the polynomial values, multiplied by their appropriate frequencies, is found as usual by multiplying the solution of the regression equations by the right-hand values. Since in this case the regression equations contain an absolute term, A, this will not give the sum of squares of deviations from the mean, but from zero. To reduce to the mean we must deduct $(13550 \cdot 4)^2 \div 988$, leaving for 3 degrees of freedom the value 1645·58. Deducting this from the 20 degrees of freedom for differences among classes, there remains 31·24 representing residual deviations from the function fitted.

	Degrees of Freedom.	Sum of Squares.	Mean Square.
Regression . . .	3	1645·58	548·53
Residual differences . .	17	31·24	1·838
Within age groups . .	967	1620·27	1·676
Total . . .	987	3297·09	

The adequacy of the form of curve chosen for representing the sequence of means observed may be judged by comparing the mean square derived from the deviations with that within age classes. The average sum of squares within age groups, derived from the standard deviations at each age given by Gray, is 1620·27. The whole variation among the 988 times recorded has thus been analysed into three portions (see preceding Table).

Since the mean square for residuals approximates closely to that observed among runners of the same age, it is evident that no curve could fit the data appreciably better. In applying this test we have anticipated the method explained in Section 44.

TABLE IV—TABLE OF *t*

n.	P = ·9	·8.	·7.	·6.	·5.	·4.	·3.	·2.	·1.	·05.	·02.	·01.
1	·158	·325	·510	·727	1·000	1·376	1·963	3·078	6·314	12·706	31·821	63·657
2	·142	·289	·445	·617	·816	1·061	1·386	1·886	2·920	4·303	6·965	9·925
3	·137	·277	·424	·584	·765	·978	1·250	1·638	2·353	3·182	4·541	5·841
4	·134	·271	·414	·569	·741	·941	1·190	1·533	2·132	2·776	3·747	4·604
5	·132	·267	·408	·559	·727	·920	1·156	1·476	2·015	2·571	3·365	4·032
6	·131	·265	·404	·553	·718	·906	1·134	1·440	1·943	2·447	3·143	3·707
7	·130	·263	·402	·549	·711	·896	1·119	1·415	1·895	2·365	2·998	3·499
8	·130	·262	·399	·546	·706	·889	1·108	1·397	1·860	2·306	2·896	3·355
9	·129	·261	·398	·543	·703	·883	1·100	1·383	1·833	2·262	2·821	3·250
10	·129	·260	·397	·542	·700	·879	1·093	1·372	1·812	2·228	2·764	3·169
11	·129	·260	·396	·540	·697	·876	1·088	1·363	1·796	2·201	2·718	3·106
12	·128	·259	·395	·539	·695	·873	1·083	1·356	1·782	2·179	2·681	3·055
13	·128	·259	·394	·538	·694	·870	1·079	1·350	1·771	2·160	2·650	3·012
14	·128	·258	·393	·537	·692	·868	1·076	1·345	1·761	2·145	2·624	2·977
15	·128	·258	·393	·536	·691	·866	1·074	1·341	1·753	2·131	2·602	2·947
16	·128	·258	·392	·535	·690	·865	1·071	1·337	1·746	2·120	2·583	2·921
17	·128	·257	·392	·534	·689	·863	1·069	1·333	1·740	2·110	2·567	2·898
18	·127	·257	·392	·534	·688	·862	1·067	1·330	1·734	2·101	2·552	2·878
19	·127	·257	·391	·533	·688	·861	1·066	1·328	1·729	2·093	2·539	2·861
20	·127	·257	·391	·533	·687	·860	1·064	1·325	1·725	2·086	2·528	2·845
21	·127	·257	·391	·532	·686	·859	1·063	1·323	1·721	2·080	2·518	2·831
22	·127	·256	·390	·532	·686	·858	1·061	1·321	1·717	2·074	2·508	2·819
23	·127	·256	·390	·532	·685	·858	1·060	1·319	1·714	2·069	2·500	2·807
24	·127	·256	·390	·531	·685	·857	1·059	1·318	1·711	2·064	2·492	2·797
25	·127	·256	·390	·531	·684	·856	1·058	1·316	1·708	2·060	2·485	2·787
26	·127	·256	·390	·531	·684	·856	1·058	1·315	1·706	2·056	2·479	2·779
27	·127	·256	·389	·531	·684	·855	1·057	1·314	1·703	2·052	2·473	2·771
28	·127	·256	·389	·530	·683	·855	1·056	1·313	1·701	2·048	2·467	2·763
29	·127	·256	·389	·530	·683	·854	1·055	1·311	1·699	2·045	2·462	2·756
30	·127	·256	·389	·530	·683	·854	1·055	1·310	1·697	2·042	2·457	2·750
∞	·12566	·25335	·38532	·52440	·67449	·84162	1·03643	1·28155	1·64485	1·95996	2·32634	2·57582

VI

THE CORRELATION COEFFICIENT

30. No quantity has been more characteristic of biometrical work than the correlation coefficient, and no method has been applied to such various data as the method of correlation. Observational data in particular, in cases where we can observe the occurrence of various possible contributory causes of a phenomenon, but cannot control them, has been given by its means an altogether new importance. In experimental work proper its position is much less central; it will be found useful in the exploratory stages of an inquiry, as when two factors which had been thought independent appear to be associated in their occurrence; but it is seldom, with controlled experimental conditions, that it is desired to express our conclusion in the form of a correlation coefficient.

One of the earliest and most striking successes of the method of correlation was in the biometrical study of inheritance. At a time when nothing was known of the mechanism of inheritance, or of the structure of the germinal material, it was possible by this method to demonstrate the existence of inheritance, and to "measure its intensity"; and this in an organism in which experimental breeding could not be practised, namely, Man. By comparison of the results obtained from the physical measurements in man with those obtained from other organisms, it was established that man's nature is not less governed by heredity than that of the rest of the animate world. The scope of the analogy was further widened by demonstrating that correlation coefficients of the same magnitude were obtained for the mental and moral qualities in man as for the physical measurements.

These results are still of fundamental importance, for not only is inheritance in man still incapable of experimental study, and existing methods of mental testing are still unable to analyse the mental disposition, but even with organisms suitable for experiment and measurement, it is only in the most favourable cases that the several factors causing fluctuating variability can be resolved, and their effects studied, by Mendelian methods. Such fluctuating variability, with an approximately normal distribution, is characteristic of the majority of the useful qualities of domestic plants and animals; and although there is strong reason to think that inheritance in such cases is ultimately Mendelian, the biometrical method of study is at present alone capable of holding out hopes of immediate progress.

That this method was once centred on the correlation coefficient gives to this statistic a certain importance, even to those who prefer to develop their analysis in other terms.

We give in Table 31 an example of a correlation table. It consists of a record in compact form of the stature of 1376 fathers and daughters. (Pearson and Lee's data.) The measurements are grouped in inches, and those whose measurement was recorded as an integral number of inches have been split; thus a father recorded as of 67 inches would appear as ½ under 66·5 and ½ under 67·5. Similarly with the daughters; in consequence, when both measurements are whole numbers the case appears in four quarters. This gives the table a confusing appearance, since the majority of entries are fractional, although they represent frequencies. The practice of splitting observations is not to be deliberately imitated. A little care in the choice of group limits will avoid all ambiguity. When many items are split, Sheppard's corrections are no longer accurate.

The most obvious feature of the table is that cases do not occur in which the father is very tall and the daughter very short, and *vice versa*; the upper right-hand and lower left-hand corners of the table are blank, so that we may conclude that such occurrences are too rare to occur in a sample of about 1400 cases. The observations recorded lie in a roughly elliptical figure lying diagonally across the table. If we mark out the region in which the frequencies exceed 10 it appears that this region, apart from natural irregularities, is similar, and similarly situated. The frequency of occurrence increases from all sides to the central region of the table, where a few frequencies over 30 may be seen. The lines of equal frequency are roughly similar and similarly situated ellipses. In the outer zone observations occur only occasionally, and therefore irregularly; beyond this we could only explore by taking a much larger sample.

The table has been divided into four quadrants by marking out central values of the two variates; these values, 67·5 inches for the fathers and 63·5 inches for the daughters, are near the means. When the table is so divided it is obvious that the lower right-hand and upper left-hand quadrants are distinctly more populous than the other two; not only are more squares occupied, but the frequencies are higher. It

TABLE

Height of Daughters in Inches.	Height of								
	58·5	59·5	60·5	61·5	62·5	63·5	64·5	65·5	66·5
52·5	...	...	...	...	·25	·25	...	...	...
53·5	...	...	...	...	·25	·25	...	...	...
54·5	...	...	...	...	...	...	...	...	...
55·5	...	...	...	...	...	...	...	1	...
56·5	·25	·25	...	·25	1·25	·5	...	1	·5
57·5	·25	·25	·5	1·5	4·5	1	1·5	1·5	2·5
58·5	·25	·75	·5	·75	·75	1	1·75	1·25	5
59·5	·5	1	2	...	6	4·75	5	6·25	11·75
60·5	·75	·75	...	2·5	8	6·25	12·5	18·25	20·25
61·5	...	·5	1·75	2	9·75	11·5	13	23·75	23·75
62·5	...	1	2·25	2	4·5	12	22·75	26	33
63·5	...	...	·25	2	6	8·25	11	27·25	35·75
64·5	...	...	·25	2·5	1·75	3·25	9·25	23	18·75
65·5	...	...	...	·5	1	·5	11	12·25	9·25
66·5	...	...	...	·5	·5	1·5	3·25	7·25	8·75
67·5	...	...	...	...	...	...	1	5·75	7
68·5	...	...	...	...	·25	·25	·25	·25	1·5
69·5	...	...	...	...	·25	·25	·25	·25	·25
70·5	...	...	...	...	...	...	...	...	...
71·5	...	...	...	...	...	...	...	...	...
72·5	...	...	...	...	...	...	...	...	...
Total	2	4·5	7·5	14·5	45	51·5	92·5	155	178

Fathers in Inches.

67·5	68·5	69·5	70·5	71·5	72·5	73·5	74·5	75·5	Total.
...	...	...	...	...	...	...	...	...	·5
...	...	...	...	...	...	...	...	...	·5
...	...	...	...	...	...	...	...	...	...
...	...	...	...	...	...	...	...	...	1
·5	...	...	...	...	...	...	...	...	4·5
...	·5	·5	...	...	...	...	...	...	14·5
2·75	·5	·25	...	...	...	...	...	...	15·5
3·5	3·5	2	1·75	·5	...	...	...	...	48·5
11	9	4·75	2·5	1·25	1·25	...	...	...	99
20·25	16·5	10·25	4·25	3	1·25	...	...	...	141·5
28·25	24·75	14·25	13·75	4·75	·75	·5	...	...	190·5
37·25	31·5	26·25	16·25	7·75	1·5	·75	·25	...	212
28·5	33	34·25	24·5	11·75	5·5	1	·25	1	198·5
19·75	30	26·5	22·25	15	4·75	3·75	2	1	159·5
16	26·25	26·75	20·5	18·5	7·75	4·25	·25	·5	142·5
4	14·25	13·25	12	11·25	4·5	3·75	·75	...	77·5
3	5·5	4·25	5·75	5·25	3·75	2·5	1·5	2	36
·25	1	2·5	6·5	2·25	2·75	2	1	...	19·5
...	1·75	·25	4·5	·75	1·25	·75	·25	...	9·5
...	·5	...	·5	·5	1·5	·75	·25	...	4
...	1	...	...	...	...	...	...	...	1
175	199·5	166	135	82·5	36·5	20	6·5	4·5	1376

is apparent that tall men have tall daughters more frequently than the short men, and *vice versa*. The method of correlation aims at measuring the degree to which this association exists.

The marginal totals show the frequency distributions of the fathers and the daughters respectively. These are both approximately normal distributions, as is frequently the case with biometrical data collected without selection. This marks a frequent difference between biometrical and experimental data. An experimenter would perhaps have bred from two contrasted groups of fathers of, for example, 63 and 72 inches in height; all his fathers would then belong to these two classes, and the correlation coefficient, if used, would be almost meaningless. Such an experiment would serve to ascertain the regression of daughter's height on father's height and so to determine the effect on the daughters of selection applied to the fathers, but it would not give us the correlation coefficient, which is a descriptive observational feature of the population as it is, and may be wholly vitiated by selection.

Just as normal variation with one variate may be specified by a frequency formula in which the logarithm of the frequency is a quadratic function of the variate, so with two variates the frequency may be expressible in terms of a quadratic function of the values of the two variates. We then have a normal correlation surface, for which the frequency may conveniently be written in the form

$$df = \frac{1}{2\pi\sigma_1\sigma_2\sqrt{1-\rho^2}} e^{-\frac{1}{2(1-\rho^2)}\left\{\frac{x^2}{\sigma_1^2} - \frac{2\rho xy}{\sigma_1\sigma_2} + \frac{y^2}{\sigma_2^2}\right\}} dxdy.$$

In this expression x and y are the deviations of

the two variates from their means, σ_1 and σ_2 are the two standard deviations, and ρ is the *correlation* between x and y. The correlation in the above expression may be positive or negative, but cannot exceed unity in magnitude; it is a pure number without physical dimensions. If $\rho = 0$, the expression for the frequency degenerates into the product of the two factors

$$\frac{1}{\sigma_1\sqrt{2\pi}} e^{-\frac{x^2}{2\sigma_1^2}} dx \cdot \frac{1}{\sigma_2\sqrt{2\pi}} e^{-\frac{y^2}{2\sigma_2^2}} dy,$$

showing that the limit of the normal correlation surface, when the correlation vanishes, is merely that of two normally distributed variates varying in complete independence. At the other extreme, when ρ is $+1$ or -1, the variation of the two variates is in strict proportion, so that the value of either may be calculated accurately from that of the other. In other words, we cease strictly to have two variates, but merely two measures of the same variable quantity.

If we pick out the cases in which one variate has an assigned value, we have what is termed an array; the columns and rows of the table may, except as regards variation within the group limits, be regarded as arrays. With normal correlation the variation within an array may be obtained from the general formula, by giving x a constant value, (say) a, and dividing by the total frequency with which this value occurs; then we have

$$df = \frac{1}{\sigma_2\sqrt{2\pi}\sqrt{1-\rho^2}} \cdot e^{-\frac{1}{2(1-\rho^2)\sigma_2^2}\left(y-\rho\frac{a\sigma_2}{\sigma_1}\right)^2} dy,$$

showing (i) that the variation of y within the array is normal; (ii) that the mean value of y for that array is

$\rho a\sigma_2/\sigma_1$, so that the regression of y on x is linear, with regression coefficient

$$\rho\frac{\sigma_2}{\sigma_1},$$

and (iii) that the variance of y within the array is $\sigma_2^2(1-\rho^2)$, and is the same within each array. We may express this by saying that of the total variance of y the fraction $(1-\rho^2)$ is independent of x, while the remaining fraction ρ^2, is determined by, or calculable from, the value of x.

These relations are reciprocal; the regression of x on y is linear, with regression coefficient $\rho\sigma_1/\sigma_2$; the correlation ρ is thus the geometric mean of the two regressions. The two regression lines representing the mean value of x for given y, and the mean value of y for given x, cannot coincide unless $\rho = \pm 1$. The variation of x within an array in which y is fixed is normal with variance equal to $\sigma_1^2(1-\rho^2)$, so that we may say that of the variance of x the fraction $(1-\rho^2)$ is independent of y, and the remaining fraction, ρ^2, is determined by, or calculable from, the value of y.

Such are the formal mathematical consequences of normal correlation. Much biometric material certainly shows a general agreement with the features to be expected on this assumption; though I am not aware that the question has been subjected to any sufficiently critical inquiry. Approximate agreement is perhaps all that is needed to justify the use of the correlation as a quantity descriptive of the population; its efficacy in this respect is undoubted, and it is not improbable that in some cases it affords, in conjunction with the means and variances, a complete description of the simultaneous variation of the variates.

31. The Statistical Estimation of the Correlation

Just as the variance of a normal population in one variate may be most satisfactorily estimated from the sum of the squares of deviations from the mean of the observed distribution, so, as we have seen, the only satisfactory estimate of the covariance, when the variates are normally correlated, is found from the sum of the products. The estimate used for the correlation is the ratio of the covariance to the geometric mean of the two variances. If x and y represent the deviations of the two variates from their means, we calculate the three statistics s_1, s_2, r by the three equations

$$ns_1^2 = \mathrm{S}(x^2), \quad ns_2^2 = \mathrm{S}(y^2), \quad nrs_1s_2 = \mathrm{S}(xy);$$

then s_1 and s_2 are estimates of the standard deviations σ_1 and σ_2, and r is an estimate of the correlation ρ. Such an estimate is called the *correlation coefficient*, or the *product moment correlation*, the latter term referring to the summation of the product terms, xy, in the last equation. The value used for n should properly be the number of degrees of freedom, or one less than the number of pairs of observations in the sample. As far as the value obtained for r is concerned, however, the value used for n is indifferent, and it is usually convenient to base the calculation directly on the sums of squares and products without dividing by n.

The method of calculation might have been derived from the consideration that the correlation of the population is the geometric mean of the two regression coefficients; for our estimates of these two regressions would be

$$\frac{\mathrm{S}(xy)}{\mathrm{S}(x^2)} \text{ and } \frac{\mathrm{S}(xy)}{\mathrm{S}(y^2)},$$

so that it is in accordance with these estimates to take as our estimate of ρ

$$r = \frac{S(xy)}{\sqrt{S(x^2) \cdot S(y^2)}},$$

which is in fact the product moment correlation.

Ex. 25. *Parental correlation in stature.*—The numerical work required to calculate the correlation coefficient is shown in Table 32.

The first eight columns require no explanation, since they merely repeat the usual process of finding the mean and variance of the two marginal distributions. It is not necessary actually to find the mean, by dividing the total of the 3rd column, 480·5, by 1376, since we may work all through with the undivided totals. The correction for the fact that our working mean is not the true mean is performed by subtracting $(480{\cdot}5)^2 \div 1376$ in the 4th column; a similar correction appears at the foot of the 8th column, and at the foot of the last column. The correction for the sum of products is performed by subtracting $480{\cdot}5 \times 260{\cdot}5 \div 1376$. This correction of the product term may be positive or negative; if the total deviations of the two variates are of opposite sign, the correction must be added. The sum of squares, with and without Sheppard's adjustment $(1376 \div 12)$, are shown separately; there is no corresponding adjustment to be made to the product term.

The 9th column shows the total deviations of the daughter's height for each of the 18 columns in which Table 31 is divided. When the numbers are small, these may usually be written down by inspection of the table. In the present case, where the numbers are large, and the entries are complicated by quartering, more care is required. The total of column 9

TABLE 32

Daughters.			
Deviation.	Frequency.		
−11	·5	5·5	60·5
−10	·5	5	50
− 9	—	—	—
− 8	1	8	64
− 7	4·5	31·5	220·5
− 6	14·5	87	522
− 5	15·5	77·5	387·5
− 4	48·5	194	776
− 3	99	297	891
− 2	141·5	283	566
− 1	190·5	190·5	190·5
0	212	−1179	...
1	198·5	198·5	198·5
2	159·5	319	638
3	142·5	427·5	1282·5
4	77·5	310	1240
5	36	180	900
6	19·5	117	702
7	9·5	66·5	465·5
8	4	32	256
9	1	9	81
	1376	+1659·5 −1179	
	Total .	+480·5	9491·5
Correction for mean . . .			−167·8
			9323·7
Sheppard's adjustment . .			114·7
			9209·0

Fathers.				Total for Daughters.	Product.
Deviation.	Frequency.				
−9	2	18	162	− 8·75	+ 78·75
−8	4·5	36	288	− 15·25	+122
−7	7·5	52·5	367·5	− 19	+133
−6	14·5	87	522	− 23	+138
−5	45	225	1125	−108·75	+543·75
−4	51·5	206	824	− 81	+324
−3	92·5	277·5	832·5	− 76·25	+228·75
−2	155	310	620	− 88·50	+177
−1	178	178	178	− 131·25	+131·25
0	175	−1390	...	+ 15·5	...
1	199·5	199·5	199·5	+183·25	+183·25
2	166	332	664	+197·25	+394·5
3	135	405	1215	+245	+735
4	82·5	330	1320	+174·75	+699
5	36·5	182·5	912·5	+105·25	+526·25
6	20	120	720	+ 71·5	+429
7	6·5	45·5	318·5	+ 25·25	+176·75
8	4·5	36	288	+ 14·5	+116
	1376	+1650·5 −1390		480·5	
	Total .	+260·5	10556·5	Total .	+5136·25
Correction for mean . .			−49·3	Correction for mean	−90·97
			10507·2		
Sheppard's adjustment . .			114·7		+5045·28
			10392·5		

checks with that of the 3rd column. In order that it shall do so, the central entry +15·5, which does not contribute to the products, has to be included. Each entry in the 9th column is multiplied by the paternal deviation to give the 10th column. In the present case all the entries in column 10 are positive; frequently both positive and negative entries occur, and it is then convenient to form a separate column for each. A useful check is afforded by repeating the work of the last two columns, interchanging the variates; we should then find the total deviation of the fathers for each array of daughters, and multiply by the daughters' deviation. The uncorrected totals, 5136·25, should then agree. This check is especially useful with small tables, in which the work of the last two columns, carried out rapidly, is liable to error.

The value of the correlation coefficient, using Sheppard's adjustment, is found by dividing 5045·28 by the geometric mean of 9209·0 and 10,392·5; its value is +·5157. If Sheppard's adjustment had not been used, we should have obtained +·5097. The difference is in this case not large compared to the errors of random sampling, and the full effects on the distribution in random samples of using Sheppard's adjustment have never been fully examined, but there can be little doubt that Sheppard's adjustment should be used, and that its use gives generally an improved estimate of the correlation. On the other hand, the distribution in random samples of the uncorrected value is simpler and better understood, so that the uncorrected value should be used in tests of significance, in which the effect of correction need not, of course, be overlooked. For simplicity coarse grouping should be avoided where such tests are intended. The fact that with small samples the correlation obtained by the use of Sheppard's adjustment may exceed unity illustrates the disturbance introduced into the random sampling distribution.

32. Partial Correlations

A great extension of the utility of the idea of correlation lies in its application to groups of more than two variates. In such cases, where the correlation between each pair of three variates is known, it is possible to eliminate any one of them, and so find what the correlation of the other two would be in a population selected so that the third variate was constant.

When estimates of the three correlations are obtainable *from the same body of data* the process of elimination shown below will give an estimate of the partial correlation exactly comparable with a direct estimate.

Ex. 26. *Elimination of age in organic correlations with growing children.*—For example, it was found (Mumford and Young's data) in a group of boys of different ages, that the correlation of *standing height* with *chest girth* was +·836. One might expect that part of this association was due to general growth with increasing age. It would be more desirable for many purposes to know the correlation between the variates for boys of a given age; but in fact only a few of the boys will be exactly of the same age, and even if we make age groups as broad as a year, we shall have in each group many fewer than the total number measured. In order to utilise the whole material, we only need to know the correlations of *standing height* with *age*, and of *chest girth* with *age*. These are given as ·714 and ·708.

The fundamental formula in calculating partial correlation coefficients may be written

$$r_{12\cdot3}=\frac{r_{12}-r_{13}r_{23}}{\sqrt{(1-r_{13}^2)(1-r_{23}^2)}}.$$

Here the three variates are numbered 1, 2, and 3, and we wish to find the correlation between 1 and 2, when 3 is eliminated; this is called the "partial" correlation between 1 and 2, and is designated by $r_{12\cdot3}$, to show that variate 3 has been eliminated. The symbols r_{12}, r_{13}, r_{23} indicate the correlations found directly between each pair of variates, these correlations being distinguished as "total" correlations.

Inserting the numerical values in the formula given we find $r_{12\cdot3}=\cdot668$, showing that when age is eliminated the correlation, though still considerable, has been markedly reduced. The mean value stated by the above-mentioned authors for the correlations found by grouping the boys by years, is ·653, not a greatly different value. In a similar manner, two or more variates may be eliminated in succession; thus with four variates, we may first eliminate variate 4, by thrice applying the formula to find $r_{12\cdot4}$, $r_{13\cdot4}$, and $r_{23\cdot4}$. Then applying the same formula again, to these three new values, we have

$$r_{12\cdot34}=\frac{r_{12\cdot4}-r_{13\cdot4}r_{23\cdot4}}{\sqrt{(1-r_{13\cdot4}^2)(1-r_{23\cdot4}^2)}}.$$

The labour increases rapidly with the number of variates to be eliminated. To eliminate s variates, the number of operations involved, each one application of the same formula, is $\frac{1}{6}s(s+1)(s+2)$; for values of s from 1 to 6 this gives 1, 4, 10, 20, 35, 56 operations. Much of this labour may be saved by using tables of $\sqrt{1-r^2}$ such as that published by J. R. Miner.

Like the independent variates in regression, the variates eliminated in correlation analysis need not be distributed even approximately in normal distributions. Equally, and this is most frequently overlooked, random errors in them introduce systematic errors in the results. For example, if the partial correlation of variates (1) and (2) were really zero, so that r_{12} were equal to $r_{13}\,r_{23}$, random errors in the measurement or evaluation of variate (3) would tend to reduce both r_{13} and r_{23} numerically, so that their product must be numerically less than r_{12}. An apparent partial correlation between the first two variates will therefore be produced by random errors in the third.

The meaning of the correlation coefficient should be borne clearly in mind. The original aim to measure the "strength of heredity" by this method was based clearly on the supposition that the whole class of factors which tend to make relatives alike, in contrast to the unlikeness of unrelated persons, may be grouped together as heredity. That this is so for all practical purposes is, I believe, admitted, but the correlation does not tell us that this is so; it merely tells us the degree of resemblance in the actual population studied, between father and daughter. It tells us to what extent the height of the father is relevant information respecting the height of the daughter, or, otherwise interpreted, it tells us the relative importance of the factors which act alike upon the heights of father and daughter, compared to the totality of factors at work. If we know that B is caused by A, together with other factors, independent of A, and that B has no influence on A, then the correlation between A and B does tell us how important, in relation to the other causes at work, is the influence of A. If we have not such knowledge, the correlation does not tell us whether A causes B, or B causes A, or whether both influences are at work, with or without the effects of common causes.

This is true equally of partial correlations. If we know that a phenomenon A is not itself influential in determining certain other phenomena B, C, D, . . ., but on the contrary is probably directly influenced by them, then the calculation of the partial correlations A with B, C, D, . . ., in each case eliminating the remaining values, will form a most valuable analysis of the causation of A. If on the contrary we choose a group of social phenomena with no antecedent knowledge of the causation or absence of causation among them, then the calculation of correlation coefficients, total or partial, will not advance us a step towards evaluating the importance of the causes at work.

The correlation between A and B measures, on a conventional scale, the importance of the factors which (on a balance of like and unlike action) act alike in both A and B, as against the remaining factors which affect A and B independently. If we eliminate a third variate C, we are removing from the comparison all those factors which become inoperative when C is fixed. If these are only those which affect A and B independently, then the correlation between A and B, whether positive or negative, will be numerically increased. We shall have eliminated irrelevant disturbing factors, and obtained, as it were, a better controlled experiment. We may also require to eliminate C if these factors act alike, or oppositely on the two variates correlated; in such a case the variability of C actually masks the effect we wish to investigate. Thirdly, C may be one of the chain of events by the mediation of which A affects B, or *vice versa*. The extent to which C is the channel through which the influence passes may be estimated by eliminating C; as one may demonstrate the small effect of latent factors in human heredity by finding the correlation of grandparent and grandchild, eliminating the intermediate parent. In no case, however, can we judge whether or not it is profitable to eliminate a certain variate unless we know, or are willing to assume, a qualitative scheme of causation. For the purely descriptive purpose of specifying a population in respect of a number of variates, either partial or total correlations are effective, and correlations of either type may be of interest.

As an illustration we may consider in what sense the coefficient of correlation does measure the "strength of heredity," assuming that heredity only is concerned in causing the resemblance between relatives; that is, that any environmental effects are distributed at haphazard. In the first place, we may note that if such environmental effects are increased in magnitude, the correlations would be reduced; thus the same population, genetically speaking, would show higher correlations if reared under relatively uniform nutritional conditions, than they would if the nutritional conditions had been very diverse, although the genetical processes in the two cases were identical. Secondly, if environmental effects were at all influential (as in the population studied seems not to be indeed the case), we should obtain higher correlations from a mixed population of genetically very diverse strains than we should from a more uniform population. Thirdly, although the influence of father on daughter is in a certain sense direct, in that the father contributes to the germinal composition of his daughter, we must not assume that this fact is necessarily the cause of the whole of the correlation ; for it has been shown that husband and wife also show considerable resemblance in stature, and consequently taller fathers tend to have taller daughters partly because they choose, or are chosen by, taller wives. For this reason, for example, we should expect to find a noticeable positive correlation between stepfathers and stepdaughters ; also that, when the stature of the wife is eliminated, the partial correlation between father and daughter will be found to be lower than the total correlation. These considerations serve to some extent to define the sense in which the somewhat vague phrase "strength of heredity" must be interpreted, in speaking of the correlation coefficient. It will readily be understood that, in less well understood cases, analogous considerations may be of some importance, and should be critically considered with all possible care.

33. Accuracy of the Correlation Coefficient

With large samples, and moderate or small correlations, the correlation obtained from a sample of n pairs of values is distributed normally about the true value ρ, with variance,

$$\frac{(1-\rho^2)^2}{n-1}$$

it is therefore usual to attach to an observed value r, a standard error $(1-r^2)/\sqrt{n-1}$, or $(1-r^2)/\sqrt{n}$. This procedure is only valid under the restrictions stated above; with small samples the value of r is often very different from the true value, ρ, and the factor $1-r^2$, correspondingly in error; in addition, the distribution of r is far from normal, so that tests of significance based on the large-sample formula are often very deceptive. Since it is with small samples, less than 100, that the practical research worker ordinarily wishes to use the correlation coefficient, we shall give an account of more accurate methods of handling the results.

In all cases the procedure is alike for total and for partial correlations. Exact account may be taken of the differences in the distributions in the two cases, by deducting unity from the sample number for each variate eliminated; thus a partial correlation found by eliminating three variates, and based on data giving 13 values for each variate, is distributed exactly as is a total correlation based on 10 pairs of values.

34. The Significance of an Observed Correlation

In testing the significance of an observed correlation we require to calculate the probability that such a correlation should arise, by random sampling, from an uncorrelated population. If the probability is low we regard the correlation as significant. The Table of t given in the preceding chapter (p. 174) may be utilised to make an exact test. If n' be the numbers of pairs of observations on which the correlation is based, and r the correlation obtained, without using Sheppard's adjustment, then we take

$$t = \frac{r}{\sqrt{1-r^2}} \cdot \sqrt{n'-2},$$

$$n = n'-2,$$

and it may be demonstrated that the distribution of t so calculated, will agree with that given in the table.

It should be observed that this test, as is obviously necessary, is identical with that given in the last chapter for testing whether or not the linear regression coefficient differs significantly from zero.

Table V.A. (p. 209) allows this test to be applied directly from the value of r, for samples up to 100 pairs of observations. Taking the four definite levels of significance, represented by P = ·10, ·05, ·02, and ·01, the table shows for each value of n, from 1 to 20, and thence by larger steps to 100, the corresponding values of r.

Ex. 27. *Significance of a correlation coefficient between autumn rainfall and wheat crop.*—For the twenty years 1885-1904, the mean wheat yield of Eastern England was found to be correlated with the autumn rainfall; the correlation found was −·629. Is this value significant? We obtain in succession

$$1-r^2 = \cdot 6044,$$
$$\sqrt{1-r^2} = \cdot 7774,$$
$$r/\sqrt{1-r^2} = -\cdot 8091,$$
$$t = -3\cdot 433.$$

For $n = 18$, this shows that P is less than ·01, and the correlation is definitely significant. The same conclusion may be read off at once from Table V.A. entered with $n = 18$.

If we had applied the standard error,

$$\sigma_r = \frac{1-r^2}{\sqrt{n'-1}},$$

we should have

$$t = \frac{r}{\sigma_r} = \frac{r}{1-r^2}\sqrt{n'-1} = -4\cdot 536,$$

a much greater value than the true one, very much exaggerating the significance. In addition, assuming that r was normally distributed ($n = \infty$), the significance of the result would be even further exaggerated. This illustration will suffice to show how deceptive, in small samples, is the use of the standard error of the correlation coefficient, on the assumption that it will be normally distributed. Without this assumption the standard error is without utility. The misleading character of the formula is increased if n' is substituted for $n'-1$, as if often done. Judging from the normal deviate 4·536, we should suppose that the correlation obtained would be exceeded in random samples from uncorrelated material only 6 times in a million trials. Actually it would be exceeded about 3000 times in a million trials, or with 500 times the frequency supposed.

It is necessary to warn the student emphatically against the misleading character of the standard error of the correlation coefficient deduced from a small sample, because the principal utility of the correlation coefficient lies in its application to subjects of which little is known, and upon which the data are relatively scanty. With extensive material appropriate for biometrical investigations there is little danger of false conclusions being drawn, whereas with the comparatively few cases to which the experimenter must often look for guidance, the uncritical application of methods standardised in biometry must be so frequently misleading as to endanger the credit of this most valuable weapon of research. It is not true, as the example above shows, that valid conclusions cannot be drawn from small samples; if accurate methods are used in calculating the probability, we thereby make full allowance for the size of the sample, and should be influenced in our judgment only by the value of the probability indicated. The great increase of certainty which accrues from increasing data is reflected in the value of P, if accurate methods are used.

Ex. 28. *Significance of a partial correlation coefficient.*—In a group of 32 poor law relief unions, Yule found that the percentage change from 1881 to 1891 in the percentage of the population in receipt of relief was correlated with the corresponding change in the ratio of the numbers given outdoor relief to the numbers relieved in the workhouse, when two other variates had been eliminated, namely, the corresponding changes in the percentage of the population over 65, and in the population itself.

The correlation found by Yule after eliminating the two variates was $+\cdot457$; such a correlation is termed a partial correlation of the second order. Test its significance.

It has been demonstrated that the distribution in random samples of partial correlation coefficients may be derived from that of total correlation coefficients merely by deducting from the number of the sample the number of variates eliminated. Deducting 2 from the 32 unions used, we have 30 as the effective number of the sample; hence

$$n = 28.$$

Calculating t from r as before, we find

$$t = 2\cdot719,$$

whence it appears from the table that P lies between ·02 and ·01. The correlation is therefore significant. This, of course, as in other cases, is on the assumption that the variates correlated (but not necessarily those eliminated) are normally distributed; economic variates seldom themselves give normal distributions, but the fact that we are here dealing with rates of change makes the assumption of normal distribution much more plausible. The values given in Table V.A. for $n = 25$, and $n = 30$, give a sufficient indication of the level of significance attained by this observation.

35. Transformed Correlations

In addition to testing the significance of a correlation, to ascertain if there is any substantial evidence of association at all, it is also frequently required to perform one or more of the following operations, for each of which the standard error would be used in the case of a normally distributed quantity. With correlations derived from large samples the standard error may, therefore, be so used, except when the correlation approaches ± 1; but with small samples such as frequently occur in practice, special methods must be applied to obtain reliable results.

(i) To test if an observed correlation differs significantly from a given theoretical value.

(ii) To test if two observed correlations are significantly different.

(iii) If a number of independent estimates of a correlation are available, to combine them into an improved estimate.

(iv) To perform tests (i) and (ii) with such average values.

Problems of these kinds may be solved by a method analogous to that by which we have solved the problem of testing the significance of an observed correlation.

In that case we were able from the given value r to calculate a quantity t which is distributed in a known manner, for which tables were available. The transformation led exactly to a distribution which had already been studied. The transformation which we shall now employ leads approximately to the normal distribution in which all the above tests may be carried out without difficulty. Let

$$z = \tfrac{1}{2}\{\log_e(1+r) - \log_e(1-r)\},$$
$$= r + \tfrac{1}{3}r^3 + \tfrac{1}{5}r^5 + \ldots,$$

then as r changes from 0 to 1, z will pass from 0 to ∞. For small values of r, z is nearly equal to r, but as r approaches unity, z increases without limit. For negative values of r, z is negative. The advantage of this transformation of r into z lies in the distribution of these two quantities in random samples. The standard deviation of r depends on the true value of the correlation, ρ, as is seen from the formula

$$\sigma_r = \frac{1-\rho^2}{\sqrt{n'-1}}.$$

Since ρ is unknown, we have to substitute for it the observed value r, and this value will not, in small samples, be a very accurate estimate of ρ. The standard error of z is simpler in form, approximately

$$\sigma_z = \frac{1}{\sqrt{n'-3}},$$

and is practically independent of the value of the correlation in the population from which the sample is drawn.

In the second place, the distribution of r is not normal in small samples, and even for large samples it remains far from normal for high correlations. The distribution of z is not strictly normal, but it tends to normality rapidly as the sample is increased, whatever may be the value of the correlation. We shall give examples to test the effect of the departure of the z distribution from normality.

Finally, the distribution of r changes its form rapidly as ρ is changed; consequently no attempt can be made, with reasonable hope of success, to allow for the skewness of the distribution. On the contrary, the distribution of z is nearly constant in form, and the accuracy of tests may be improved by small corrections for departure from normality; such corrections are, however, too small to be of practical importance, and we shall not deal with them. The simple assumption that z is normally distributed will in all ordinary cases be sufficiently accurate.

These three advantages of the transformation from r to z may be seen by comparing Figs. 7 and 8. In Fig. 7 are shown the actual distributions of r, for 8 pairs of observations, from populations having correlations 0 and 0·8; Fig. 8 shows the corresponding distribution curves for z. The two curves in Fig. 7 are widely different in their modal heights; both are distinctly non-normal curves; in form also they are strongly contrasted, the one being symmetrical, the other highly unsymmetrical. On the contrary, in Fig. 8 the two curves do not differ greatly in height; although not exactly normal in form, they come so close to it, even for a small sample of 8 pairs of observations, that the eye cannot detect the difference; and this approximate normality holds up to the extreme limits $\rho = \pm 1$. One additional feature is brought out by Fig. 8; in the distribution for $\rho = 0·8$, although the curve itself is as symmetrical as the eye can judge of, yet the ordinate of zero error is not centrally placed.

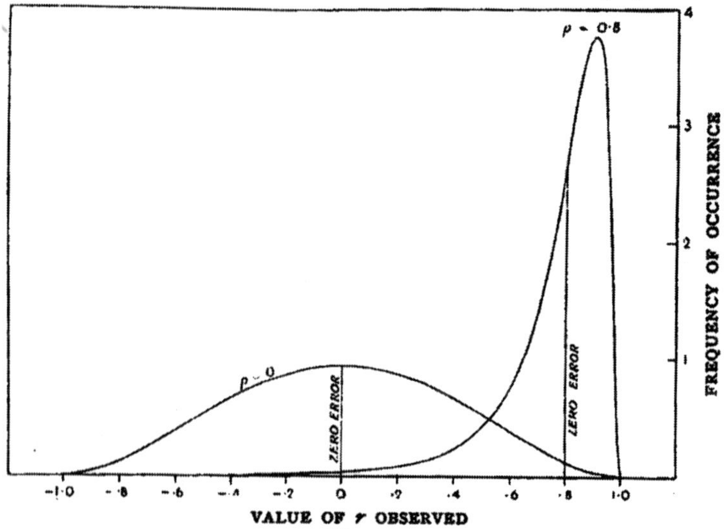

Fig. 7.

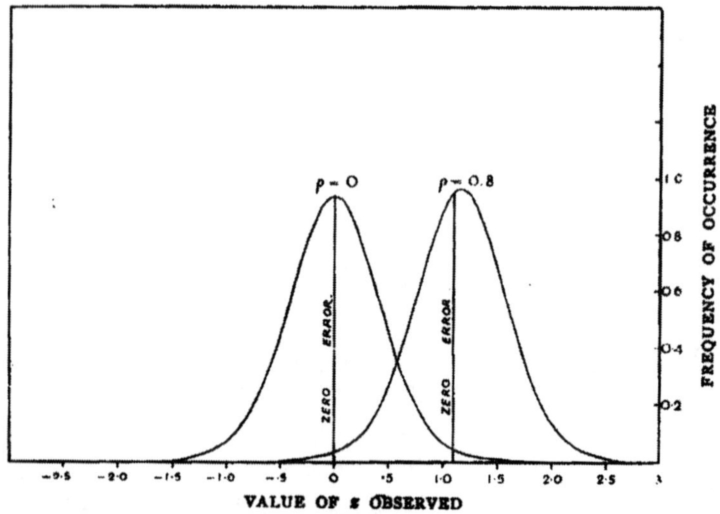

Fig. 8.

The figure, in fact, reveals the small bias which is introduced into the estimate of the correlation coefficient as ordinarily calculated: we shall treat further of this bias in the next section, and in the following chapter shall deal with a similar bias introduced in the calculation of intraclass correlations.

To facilitate the transformation we give in Table V.B. (p. 210) the values of r corresponding to values of z, proceeding by intervals of ·01, from 0 to 3. In the earlier part of this table it will be seen that the values of r and z do not differ greatly; but with higher correlations small changes in r correspond to relatively large changes in z. In fact, measured on the z-scale, a correlation of ·99 differs from a correlation ·95 by more than a correlation ·6 exceeds zero. The values of z give a truer picture of the relative importance of correlations of different sizes than do the values of r.

To find the value of z corresponding to a given value of r, say ·6, the entries in the table lying on either side of ·6 are first found, whence we see at once that z lies between ·69 and ·70; the interval between these entries is then divided proportionately to find the fraction to be added to 69. In this case we have 20/64, or ·31, so that $z = ·6931$. Similarly, in finding the value of r corresponding to any value of z, say ·9218, we see at once that it lies between ·7259 and ·7306; the difference is 47, and 18 per cent. of this gives 8 to be added to the former value, giving us finally $r = ·7267$. The same table may thus be used to transform r into z, and to reverse the process.

Ex. 29. *Test of the approximate normality of the distribution of z.*—In order to illustrate the kind of accuracy obtainable by the use of z, let us take the case that has already been treated by an exact method in Ex. 27. A correlation of $-\cdot629$ has been obtained from 20 pairs of observations; test its significance.

For $r = -\cdot629$ we have, using either a table of natural logarithms, or the special table for z, $z = -\cdot7398$. To divide this by its standard error is equivalent to multiplying it by $\sqrt{17}$. This gives $-3\cdot050$, which we interpret as a normal deviate. From the table of normal deviates it appears that this value will be exceeded about 23 times in 10,000 trials. The true frequency, as we have seen, is about 30 times in 10,000 trials. The error tends only slightly to exaggerate the significance of the result.

Ex. 30. *Further test of the normality of the distribution of z.*—A partial correlation $+\cdot457$ was obtained from a sample of 32, after eliminating two variates. Does this differ significantly from zero? Here $z = \cdot4935$; deducting the two eliminated variates the effective size of the sample is 30, and the standard error of z is $1/\sqrt{27}$; multiplying z by $\sqrt{27}$, we have as a normal variate $2\cdot564$. Table I (or the bottom line of Table IV) shows, as before, that P is just over $\cdot01$. There is a slight exaggeration of significance, but it is even slighter than in the previous example.

These examples indicate that the z transformation will give a variate which, for most practical purposes, may be taken to be normally distributed. In the case of simple tests of significance the use of the Table of t is to be preferred; in the following examples this method is not available, and the only method available which is both tolerably accurate and sufficiently rapid for practical use lies in the use of z.

Ex. 31. *Significance of deviation from expectation of an observed correlation coefficient.*—In a sample of 25 pairs of parent and child the correlation was found to be ·60. Is this value consistent with the view that the true correlation in that character was ·46 ?

The first step is to find the difference of the corresponding values of z. This is shown in Table 33.

To obtain the normal deviate we multiply by $\sqrt{22}$, and obtain ·918. The deviation is less than the standard deviation, and the value obtained is therefore quite in accordance with the hypothesis.

TABLE 33

	r.	z.
Sample value . .	·60	·6931
Population value . .	·46	·4973
Difference . .		·1958

Ex. 32. *Significance of difference between two observed correlations.*—Of two samples the first, of 20 pairs, gives a correlation ·6, the second, of 25 pairs, gives a correlation ·8 : are these values significantly different ?

In this case we require not only the difference of the values of z, but the standard error of the difference. The variance of the difference is the sum of the reciprocals of 17 and 22 ; the work is shown below.

TABLE 34

	r.	z.	$n'-3$.	Reciprocal.
1st sample .	·60	·6931	17	·05882
2nd sample .	·80	1·0986	22	·04545
Difference .		·4055±·3230	Sum .	·10427

The standard error which is appended to the difference of the values of z is the square root of the variance found on the same line. The difference does not exceed twice the standard error, and cannot therefore be judged significant. There is thus no sufficient evidence to conclude that the two samples are not drawn from equally correlated populations.

Ex. 33. *Combination of values from small samples.*—Assuming that the two samples in the last example were drawn from equally correlated populations, estimate the value of the correlation.

The two values of z must be given weight inversely proportional to their variance. We therefore multiply the first by 17, the second by 22 and add, dividing the total by 39. This gives an estimated value of z for the population, and the corresponding value of r may be found from the table.

TABLE 35

	r.	z.	$n'-3$.	$(n'-3)z$.
1st sample . .	·60	·6931	17	11·7827
2nd sample . .	·80	1·0986	22	24·1692
	·7267	·9218	39	35·9519

The weighted average value of z is ·9218, to which corresponds the value $r = ·7267$; the value of z so obtained may be regarded as subject to normally distributed errors of random sampling with variance equal to 1/39. The accuracy is therefore equivalent to that of a single value obtained from 42 pairs of observations. Tests of significance may thus be applied to such averaged values of z, as to individual values.

36. Systematic Errors

In connexion with the averaging of correlations obtained from small samples it is worth while to consider the effects of two classes of systematic errors, which, although of little or no importance when single values only are available, become of increasing importance as larger numbers of samples are averaged.

The value of z obtained from any sample is an estimate of a true value, ζ, belonging to the sampled population, just as the value of r obtained from a sample is an estimate of a population value, ρ. If the method of obtaining the correlation were free from bias, the values of z would be normally distributed about a mean $\bar{z}$, which would agree in value with ζ. Actually there is a small bias which makes the mean value of z somewhat greater numerically than ζ; thus the correlation, whether positive or negative, is slightly exaggerated. This bias may effectively be corrected by subtracting from the value of z the correction

$$\frac{\rho}{2(n'-1)}.$$

For single samples this correction is unimportant, being small compared to the standard error of z. For example, if $n' = 10$, the standard error of z is ·378, while the correction is $\rho/18$ and cannot exceed ·056. If, however, $\bar{z}$ were the mean of 1000 such values of z, derived from samples of 10, the standard error of $\bar{z}$ is only ·012, and the correction, which is unaltered by taking the mean, may well be of great importance.

The second type of systematic error is that introduced by neglecting Sheppard's adjustment. In calculating the value z, we must always take the value of

r found without using Sheppard's adjustment, since the latter complicates the distribution.

But the omission of Sheppard's adjustment introduces a systematic error, in the opposite direction to that mentioned above; and which, though normally very small, appears in large as well as in small samples. In the case of averaging the correlations from a number of coarsely grouped small samples, the average z should be obtained from values of r found without Sheppard's adjustment, and to the result a correction, representing the average effect of Sheppard's adjustment, may be applied.

37. Correlation between Series

The extremely useful case in which it is required to find the correlation between two series of quantities, such as annual figures, arranged in order at equal intervals of time, may be regarded as a case of partial correlation, although it may be treated more directly by the method of fitting curved regression lines given in Section 27 (p. 147).

If, for example, we had a record of the number of deaths from a certain disease for successive years, and wished to study if this mortality were associated with meteorological conditions, or the incidence of some other disease, or the mortality of some other age group, the outstanding difficulty in the direct application of the correlation coefficient is that the number of deaths considered probably exhibits a progressive change during the period available. Such changes may be due to changes in the population among which the deaths occur, whether it be the total population of a district, or that of a particular age group, or to changes in the sanitary conditions in which the population lives, or in the skill and availability of medical assistance, or to changes in the racial or genetic composition of the population. In any case, it is usually found that the changes are still apparent when the number of deaths is converted into a death-rate on the existing population in each year, by which means one of the direct effects of changing population is eliminated.

If the progressive change could be represented effectively by a straight line it would be sufficient to consider the *time* as a third variate, and to eliminate it by calculating the corresponding partial correlation coefficient. Usually, however, the change is not so simple, and would need an expression involving the square and higher powers of the time adequately to represent it. The partial correlation required is one found by eliminating not only t, but t^2, t^3, t^4, . . ., regarding these as separate variates; for if we have eliminated all of these up to (say) the 4th degree, we have incidentally eliminated from the correlation any function of the time of the 4th degree, including that by which the progressive change is best represented.

This partial correlation may be calculated directly from the coefficients of the regression function obtained as in Section 28 (p. 151). If y and y' are the two quantities to be correlated, we obtained for y the coefficients A, B, C, . . ., and for y' the corresponding coefficients A′, B′, C′, . . .; the sums of the squares of the deviations of the variates from the curved regression lines are obtained as before, from the equations

$$S(y-Y)^2 = S(y^2) - n'A^2 - \frac{n'(n'^2-1)}{12}B^2 - \ldots,$$

$$S(y'-Y')^2 = S(y'^2) - n'A'^2 - \frac{n'(n'^2-1)}{12}B'^2 - \ldots;$$

while the sum of the products may be obtained from the similar equation

$$S\{(y-Y)(y'-Y')\} = S(yy') - n'AA' - \frac{n'(n'^2-1)}{12}BB' - \ldots;$$

the required partial correlation being, then,

$$r = \frac{S\{(y-Y)(y'-Y')\}}{\sqrt{S(y-Y)^2 \,.\, S(y'-Y')^2}}$$

In this process the number of variates eliminated is equal to the degree of t to which the fitting has been carried; it will be understood that both variates must be fitted to the same degree, even if one of them is capable of adequate representation by a curve of lower degree than is the other.

TABLE V.A.—VALUES OF THE CORRELATION COEFFICIENT FOR DIFFERENT LEVELS OF SIGNIFICANCE

n.	P = ·1.	·05.	·02.	·01.
1	·98769	·996917	·9995066	·9998766
2	·90000	·95000	·98000	·990000
3	·8054	·8783	·93433	·95873
4	·7293	·8114	·8822	·91720
5	·6694	·7545	·8329	·8745
6	·6215	·7067	·7887	·8343
7	·5822	·6664	·7498	·7977
8	·5494	·6319	·7155	·7646
9	·5214	·6021	·6851	·7348
10	·4973	·5760	·6581	·7079
11	·4762	·5529	·6339	·6835
12	·4575	·5324	·6120	·6614
13	·4409	·5139	·5923	·6411
14	·4259	·4973	·5742	·6226
15	·4124	·4821	·5577	·6055
16	·4000	·4683	·5425	·5897
17	·3887	·4555	·5285	·5751
18	·3783	·4438	·5155	·5614
19	·3687	·4329	·5034	·5487
20	·3598	·4227	·4921	·5368
25	·3233	·3809	·4451	·4869
30	·2960	·3494	·4093	·4487
35	·2746	·3246	·3810	·4182
40	·2573	·3044	·3578	·3932
45	·2428	·2875	·3384	·3721
50	·2306	·2732	·3218	·3541
60	·2108	·2500	·2948	·3248
70	·1954	·2319	·2737	·3017
80	·1829	·2172	·2565	·2830
90	·1726	·2050	·2422	·2673
100	·1638	·1946	·2301	·2540

For a total correlation, *n* is 2 less than the number of pairs in the sample; for a partial correlation, the number of eliminated variates also should be subtracted.

TABLE V.B.—TABLE OF r, FOR VALUES OF z FROM 0 TO 3

z.	·01.	·02.	·03.	·04.	·05.	·06.	·07.	·08.	·09.	·10.
·0	·0100	·0200	·0300	·0400	·0500	·0599	·0699	·0798	·0898	·0997
·1	·1096	·1194	·1293	·1391	·1489	·1586	·1684	·1781	·1877	·1974
·2	·2070	·2165	·2260	·2355	·2449	·2543	·2636	·2729	·2821	·2913
·3	·3004	·3095	·3185	·3275	·3364	·3452	·3540	·3627	·3714	·3800
·4	·3885	·3969	·4053	·4136	·4219	·4301	·4382	·4462	·4542	·4621
·5	·4699	·4777	·4854	·4930	·5005	·5080	·5154	·5227	·5299	·5370
·6	·5441	·5511	·5580	·5649	·5717	·5784	·5850	·5915	·5980	·6044
·7	·6107	·6169	·6231	·6291	·6351	·6411	·6469	·6527	·6584	·6640
·8	·6696	·6751	·6805	·6858	·6911	·6963	·7014	·7064	·7114	·7163
·9	·7211	·7259	·7306	·7352	·7398	·7443	·7487	·7531	·7574	·7616
1·0	·7658	·7699	·7739	·7779	·7818	·7857	·7895	·7932	·7969	·8005
1·1	·8041	·8076	·8110	·8144	·8178	·8210	·8243	·8275	·8306	·8337
1·2	·8367	·8397	·8426	·8455	·8483	·8511	·8538	·8565	·8591	·8617
1·3	·8643	·8668	·8692	·8717	·8741	·8764	·8787	·8810	·8832	·8854
1·4	·8875	·8896	·8917	·8937	·8957	·8977	·8996	·9015	·9033	·9051
1·5	·9069	·9087	·9104	·9121	·9138	·9154	·9170	·9186	·9201	·9217
1·6	·9232	·9246	·9261	·9275	·9289	·9302	·9316	·9329	·9341	·9354
1·7	·9366	·9379	·9391	·9402	·9414	·9425	·9436	·9447	·9458	·94681
1·8	·94783	·94884	·94983	·95080	·95175	·95268	·95359	·95449	·95537	·95624
1·9	·95709	·95792	·95873	·95953	·96032	·96109	·96185	·96259	·96331	·96403
2·0	·96473	·96541	·96609	·96675	·96739	·96803	·96865	·96926	·96986	·97045
2·1	·97103	·97159	·97215	·97269	·97323	·97375	·97426	·97477	·97526	·97574
2·2	·97622	·97668	·97714	·97759	·97803	·97846	·97888	·97929	·97970	·98010
2·3	·98049	·98087	·98124	·98161	·98197	·98233	·98267	·98301	·98335	·98367
2·4	·98399	·98431	·98462	·98492	·98522	·98551	·98579	·98607	·98635	·98661
2·5	·98688	·98714	·98739	·98764	·98788	·98812	·98835	·98858	·98881	·98903
2·6	·98924	·98945	·98966	·98987	·99007	·99026	·99045	·99064	·99083	·99101
2·7	·99118	·99136	·99153	·99170	·99186	·99202	·99218	·99233	·99248	·99263
2·8	·99278	·99292	·99306	·99320	·99333	·99346	·99359	·99372	·99384	·99396
2·9	·99408	·99420	·99431	·99443	·99454	·99464	·99475	·99485	·99495	·99505

For greater accuracy, and for values beyond the table,

$$r=(e^{2z}-1)\div(e^{2z}+1);$$

$$z=\tfrac{1}{2}\{\log(1+r)-\log(1-r)\}.$$

VII

INTRACLASS CORRELATIONS AND THE ANALYSIS OF VARIANCE

38. A type of data, which is of very common occurrence, may be treated by methods closely analogous to that of the correlation table, while at the same time it may be more usefully and accurately treated by the analysis of variance, that is by the separation of the variance ascribable to one group of causes from the variance ascribable to other groups. We shall in this chapter treat first of those cases, arising in biometry, in which the analogy with the correlations treated in the last chapter may most usefully be indicated, and then pass to more general cases, prevalent in experimental results, in which the treatment by correlation appears artificial, and in which the analysis of variance appears to throw a real light on the problems before us. A comparison of the two methods of treatment illustrates the general principle, so often lost sight of, that tests of significance, in so far as they are accurately carried out, are bound to agree, whatever process of statistical reduction may be employed.

If we have measurements of n' pairs of brothers, we may ascertain the correlation between brothers in two slightly different ways. In the first place we may divide the brothers into two classes, as for instance elder brother and younger brother, and find the correlation between these two classes exactly as we do with parent and child. If we proceed in this manner we shall find the mean of the measurements of the elder brothers, and separately that of the younger brothers. Equally the standard deviations about the mean are found separately for the two classes. The correlation so obtained, being that between two classes of measurements, is termed for distinctness an **interclass** correlation. Such a procedure would be imperative if the quantities to be correlated were, for example, the *ages*, or some characteristic sensibly dependent upon age, at a fixed date. On the other hand, we may not know, in each case, which measurement belongs to the elder and which to the younger brother, or, such a distinction may be quite irrelevant to our purpose; in these cases it is usual to use a common mean derived from all the measurements, and a common standard deviation about that mean. If x_1, x'_1; x_2, x'_2; . . . ; $x_{n'}, x'_{n'}$ are the pairs of measurements given, we calculate

$$\bar{x} = \frac{1}{2n'} S(x+x'),$$

$$s^2 = \frac{1}{2n}\{S(x-\bar{x})^2 + S(x'-\bar{x})^2\},$$

$$r = \frac{1}{ns^2} S\{(x-\bar{x})(x'-\bar{x})\}.$$

When this is done, r is distinguished as an **intraclass** correlation, since we have treated all the brothers as belonging to the same class, and having the same mean and standard deviation. The intraclass correlation, when its use is justified by the irrelevance of any such distinction as age, may be expected to give a more accurate estimate of the true value than does any of the possible interclass correlations derived from the same material, for we have used estimates of the mean and standard deviation founded on $2n'$ instead of on n' values. This is in fact found to be the case; the intraclass correlation is not an estimate equivalent to an interclass correlation, but is somewhat more accurate. The error distribution is, however, as we shall see, affected also in other ways, which require the intraclass correlation to be treated separately.

The analogy of this treatment with that of interclass correlations may be further illustrated by the construction of what is called a symmetrical table. Instead of entering each pair of observations once in such a correlation table, it is entered twice, the co-ordinates of the two entries being, for instance, (x_1, x'_1) and (x'_1, x_1). The total entries in the table will then be $2n'$, and the two marginal distributions will be identical, each representing the distribution of the whole $2n'$ observations. The equations given, for calculating the intraclass correlation, bear the same relation to the symmetrical table as the equations for the interclass correlation bear to the corresponding unsymmetrical table with n' entries. Although the intraclass correlation is somewhat the more accurate, it is by no means so accurate as is an interclass correlation with $2n'$ independent pairs of observations.

The contrast between the two types of correlation becomes more obvious when we have to deal not with pairs, but with sets of three or more measurements; for example, if three brothers in each family have been measured. In such cases also a symmetrical table can be constructed. Each trio of brothers will provide three pairs, each of which gives two entries, so that each trio provides 6 entries in the table. To calculate the correlation from such a table is equivalent to the following equations:

$$\bar{x} = \frac{1}{3n'} S(x+x'+x''),$$

$$s^2 = \frac{1}{3n} S\{(x-\bar{x})^2+(x'-\bar{x})^2+(x''-\bar{x})^2\},$$

$$r = \frac{1}{3ns^2} S\{(x'-\bar{x})(x''-\bar{x})+(x''-\bar{x})(x-\bar{x})+(x-\bar{x})(x'-\bar{x})\}.$$

In many instances of the use of intraclass correlations the number of observations in the same "family" is large, as when the resemblance between leaves on the same tree was studied by picking 26 leaves from a number of different trees, or when 100 pods were taken from each tree in another group of correlation studies. If k is the number in each family, then each set of k values will provide $k(k-1)$ values for the symmetrical table, which thus may contain an enormous number of entries, and be very laborious to construct. To obviate this difficulty Harris introduced an abbreviated method of calculation by which the value of the correlation given by the symmetrical table may be obtained directly from two distributions: (i) the distribution of the whole group of kn' observations, from which we obtain, as above, the values of $\bar{x}$ and s; (ii) the distribution of the n' means of families. If $\bar{x}_1, \bar{x}_2, \ldots, \bar{x}_{n'}$, represent these means each derived from k values, then

$$kS(\bar{x}_p-\bar{x})^2 = ns^2\{1+(k-1)r\}$$

is an equation from which can be calculated the value of r, the intraclass correlation derived from the symmetrical table. It is instructive to verify this fact, for the case $k = 3$, by deriving from it the full formula for r given above for that case.

One salient fact appears from the above relation:

the sum of a number of squares, and therefore the left hand of this equation, is necessarily positive. Consequently r cannot have a negative value less than $-1/(k-1)$. There is no such limitation to positive values, all values up to $+1$ being possible. Further, if k, the number in any family, is not necessarily less than some fixed value, the correlation in the population cannot be negative at all. For example, in card games, where the number of suits is limited to four, the correlation between the number of cards in different suits in the same hand may have negative values down to $-\frac{1}{3}$; but there is probably nothing in the production of a leaf or a child which necessitates that the number in such a family should be less than any number however great, and in the absence of such a necessary restriction we cannot expect to find negative correlations within such families. This is in the sharpest contrast to the unrestricted occurrence of negative values among interclass correlations, and it is obvious, since the extreme limits of variation are different in the two cases, that the distribution of values in random samples must be correspondingly modified.

39. Sampling Errors of Intraclass Correlations

The case $k = 2$, which is closely analogous to an interclass correlation, may be treated by the transformation previously employed, namely

$$z = \tfrac{1}{2}\{\log(1+r) - \log(1-r)\};$$

z is then distributed very nearly in a normal distribution, the distribution is wholly independent of the value of the correlation ρ in the population from which the sample is drawn, and the variance of z

consequently depends only on the size of the sample, being given by the formula

$$\sigma_z^2 = \frac{1}{n'-3/2}.$$

The transformation has, therefore, the same advantages in this case as for interclass correlations. It will be observed that the slightly greater accuracy of the intraclass correlation, compared to an interclass correlation based on the same number of pairs, is indicated by the use of $n'-3/2$ in place of $n'-3$. The advantage is, therefore, equivalent to $1\frac{1}{2}$ additional pairs of observations. A second difference lies in the bias to which such estimates are subject. For interclass correlations the value found in samples, whether positive or negative, is exaggerated to the extent of requiring a correction,

$$-\frac{\rho}{2(n'-1)},$$

to be applied to the average value of z. With intraclass correlations the bias is always in the negative direction, and is independent of ρ; the correction necessary in these cases being $+\frac{1}{2}\log\frac{n'}{n'-1}$, or, approximately, $+\frac{1}{2n'-1}$. This bias is characteristic of intraclass correlations for all values of k, and arises from the fact that the symmetrical table does not provide us with quite the best estimate of the correlation.

The effect of the transformation upon the error curves may be seen by comparing Figs. 9 and 10. Fig. 9 shows the actual error curves of r derived from a symmetrical table formed from 8 pairs of observations.

drawn from populations having correlations 0 and 0·8. Fig. 10 shows the corresponding error curves for the

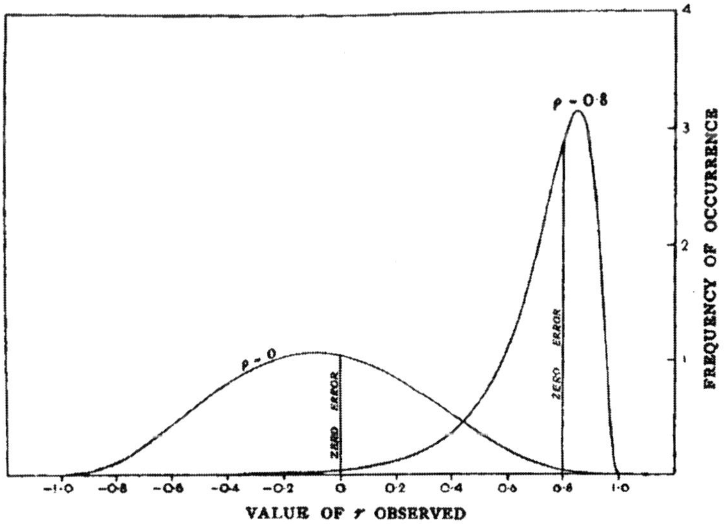

Fig. 9.

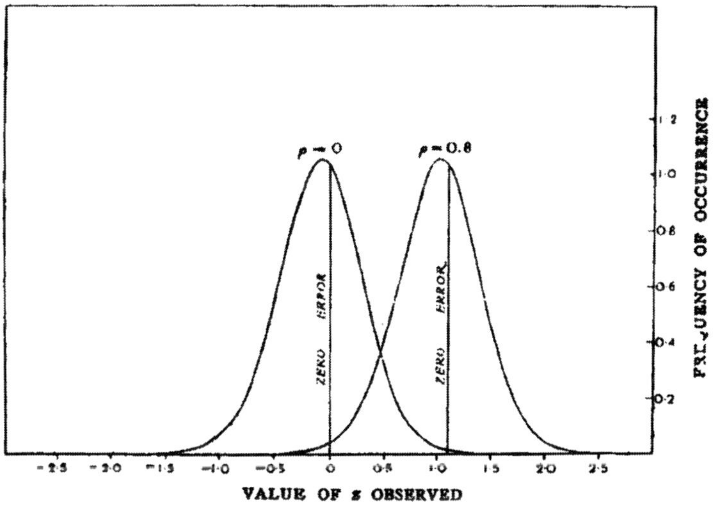

Fig. 10.

distribution of z. The three chief advantages noted in Figs. 7 and 8 are equally visible in the comparison of Figs. 9 and 10. Curves of very unequal variance are replaced by curves of equal variance, skew curves by approximately normal curves, curves of dissimilar form by curves of similar form. In one respect the effect of the transformation is more perfect for the intraclass than it is for the interclass correlations, for, although in both cases the curves are not precisely normal, with the intraclass correlations they are entirely constant in variance and form, whereas with interclass correlations there is a slight variation in both respects, as the correlation in the population is varied. Fig. 10 shows clearly the effect of the bias introduced in estimating the correlation from the symmetrical table; the bias, like the other features of these curves, is absolutely constant in the scale of z.

Ex. 34. *Accuracy of an observed intraclass correlation.*—An intraclass correlation ·6000 is derived from 13 pairs of observations: estimate the correlation in the population from which it was drawn, and find the limits within which it probably lies.

Placing the values of r and z in parallel columns, we have

TABLE 36

	r.	z.
Calculated value . .	+·6000	+ ·6931
Correction . . .	...	+ ·0400
Estimate . . .	+·6250	+ ·7331
Standard error . .	...	± ·2949
Upper limit . . .	+·8675	+1·3229
Lower limit . . .	+·1423	+ ·1433

The calculation is carried through in the z column, and the corresponding values of r found as required from the Table V.B. (p. 210). The value of r is obtained from the symmetrical table, and the corresponding value of z calculated. These values suffer from a small negative bias, and this is removed by adding to z the correction; the unbiased estimate of z is therefore ·7331, and the corresponding value of r, ·6250, is an unbiased estimate, based upon the sample, of the correlation in the population from which the sample was drawn. To find the limits within which this correlation may be expected to lie, the standard error of z is calculated, and twice this value is added and subtracted from the estimated value to obtain the values of z at the upper and lower limits. From these we obtain the corresponding values of r. The observed correlation must in this case be judged significant, since the lower limit is positive; we shall seldom be wrong in concluding that it exceeds ·14 and is less than ·87.

The sampling errors for the cases in which k exceeds 2 may be more satisfactorily treated from the standpoint of the analysis of variance; but whenever it is preferred to think in terms of correlation, it is possible to use an analogous transformation suitable for all values of k. Let

$$z = \frac{1}{2} \log \frac{1+(k-1)r}{1-r},$$

a transformation, which reduces to the form previously used when $k = 2$. Then, in random samples of sets of k observations the distribution of errors in z is independent of the true value, and approaches normality as n' is increased, though not so rapdily as when $k = 2$. The variance of z may be taken, when n' is sufficiently large, to be approximately

$$\frac{k}{2(k-1)(n'-2)}.$$

To find r for a given value of z in this transformation, Table V.B. may still be utilised, as in the following example.

Ex. 35. *Extended use of Table V.B.*—Find the value of r corresponding to $z = +1 \cdot 0605$, when $k = 100$.

First deduct from the given value of z half the natural logarithm of $(k-1)$; enter the difference as "z" in the table and multiply the corresponding value of "r" by k; add $k-2$ and divide by $2(k-1)$. The numerical work is shown below:

TABLE 37

z	$+1 \cdot 0605$
$\frac{1}{2}\log(k-1) = \frac{1}{2}\log 99$ . . .	$2 \cdot 2975$
"z"	$-1 \cdot 2370$
"r"	$-\cdot 8446$
k "r" = 100 "r" . . .	$-84 \cdot 46$
$k-2$	98
$2r(k-1) = 198r$	$13 \cdot 54$
r	$+\cdot 0684$

Ex. 36. *Significance of intraclass correlation from large samples.*—A correlation $+\cdot 0684$ was found between the "ovules failing" in the different pods from the same tree of *Cercis Canadensis*. 100 pods were taken from each of 60 trees (Harris's data). Is this a significant correlation?

As the last example shows, $z = 1 \cdot 0605$; the standard error of z is $\cdot 0933$. The value of z exceeds its standard error over 11 times, and the correlation is undoubtedly significant.

When n' is sufficiently large we have seen that, subject to somewhat severe limitations, it is possible to assume that the interclass correlation is normally distributed in random samples with standard error

$$\frac{1-\rho^2}{\sqrt{n'-1}}.$$

The corresponding formula for intraclass correlations, using k in a class, is

$$\frac{(1-\rho)\{1+(k-1)\rho\}}{\sqrt{\frac{1}{2}k(k-1)n'}}.$$

The utility of this formula is subject to even more drastic limitations than is that for the interclass correlation, for n' is more often small. In addition, the regions for which the formula is inapplicable, even when n' is large, are now not in the neighbourhood of ± 1, but in the neighbourhood of $+1$ and $-\frac{1}{k-1}$. When k is large the latter approaches zero, so that an extremely skew distribution for r is found not only with high correlations but also with very low ones. It is therefore not usually an accurate formula to use in testing significance. This abnormality in the neighbourhood of zero is particularly to be noticed, since it is only in this neighbourhood that much is to be gained by taking high values of k. Near zero, as the formula above shows, the accuracy of an intraclass correlation is with large samples equivalent to that of $\frac{1}{2}k(k-1)n'$ independent pairs of observations; which gives to high values of k an enormous advantage in accuracy. For correlations near ·5, however great k be made, the accuracy is no higher than that obtainable from $9n'/2$ pairs; while near $+1$ it tends to be no more accurate than would be n' pairs.

40. Intraclass Correlation as an Example of the Analysis of Variance

A very great simplification is introduced into questions involving intraclass correlation when we recognise that in such cases the correlation merely measures the relative importance of two groups of factors causing variation. We have seen that in the practical calculation of the intraclass correlation we merely obtain the two necessary quantities kns^2 and $ns^2\{1+(k-1)r\}$, by equating them to the two quantities

$$\overset{kn'}{\underset{1}{S}}(x-\bar{x})^2, \quad k\overset{n'}{\underset{1}{S}}(\bar{x}_p-\bar{x})^2,$$

of which the first is the sum of the squares (kn' in number) of the deviations of all the observations from their general mean, and the second is k times the sum of the squares of the n' deviations of the mean of each family from the general mean. Now it may easily be shown that

$$\overset{kn'}{\underset{1}{S}}(x-\bar{x})^2 = k\overset{n'}{\underset{1}{S}}(\bar{x}_p-\bar{x})^2+\overset{kn'}{\underset{1}{S}}(x-\bar{x}_p)^2,$$

in which the last term is the sum of the squares of the deviations of each individual measurement from the mean of the family to which it belongs. The following table summarises these relations by showing the number of degrees of freedom involved in each case, and, in the last column, the interpretation put upon each expression in the calculation of an intraclass correlation from a symmetrical table.

TABLE 38

	Degrees of Freedom.	Sum of Squares.	
Within families .	$n'(k-1)$	$\overset{kn'}{\underset{1}{S}}(x-\bar{x}_p)^2$	$ns^2(k-1)(1-r)$
Between families .	$n'-1$	$k\overset{n'}{\underset{1}{S}}(\bar{x}_p-\bar{x})^2$	$ns^2\{1+(k-1)r\}$
Total . .	$n'k-1$	$\overset{kn'}{\underset{1}{S}}(x-\bar{x})^2$	ns^2k

It will now be observed that z of the preceding section is, apart from a constant, half the difference of the logarithms of the two parts into which the sum of squares has been analysed. The fact that the form of the distribution of z in random samples is independent of the correlation of the population sampled, is thus a consequence of the fact that deviations of the individual observations from the means of their families are *independent* of the deviations of those means from the general mean. The data provide us with independent estimates of two variances; if these variances are equal the correlation is zero; if our estimates do not differ significantly the correlation is insignificant. If, however, they are significantly different, we may if we choose express the fact in terms of a correlation.

The interpretation of such an inequality of variance in terms of a correlation may be made clear as follows, by a method which also serves to show that the interpretation made by the use of the symmetrical table is slightly defective. Let a quantity be made up of two parts, each normally and independently distributed;

let the variance of the first part be A, and that of the second part B; then it is easy to see that the variance of the total quantity is A+B. Consider a sample of n' values of the first part, and to each of these add a sample of k values of the second part, taking a fresh sample of k in each case. We then have n' families of values with k in each family. In the infinite population from which these are drawn the correlation between pairs of members of the same family will be

$$\rho = \frac{A}{A+B}.$$

From such a set of kn' values we may make estimates of the values of A and B, or in other words we may analyse the variance into the portions contributed by the two causes; the intraclass correlation will be merely the fraction of the total variance due to that cause which observations in the same family have in common. The value of B may be estimated directly, for variation within each family is due to this cause alone, consequently

$$\overset{kn'}{\underset{1}{S}}(x-\bar{x}_p)^2 = n'(k-1)B.$$

The mean of the observations in any family is made up of two parts, the first part with variance A, and a second part, which is the mean of k values of the second parts of the individual values, and has therefore a variance B/k; consequently from the observed variation of the means of the families, we have

$$k\overset{n'}{\underset{1}{S}}(\bar{x}_p-\bar{x})^2 = (n'-1)(kA+B).$$

Table 38 may therefore be rewritten, writing in the

last column s^2 for A+B, and r for the unbiased estimate of the correlation.

TABLE 39

	Degrees of Freedom.	Sum of Squares.	
Within families	$n'(k-1)$	$\overset{kn'}{\underset{1}{S}}(x-\bar{x}_p)^2$	$n'(k-1)B = n's^2(k-1)(1-r)$
Between families	$n'-1$	$k\overset{n'}{\underset{1}{S}}(\bar{x}_p-\bar{x})^2$	$(n'-1)(kA+B) = (n'-1)s^2\{1+(k-1)r\}$
Total	$n'k-1$	$\overset{kn'}{\underset{1}{S}}(x-\bar{x})^2$	$(n'-1)kA+(n'k-1)B = s^2\{n'k-1-(k-1)r\}$

Comparing the last column with that of Table 38 it is apparent that the difference arises solely from putting n' for n in the first line and $n'-1$ for n in the second; the ratio between the sums of squares is altered in the ratio n' : $(n'-1)$, which precisely eliminates the negative bias observed in z derived by the previous method. The error of that method consisted in assuming that the total variance derived from n' sets of related individuals could be accurately estimated by equating the sum of squares of all the individuals from their mean, to ns^2k just as if they were all unrelated; this error is unimportant when n' is large, as it usually is when $k = 2$, but with higher values of k, data may be of great value even when n' is very small, and in such cases serious discrepancies arise from the use of the uncorrected values.

The direct test of the significance of an intraclass correlation may be applied to such a table of the analysis of variance without actually calculating r. If there is no correlation, then A is not significantly different from zero; there is no difference between the several families which is not accounted for, as a random sampling effect of the differences within each family. In fact the whole group of observations is a homogeneous group with variance equal to B.

41. Test of Significance of Difference of Variance

The test of significance of intraclass correlations is thus simply an example of the much wider class of tests of significance which arise in the analysis of variance. These tests are all reducible to the single problem of testing whether one estimate of variance derived from n_1 degrees of freedom is significantly greater than a second such estimate derived from n_2 degrees of freedom. This problem is reduced to its simplest form by calculating z equal to half the difference of the *natural* logarithms of the estimates of the variance, or to the difference of the logarithms of the corresponding standard deviations. Then if P is the probability of exceeding this value by chance, it is possible to calculate the value of z corresponding to different values of P, n_1, and n_2.

A full table of this kind, involving three variables, would be very extensive; we therefore give tables for three especially important values of P, and for a number of combinations of n_1 and n_2, sufficient to indicate the values for other combinations (Table VI, pp. 242-247). We shall give various examples of the use of this table. When both n_1 and n_2 are large, and also for moderate values when they are equal or nearly equal, the distribution of z is sufficiently near normal for effective use to be made of its standard deviation, which may be written

$$\sqrt{\frac{1}{2}\left(\frac{1}{n_1}+\frac{1}{n_2}\right)}.$$

This includes the case of the intraclass correlation, when $k = 2$, for if we have n' pairs of values, the variation between classes is based on $n'-1$ degrees of freedom, and that within classes is based on n' degrees of freedom, so that

$$n_1 = n'-1, \quad n_2 = n',$$

and for moderately large values of n' we may take z to be normally distributed as above explained. When k exceeds 2 we have

$$n_1 = n'-1, \quad n_2 = (k-1)n';$$

these may be very unequal, so that unless n' be quite large, the distribution of z will be perceptibly asymmetrical, and the standard deviation will not provide a satisfactory test of significance.

Ex. 37. *Sex difference in variance of stature.*—From 1164 measurements of males the sum of squares of the deviations was found to be 8590; while from 1456 measurements of females it was 9870: is there a significant difference in absolute variability?

TABLE 40

	Degrees of Freedom.	Sum of Squares.	Mean Square.	Log (Mean Square).	$1/n$.
Men	1163	8590	7·386	1·9996	·0008598
Women	1455	9870	6·783	1·9145	·0006873
				Difference ·0851	Sum ·0015471

The mean squares are calculated from the sum of squares by dividing by the degrees of freedom; the difference of the logarithms is ·0851, so that z is ·0426. The variance of z is half the sum of the last column, so that the standard deviation of z is ·02781. The difference in variability, though suggestive of a real effect, cannot be judged significant on these data.

Ex. 38. *Homogeneity of small samples.*—In an experiment on the accuracy of counting soil bacteria, a soil sample was divided into four parallel samples, and from each of these after dilution seven plates were inoculated. The number of colonies on each plate is shown below. Do the results from the four samples agree within the limits of random sampling? In other words, is the whole set of 28 values homogeneous, or is there any perceptible intraclass correlation?

TABLE 41

Plate.	Sample.			
	I.	II.	III.	IV.
1	72	74	78	69
2	69	72	74	67
3	63	70	70	66
4	59	69	58	64
5	59	66	58	62
6	53	58	56	58
7	51	52	56	54
Total .	426	461	450	440
Mean .	60·86	65·86	64·28	62·86

From these values we obtain

TABLE 42

	Degrees of Freedom.	Sum of Squares.	Mean Square.	S.D.	Log S.D.
Within classes .	24	1446	60·25	7·762	2·0493
Between classes .	3	94·96	31·65	5·626	1·7274
Total . .	27	1540·96	57·07	7·55	—·3219
				(Difference) = z	

The variation within classes is actually the greater, so that if any correlation is indicated it must be negative. The numbers of degrees of freedom are small and unequal, so we shall use Table VI. This is entered with n_1 equal to the degrees of freedom corresponding to the larger variance, in this case 24; also, $n_2 = 3$. The table gives 1·0781 for the 5 per cent. point; so that the observed difference, ·3219, is really very moderate, and quite insignificant. The whole set of 28 values appears to be homogeneous with variance about 57·07.

It should be noticed that if only two samples had been present, the test of homogeneity would have been equivalent to testing the significance of t, as explained in Chapter V. In fact the values for $n_1 = 1$ in the table of z (p. 242) are nothing but the logarithms of the values, for P = ·05 and ·01, in the Table of t (p. 174). Similarly, the values for $n_2 = 1$ in Table VI are the logarithms of the reciprocals of the values, which would appear in Table IV under P = ·95 and ·99. The present method may be regarded as an extension of the method of Chapter V, appropriate when we wish to compare more than two means. Equally it may be regarded as an extension of the methods of Chapter IV, for if n_2 were infinite z would equal $\frac{1}{2}\log\frac{\chi^2}{n}$ of Table III for P = ·05 and ·01, and if n_1 were infinite it would equal $-\frac{1}{2}\log\frac{\chi^2}{n}$ for P = ·95 and ·99. Tests of goodness of fit, in which the sampling variance is not calculable *a priori*, but may be estimated from the data, may therefore be made by means of Table VI. (See Chap. VIII.)

Ex. 39. *Comparison of intraclass correlations.*—

The following correlations are given (Harris's data) for the number of ovules in different pods of the same tree, 100 pods being counted on each tree (*Cercis Canadensis*) :

Meramec Highlands . .	60 trees	+·3527
Lawrence, Kansas . .	22 trees	+·3999

Is the correlation at Lawrence significantly greater than that in the Meramec Highlands?

First we find z in each case from the formula

$$z=\tfrac{1}{2}\{\log(1+99r)-\log(1-r)\}$$

(p. 219); this gives $z=2{\cdot}0081$ for Meramec and 2·1071 for Lawrence; since these were obtained by the method of the symmetrical table we shall insert the small correction $1/(2n'-1)$ and obtain 2·0165 for Meramec, and 2·1304 for Lawrence, as the values which would have been obtained by the method of the analysis of variance.

To ascertain to what errors these determinations are subject, consider first the case of Lawrence, which being based on only 22 trees is subject to the larger errors. We have $n_1=21$, $n_2=22\times 99=2178$. These values are not given in the table, but from the value for $n_1=24$, $n_2=\infty$ it appears that positive errors exceeding ·2085 will occur in rather more than 5 per cent. of samples. This fact alone settles the question of significance, for the value for Lawrence only exceeds that obtained for Meramec by ·1139.

In other cases greater precision may be required. In the Table for z the five values 6, 8, 12, 24, ∞ are chosen for being in harmonic progression, and so facilitating interpolation, if we use $1/n$ as the variable. If we have to interpolate both for n_1 and n_2, we proceed in three steps. We find first the values of z for $n_1 = 12$, $n_2 = 2178$, and for $n_1 = 24$, $n_2 = 2178$, and from these obtain the required value for $n_1 = 21$, $n_2 = 2178$.

To find the value for $n_1 = 12$, $n_2 = 2178$, observe that

$$\frac{60}{2178} = \cdot 0275,$$

for $n_2 = \infty$ we have ·2804, and for $n_2 = 60$ a value higher by ·0450, so that $\cdot 2804 + \cdot 0275 \times \cdot 0450 = \cdot 2816$ gives the approximate value for $n_2 = 2178$.

Similarly for $n_1 = 24$

$$\cdot 2085 + \cdot 0275 \times \cdot 0569 = \cdot 2101.$$

From these two values we must find the value for $n_1 = 21$; now

$$\frac{24}{21} = 1 + \frac{1}{7},$$

so that we must add to the value for $n_1 = 24$ one-seventh of its difference from the value for $n_1 = 12$; this gives

$$\cdot 2101 + \frac{\cdot 0715}{7} = \cdot 2203,$$

which is approximately the positive deviation which would be exceeded by chance in 5 per cent. of random samples.

Just as we have found the 5 per cent. point for positive deviations, so the 5 per cent. point for negative deviations may be found by interchanging n_1 and n_2; this turns out to be ·2978. If we assume that our observed value does not transgress the 5 per cent. point in either deviation, that is to say that it lies in the central nine-tenths of its frequency distribution, we may say that the value of z for Lawrence, Kansas, lies between 1·9101 and 2·4282; these fiducial limits being found respectively by subtracting the positive deviation and adding the negative deviation to the observed value.

The fact that the two deviations are distinctly unequal, as is generally the case when n_1 and n_2 are unequal and not both large, shows that such a case cannot be treated accurately by means of a probable error.

Somewhat more accurate values than the above may be obtained by improved methods of interpolation; the method given will, however, suffice for all ordinary requirements, except in the corner of the table where n_1 exceeds 24 and n_2 exceeds 30. For cases which fall into this region, the following formula gives the 5 per cent. point within one-hundredth of its value. If h is the harmonic mean of n_1 and n_2, so that

$$\frac{2}{h} = \frac{1}{n_1} + \frac{1}{n_2},$$

then

$$z = \frac{1 \cdot 6449}{\sqrt{h-1}} - \cdot 7843 \left(\frac{1}{n_1} - \frac{1}{n_2}\right).$$

Similarly, the 1 per cent. point is given approximately by the formula

$$z = \frac{2 \cdot 3263}{\sqrt{h-1 \cdot 4}} - 1 \cdot 235 \left(\frac{1}{n_1} - \frac{1}{n_2}\right).$$

For the 0·1% point we may use

$$z = \frac{3 \cdot 0902}{\sqrt{h-2 \cdot 1}} - 1 \cdot 925 \left(\frac{1}{n_1} - \frac{1}{n_2}\right).$$

The modification of the $\sqrt{h-1}$, which is good for the 5% point, used for the higher levels of significance, is due to W. G. Cochran.

Let us apply this formula to find the 5 per cent. points for the Meramec Highlands, $n_1 = 59$, $n_2 = 5940$; the calculation is as follows:

TABLE 43

$1/n_1$	·01695	$\sqrt{h-1}$	10·76		
$1/n_2$	·00017	$1/\sqrt{h-1}$	·09294	First term	·15288
$2/h$	·01712	$1/n_1-1/n_2$	·01678	Second term	·01316
$1/h$	·00856			Difference	·1397
h	116·8			Sum	·1660

The 5 per cent. point for positive deviations is therefore ·1397, and for negative deviations ·1660; with the same standards as before, therefore, we may say that the value for Meramec lies between 1·8768 and 2·1825 with a fiducial probability of 90 per cent.; the large overlap of this range with that of Lawrence shows that the correlations found in the two districts are not significantly different.

42. Analysis of Variance into more than Two Portions

It is often necessary to divide the total variance into more than two portions; it sometimes happens both in experimental and in observational data that the observations may be grouped into classes in more than one way; each observation belongs to one class of type A and to a different class of type B. In such a case we can find separately the variance between classes of type A and between classes of type B; the balance of the total variance may represent only the variance within each subclass, or there may be in addition an interaction of causes so that a change in class of type A does not have the same effect in all B classes. If the observations do not occur singly in the subclasses, the variance within the subclasses may be determined independently, and the presence or absence of interaction verified. Sometimes also, for example, if the observations are frequencies, it is possible to calculate the variance to be expected in the subclasses.

Ex. 40. *Diurnal and annual variation of rain*

TABLE 44

Hour.	Jan.	Feb.	Mar.	Apr.	May.	June.	July.	Aug.	Sept.	Oct.	Nov.	Dec.	Total.
1	19	16	34	17	21	26	18	18	11	27	31	28	266
2	27	16	32	21	18	25	17	24	14	37	27	29	287
3	27	19	27	22	21	31	15	32	16	36	27	33	306
4	19	20	23	25	26	28	15	31	20	39	28	34	308
5	23	18	23	19	28	31	23	23	16	42	28	31	305
6	20	23	33	19	22	29	15	22	17	42	24	26	292
7	20	22	35	25	19	33	15	18	20	36	19	23	285
8	22	22	28	26	24	23	15	18	20	32	21	31	282
9	22	20	25	21	24	28	11	22	16	35	24	28	276
10	21	19	19	15	18	22	16	19	16	31	20	24	240
11	17	19	23	18	26	25	17	13	14	33	22	21	248
12	20	21	31	19	25	27	24	25	20	36	31	25	304
13	16	18	35	28	23	32	24	25	18	29	29	28	305
14	21	20	35	28	23	32	20	27	15	28	24	28	301
15	17	18	39	32	22	27	25	30	20	28	31	32	321
16	18	31	38	38	31	32	31	28	15	37	27	34	360
17	26	29	37	30	22	32	24	31	20	38	24	38	351
18	21	25	41	24	24	28	25	27	21	37	26	33	332
19	26	18	35	25	23	30	25	27	20	36	26	31	322
20	24	18	30	21	28	25	28	18	16	34	30	25	297
21	23	20	27	23	18	21	25	20	14	35	27	39	292
22	25	16	33	22	29	23	22	22	14	22	26	36	290
23	22	15	33	18	24	23	21	19	11	31	28	28	273
24	22	18	30	19	26	27	18	22	14	22	28	27	273
Total	518	481	746	555	565	660	489	561	398	803	628	712	7116

frequency.—The frequencies of rain at different hours in different months (Table 44) were observed at Richmond during 10 years (quoted from Shaw, with two corrections in the totals).

The variance may be analysed as follows :

TABLE 45

	Degrees of Freedom.	Sum of Squares.	Mean Square.
Months . .	11	6,568·58	597·144
Hours . . .	23	1,539·33	66·928
Remainder . .	253	3,819·58	15·097
Total . .	287	11,927·50	

The mean of the 288 values given in the table is 24·7, and if the original data had represented independent sampling chances, we should expect the mean square residue to be nearly as great as this, or greater, if the rain distribution during the day differs in different months. Clearly the residual variance is subnormal, and the reason for this is obvious when we consider that the probability that it should be raining in the 2nd hour is not independent of whether it is raining or not in the 1st hour of the *same day*. Each shower will thus often have been entered twice or more often, and the values for neighbouring hours in the same month will be positively correlated. Much of the random variation has thus been included in that ascribed to the months, and probably accounts for the very irregular sequence of the monthly totals. The variance between the 24 hours is, however, quite significantly greater than the residual variance, and this shows that the rainy hours have been on the whole similar in the different months, so that the figures clearly indicate the influence of time of day. From the data it is not possible to estimate the influence of time of year, or to discuss whether the effect of time of day is the same in all months.

Ex. 41. *Analysis of variation in experimental field trials.*—The table on the following page gives the yield in lb. per plant in an experiment with potatoes (Rothamsted data). A plot of land, the whole of which had received a dressing of dung, was divided into 36 patches, on which 12 varieties were grown, each variety having 3 patches scattered over the area. Each patch was divided into three lines, one of which received, in addition to dung, a basal dressing only, containing no potash, while the other two received additional dressings of sulphate and chloride of potash respectively.

From data of this sort a variety of information may be derived. The total yields of the 36 patches give us 35 degrees of freedom, of which 11 represent differences among the 12 varieties, and 24 represent the differences between different patches growing the same variety. By comparing the variance in these two classes we may test the significance of the varietal differences in yield for the soil and climate of the experiment. The 72 additional degrees of freedom given by the yields of the separate rows consist of 2 due to manurial treatment, which we can subdivide into one representing the differences due to a potash dressing as against the basal dressing, and a second representing the manurial difference between the sulphate and the chloride; and 70 more representing the differences observed in manurial response in the different patches. These latter may in turn be divided into 22 representing the difference in manurial response of the different varieties, and 48 representing the differences in manurial response in different patches

TABLE 46

Variety.	Sulphate Row.	Sulphate Row.	Sulphate Row.	Chloride Row.	Chloride Row.	Chloride Row.	Basal Row.	Basal Row.	Basal Row.
Ajax	3·20	4·00	3·86	2·55	3·04	4·13	2·82	1·75	4·71
Arran Comrade	2·25	2·56	2·58	1·96	2·15	2·10	2·42	2·17	2·17
British Queen	3·21	2·82	3·82	2·71	2·68	4·17	2·75	2·75	3·32
Duke of York	1·11	1·25	2·25	1·57	2·00	1·75	1·61	2·00	2·46
Epicure	2·36	1·64	2·29	2·11	1·93	2·64	1·43	2·25	2·79
Great Scot	3·38	3·07	3·89	2·79	3·54	4·14	3·07	3·25	3·50
Iron Duke	3·43	3·00	3·96	3·33	3·08	3·32	3·50	2·32	3·29
K. of K.	3·71	4·07	4·21	3·39	4·63	4·21	2·89	4·20	4·32
Kerr's Pink	3·04	3·57	3·82	2·96	3·18	4·32	2·00	3·00	3·88
Nithsdale	2·57	2·21	3·58	2·04	2·93	3·71	1·96	2·86	3·56
Tinwald Perfection	3·46	3·11	2·50	2·83	2·96	3·21	2·55	3·39	3·36
Up-to-Date	4·29	2·93	4·25	3·39	3·68	4·07	4·21	3·64	4·11

TABLE 47

Variety.	Manuring.			Total.	Plot.		
	Sulphate.	Chloride.	Basal.		I.	II.	III.
Ajax	11·06	9·72	9·28	30·06	8·57	8·79	12·70
Arran Comrade	7·39	6·21	6·76	20·36	6·63	6·88	6·85
British Queen	9·85	9·56	8·82	28·23	8·67	8·25	11·31
Duke of York	4·61	5·32	6·07	16·00	4·29	5·25	6·46
Epicure	6·29	6·68	6·47	19·44	5·90	5·82	7·72
Great Scot	10·34	10·47	9·82	30·63	9·24	9·86	11·53
Iron Duke	10·39	9·73	9·11	29·23	10·26	8·40	10·57
K. of K.	11·99	12·23	11·41	35·63	9·99	12·90	12·74
Kerr's Pink	10·43	10·46	8·88	29·77	8·00	9·75	12·02
Nithsdale	8·36	8·68	8·38	25·42	6·57	8·00	10·85
Tinwald Perfection	9·07	9·00	9·30	27·37	8·84	9·46	9·07
Up-to-Date	11·47	11·14	11·96	34·57	11·89	10·25	12·43
Total	111·25	109·20	106·26	326·71	...	...	...

growing the same variety. To test the significance of the manurial effects, we may compare the variance in each of the two manurial degrees of freedom with that in the remaining 48; to test the significance of the differences in varietal response to manure, we compare the variance in the 22 degrees of freedom with that in the 48; while to test the significance of the difference in yield of the same variety in different patches, we compare the 24 degrees of freedom representing the differences in the yields of different patches growing the same variety with the 48 degrees representing the differences of manurial response on different patches growing the same variety.

For each variety we shall require the total yield for the whole of each patch, the total yield for the 3 patches and the total yield for each manure; we shall also need the total yield for each manure for the aggregate of the 12 varieties; these values are given on page 238 (Table 47).

The sum of the squares of the deviations of all the 108 values from their mean is 71·699; divided, according to patches, in 36 classes of 3, the value for the 36 patches is 61·078; dividing this again according to varieties into 12 classes of 3, the value for the 12 varieties is 43·638. We may express the facts so far as follows:

TABLE 48

Variance.	Degrees of Freedom.	Sum of Squares.	Mean Square.	Log (S.D.)
Between varieties .	11	43·6384	3·967	·6890
Between patches for same variety .	24	17·4401	·727	−·1594
Within patches .	72	10·6204	...	...
Total . .	107	71·6989		

The value of z, found as the difference of the logarithms in the last column, is ·8484, the corresponding 1 per cent. value being about ·564; the effect of variety is therefore very significant.

Of the variation within the patches the portion ascribable to the two differences of manurial treatment may be derived from the totals for the three manurial treatments. The sum of the squares of the three deviations, divided by 36, is ·3495; of this the square of the difference of the totals for the two potash dressings, divided by 72, contributes ·0584, while the square of the difference between their mean and the total for the basal dressing, divided by 54, gives the remainder, ·2911. It is possible, however, that the whole effect of the dressings may not appear in these figures, for if the different varieties had responded in different ways, or to different extents, to the dressings, the whole effect would not appear in the totals. The 70 remaining degrees of freedom would not be homogeneous. The 36 values, giving the totals for each manuring and for each variety, give us 35 degrees of freedom, of which 11 represent the differences of variety, 2 the differences of manuring, and the remaining 22 show the differences in manurial response of the different varieties. The analysis of this group is shown below:

TABLE 49

Variance due to	Degrees of Freedom.	Sum of Squares.	Mean Square.
Potash dressing . . .	1	·2911	·2911
Sulphate *v.* chloride . .	1	·0584	·0584
Differential response of varieties	22	2·1911	·0996
Differential response in patches with same variety . .	48	8·0798	·1683
Total . . .	72	10·6204	

To test the significance of the variation observed in the yield of patches bearing the same variety, we may compare the value ·727 found above from 24 degrees of freedom, with ·1683 just found from 48 degrees. The value of z, half the difference of the logarithms, is ·7316, while the 1 per cent. point is about ·394. The evidence for unequal fertility of the different patches is therefore unmistakable. As is always found in careful field trials, local irregularities in the nature or depth of the soil materially affect the yields. In this case the soil irregularity was perhaps combined with unequal quality or quantity of the dung supplied.

There is no sign of differential response among the varieties; indeed, the difference between patches with different varieties is less than that found for patches with the same variety. The difference between the values is not significant; $z = ·2623$, while the 5 per cent. point is about ·33.

Finally, the effect of the manurial dressings tested is small; the difference due to potash is indeed greater than the value for the differential effects, which we may now call random fluctuations, but z is only ·3427, and would require to be about ·7 to be significant. With no total response, it is of course to be expected, though not as a necessary consequence, that the differential effects should be insignificant. Evidently the plants with the basal dressing had all the potash necessary, and in addition no apparent effect on the yield was produced by the difference between chloride and sulphate ions.

[TABLE

TABLE

5 PER CENT. POINTS OF

	Values			
	1.	2.	3.	4.
Values of n_2 1	2·5421	2·6479	2·6870	2·7071
2	1·4592	1·4722	1·4765	1·4787
3	1·1577	1·1284	1·1137	1·1051
4	1·0212	·9690	·9429	·9272
5	·9441	·8777	·8441	·8236
6	·8948	·8188	·7798	·7558
7	·8606	·7777	·7347	·7080
8	·8355	·7475	·7014	·6725
9	·8163	·7242	·6757	·6450
10	·8012	·7058	·6553	·6232
11	·7889	·6909	·6387	·6055
12	·7788	·6786	·6250	·5907
13	·7703	·6682	·6134	·5783
14	·7630	·6594	·6036	·5677
15	·7568	·6518	·5950	·5585
16	·7514	·6451	·5876	·5505
17	·7466	·6393	·5811	·5434
18	·7424	·6341	·5753	·5371
19	·7386	·6295	·5701	·5315
20	·7352	·6254	·5654	·5265
21	·7322	·6216	·5612	·5219
22	·7294	·6182	·5574	·5178
23	·7269	·6151	·5540	·5140
24	·7246	·6123	·5508	·5106
25	·7225	·6097	·5478	·5074
26	·7205	·6073	·5451	·5045
27	·7187	·6051	·5427	·5017
28	·7171	·6030	·5403	·4992
29	·7155	·6011	·5382	·4969
30	·7141	·5994	·5362	·4947
60	·6933	·5738	·5073	·4632
∞	·6729	·5486	·4787	·4319

VI

THE DISTRIBUTION OF z

of n_1.

5.	6.	8.	12.	24.	∝.
2·7194	2·7276	2·7380	2·7484	2·7588	2·7693
1·4800	1·4808	1·4819	1·4830	1·4840	1·4851
1·0994	1·0953	1·0899	1·0842	1·0781	1·0716
·9168	·9093	·8993	·8885	·8767	·8639
·8097	·7997	·7862	·7714	·7550	·7368
·7394	·7274	·7112	·6931	·6729	·6499
·6896	·6761	·6576	·6369	·6134	·5862
·6525	·6378	·6175	·5945	·5682	·5371
·6238	·6080	·5862	·5613	·5324	·4979
·6009	·5843	·5611	·5346	·5035	·4657
·5822	·5648	·5406	·5126	·4795	·4387
·5666	·5487	·5234	·4941	·4592	·4156
·5535	·5350	·5089	·4785	·4419	·3957
·5423	·5233	·4964	·4649	·4269	·3782
·5326	·5131	·4855	·4532	·4138	·3628
·5241	·5042	·4760	·4428	·4022	·3490
·5166	·4964	·4676	·4337	·3919	·3366
·5099	·4894	·4602	·4255	·3827	·3253
·5040	·4832	·4535	·4182	·3743	·3151
·4986	·4776	·4474	·4116	·3668	·3057
·4938	·4725	·4420	·4055	·3599	·2971
·4894	·4679	·4370	·4001	·3536	·2892
·4854	·4636	·4325	·3950	·3478	·2818
·4817	·4598	·4283	·3904	·3425	·2749
·4783	·4562	·4244	·3862	·3376	·2685
·4752	·4529	·4209	·3823	·3330	·2625
·4723	·4499	·4176	·3786	·3287	·2569
·4696	·4471	·4146	·3752	·3248	·2516
·4671	·4444	·4117	·3720	·3211	·2466
·4648	·4420	·4090	·3691	·3176	·2419
·4311	·4064	·3702	·3255	·2654	·1644
·3974	·3706	·3309	·2804	·2085	0

TABLE

1 PER CENT. POINTS OF

	Values			
Values of n_2	1.	2.	3.	4.
1	4·1535	4·2585	4·2974	4·3175
2	2·2950	2·2976	2·2984	2·2988
3	1·7649	1·7140	1·6915	1·6786
4	1·5270	1·4452	1·4075	1·3856
5	1·3943	1·2929	1·2449	1·2164
6	1·3103	1·1955	1·1401	1·1068
7	1·2526	1·1281	1·0672	1·0300
8	1·2106	1·0787	1·0135	·9734
9	1·1786	1·0411	·9724	·9299
10	1·1535	1·0114	·9399	·8954
11	1·1333	·9874	·9136	·8674
12	1·1166	·9677	·8919	·8443
13	1·1027	·9511	·8737	·8248
14	1·0909	·9370	·8581	·8082
15	1·0807	·9249	·8448	·7939
16	1·0719	·9144	·8331	·7814
17	1·0641	·9051	·8229	·7705
18	1·0572	·8970	·8138	·7607
19	1·0511	·8897	·8057	·7521
20	1·0457	·8831	·7985	·7443
21	1·0408	·8772	·7920	·7372
22	1·0363	·8719	·7860	·7309
23	1·0322	·8670	·7806	·7251
24	1·0285	·8626	·7757	·7197
25	1·0251	·8585	·7712	·7148
26	1·0220	·8548	·7670	·7103
27	1·0191	·8513	·7631	·7062
28	1·0164	·8481	·7595	·7023
29	1·0139	·8451	·7562	·6987
30	1·0116	·8423	·7531	·6954
60	·9784	·8025	·7086	·6472
∞	·9462	·7636	·6651	·5999

VI.—*Continued*

THE DISTRIBUTION OF z

of n_1.

5.	6.	8.	12	24.	∞.
4·3297	4·3379	4·3482	4·3585	4·3689	4·3794
2·2991	2·2992	2·2994	2·2997	2·2999	2·3001
1·6703	1·6645	1·6569	1·6489	1·6404	1·6314
1·3711	1·3609	1·3473	1·3327	1·3170	1·3000
1·1974	1·1838	1·1656	1·1457	1·1239	1·0997
1·0843	1·0680	1·0460	1·0218	·9948	·9643
1·0048	·9864	·9614	·9335	·9020	·8658
·9459	·9259	·8983	·8673	·8319	·7904
·9006	·8791	·8494	·8157	·7769	·7305
·8646	·8419	·8104	·7744	·7324	·6816
·8354	·8116	·7785	·7405	·6958	·6408
·8111	·7864	·7520	·7122	·6649	·6061
·7907	·7652	·7295	·6882	·6386	·5761
·7732	·7471	·7103	·6675	·6159	·5500
·7582	·7314	·6937	·6496	·5961	·5269
·7450	·7177	·6791	·6339	·5786	·5064
·7335	·7057	·6663	·6199	·5630	·4879
·7232	·6950	·6549	·6075	·5491	·4712
·7140	·6854	·6447	·5964	·5366	·4560
·7058	·6768	·6355	·5864	·5253	·4421
·6984	·6690	·6272	·5773	·5150	·4294
·6916	·6620	·6196	·5691	·5056	·4176
·6855	·6555	·6127	·5615	·4969	·4068
·6799	·6496	·6064	·5545	·4890	·3967
·6747	·6442	·6006	·5481	·4816	·3872
·6699	·6392	·5952	·5422	·4748	·3784
·6655	·6346	·5902	·5367	·4685	·3701
·6614	·6303	·5856	·5316	·4626	·3624
·6576	·6263	·5813	·5269	·4570	·3550
·6540	·6226	·5773	·5224	·4519	·3481
·6028	·5687	·5189	·4574	·3746	·2352
·5522	·5152	·4604	·3908	·2913	0

TABLE

0·1 PER CENT. POINTS OF

Values of n_2.	Values 1.	2.	3.	4.
1	6·4577	6·5612	6·5966	6·6201
2	3·4531	3·4534	3·4535	3·4535
3	2·5604	2·5003	2·4748	2·4603
4	2·1529	2·0574	2·0143	1·9892
5	1·9255	1·8002	1·7513	1·7184
6	1·7849	1·6479	1·5828	1·5433
7	1·6874	1·5384	1·4662	1·4221
8	1·6177	1·4587	1·3809	1·3332
9	1·5646	1·3982	1·3160	1·2653
10	1·5232	1·3509	1·2650	1·2116
11	1·4900	1·3128	1·2238	1·1683
12	1·4627	1·2814	1·1900	1·1326
13	1·4400	1·2553	1·1616	1·1026
14	1·4208	1·2332	1·1376	1·0772
15	1·4043	1·2141	1·1169	1·0553
16	1·3900	1·1976	1·0989	1·0362
17	1·3775	1·1832	1·0832	1·0195
18	1·3665	1·1704	1·0693	1·0047
19	1·3567	1·1591	1·0569	·9915
20	1·3480	1·1489	1·0458	·9798
21	1·3401	1·1398	1·0358	·9691
22	1·3329	1·1315	1·0268	·9595
23	1·3264	1·1240	1·0186	·9507
24	1·3205	1·1171	1·0111	·9427
25	1·3151	1·1108	1·0041	·9354
26	1·3101	1·1050	·9978	·9286
27	1·3055	1·0997	·9920	·9223
28	1·3013	1·0947	·9866	·9165
29	1·2973	1·0903	·9815	·9112
30	1·2936	1·0859	·9768	·9061
60	1·2413	1·0248	·9100	·8345
∞	1·1910	·9663	·8453	·7648

The author is indebted to Dr Deming

VI.—*Continued*

THE DISTRIBUTION OF z

of n_1.

5.	6.	8.	12.	24.	∞.
6·6323	6·6405	6·6508	6·6611	6·6715	6·6819
3·4535	3·4535	3·4536	3·4537	3·4536	3·4536
2·4511	2·4446	2·4361	2·4272	2·4179	2·4081
1·9728	1·9612	1·9459	1·9294	1·9118	1·8927
1·6964	1·6808	1·6596	1·6370	1·6123	1·5845
1·5177	1·4986	1·4730	1·4449	1·4134	1·3783
1·3927	1·3711	1·3417	1·3090	1·2721	1·2296
1·3008	1·2770	1·2443	1·2077	1·1662	1·1169
1·2304	1·2047	1·1694	1·1293	1·0830	1·0279
1·1748	1·1475	1·1098	1·0668	1·0165	·9557
1·1297	1·1012	1·0614	1·0157	·9619	·8957
1·0926	1·0628	1·0213	·9733	·9162	·8450
1·0614	1·0306	·9875	·9374	·8774	·8014
1·0348	1·0031	·9586	·9066	·8439	·7635
1·0119	·9795	·9336	·8800	·8147	·7301
·9920	·9588	·9119	·8567	·7891	·7005
·9745	·9407	·8927	·8361	·7664	·6740
·9590	·9246	·8757	·8178	·7462	·6502
·9442	·9103	·8605	·8014	·7277	·6285
·9329	·8974	·8469	·7867	·7115	·6086
·9217	·8858	·8346	·7735	·6964	·5904
·9116	·8753	·8234	·7612	·6828	·5738
·9024	·8657	·8132	·7501	·6704	·5583
·8939	·8569	·8038	·7400	·6589	·5440
·8862	·8489	·7953	·7306	·6483	·5307
·8791	·8415	·7873	·7220	·6385	·5183
·8725	·8346	·7800	·7140	·6294	·5066
·8664	·8282	·7732	·7066	·6209	·4957
·8607	·8223	·7679	·6997	·6129	·4853
·8554	·8168	·7610	·6932	·6056	·4756
·7798	·7377	·6760	·5992	·4955	·3198
·7059	·6599	·5917	·5044	·3786	0

for this section of the Table of z.

VIII

FURTHER APPLICATIONS OF THE ANALYSIS OF VARIANCE

43. We shall in this chapter give examples of the further applications of the method of the analysis of variance developed in the last chapter in connexion with the theory of intraclass correlations. It is impossible in a short space to give examples of all the different applications which may be made of this method; we shall therefore limit ourselves to those of the most immediate practical importance, paying especial attention to those cases where erroneous methods have been largely used, or where no alternative method of attack has hitherto been put forward.

44. Fitness of Regression Formulæ

There is no more pressing need in connexion with the examination of experimental results than to test whether a given body of data is or is not in agreement with any suggested hypothesis. The previous chapters have largely been concerned with such tests appropriate to hypotheses involving frequency of occurrence, such as the Mendelian hypothesis of segregating genes, or the hypothesis of linear arrangement in linkage groups, or the more general hypotheses of the independence or correlation of variates. More frequently, however, it is desired to test hypotheses involving, in statistical language, the form of regression lines. We may wish to test, for example, if the growth of an animal, plant or population follows an assigned law, if for example it increases with time in arithmetic or geometric progression, or according to the so-called "autocatalytic," or "logistic," law of increase; we may wish to test if with increasing applications of manure, plant growth increases in accordance with the laws which have been put forward, or whether in fact the data in hand are inconsistent with such a supposition. Such questions arise not only in crucial tests of widely recognised laws, but in every case where a relation, however empirical, is believed to be descriptive of the data, and are of value not only in the final stage of establishing the laws of nature, but in the early stages of testing the efficiency of a technique. The methods we shall put forward for testing the Goodness of Fit of regression lines are aimed both at simplifying the calculations by reducing them to a standard form, and so making *accurate* tests possible, and at so displaying the whole process that it may be apparent exactly what questions can be answered by such a statistical examination of the data.

If for each of a number of selected values of the independent variate x a number of observations of the dependent variate y is made, let the number of values of x available be a; then a is the number of arrays in our data. Designating any particular array by means of the suffix p, the number of observations in any array will be denoted by n_p, and the mean of their values by $\bar{y}_p$; $\bar{y}$ being the general mean of all the values of y. Then whatever be the nature of the data, the purely algebraic identity

$$S(y-\bar{y})^2 = S\{n_p(\bar{y}_p-\bar{y})^2\}+SS(y-\bar{y}_p)^2$$

expresses the fact that the sum of the squares of the deviations of all the values of y from their general mean may be broken up into two parts, one representing the sum of the squares of the deviations of the means of the arrays from the general mean, each multiplied by the number in the array, while the second is the sum of the squares of the deviations of each observation from the mean of the array in which it occurs. This resembles the analysis used for intraclass correlations, save that now the number of observations may be different in each array. The deviations of the observations from the means of the arrays are due to causes of variation, including errors of grouping, errors of observation, and so on, which are not dependent upon the value of x; the standard deviation due to these causes thus provides a basis for comparison by which we can test whether the deviations of the means of the arrays from the values expected by hypothesis are or are not significant.

Let Y_p represent in any array the mean value expected on the hypothesis to be tested, then

$$S\{n_p(\bar{y}_p - Y_p)^2\}$$

will measure the discrepancy between the data and the hypothesis. In comparing this with the variation within the arrays, we must of course consider how many degrees of freedom are available, in which the observations may differ from the hypothesis. In some cases, which are relatively rare, the hypothesis specifies the actual mean value to be expected in each array; in such cases a degrees of freedom are available, a being the number of the arrays. More frequently, the hypothesis specifies only the form of the regression line, having one or more parameters to be determined from the observations, as when we wish to test if the regression can be represented by a straight line, so that our hypothesis is justified if any straight line fits the data. In such cases to find the number of degrees of freedom we must deduct from *a* the number of parameters obtained from the data.

Ex. 42. *Test of straightness of regression line.*—The following data are taken from a paper by A. H. Hersh on the influence of temperature on the number of eye facets in *Drosophila melanogaster*, in various homozygous and heterozygous phases of the " bar " factor. They represent females heterozygous for " full " and " double-bar," the facet number being measured in factorial units, effectively a logarithmic scale. Can the influence of temperature on facet number be represented by a straight line, in these units ?

[TABLE

TABLE 50

Temperature °C.	15°.	17°.	19°.	21°.	23°.	25°.	27°.	29°.	31°.	Total.
+ 8·07	3	1	1	...	...	...	...	...	...	5
+ 7·07	5	2	5	1	...	...	...	...	...	13
+ 6·07	13	7	3	...	...	...	...	...	...	23
+ 5·07	25	9	2	1	...	...	...	...	...	37
+ 4·07	22	10	16	...	...	2	...	...	...	50
+ 3·07	12	10	12	6	1	3	...	...	...	44
+ 2·07	7	5	14	16	2	2	...	...	...	46
+ 1·07	3	4	14	21	8	9	...	...	...	59
+ ·07	...	3	7	26	7	19	1	...	...	63
− ·93	...	1	7	12	11	24	3	1	...	59
− 1·93	...	...	1	9	14	22	8	6	...	60
− 2·93	...	2	1	5	12	15	15	4	...	54
− 3·93	...	...	...	2	19	18	44	10	1	94
− 4·93	...	...	...	1	4	4	26	6	6	47
− 5·93	...	...	...	...	2	2	19	14	13	50
− 6·93	...	...	...	...	2	...	11	28	9	50
− 7·93	...	...	...	...	3	1	8	8	8	28
− 8·93	...	...	...	...	1	...	2	5	5	13
− 9·93	...	...	...	...	...	...	...	4	4	8
−10·93	...	...	...	...	...	...	...	10	2	12
−11·93	...	...	...	...	...	1	...	1	2	4
−12·93	...	...	...	...	...	...	...	·5	1·5	2
−13·93	...	...	...	...	...	...	...	·5	·5	1
−14·93	...	...	...	...	...	...	...	...	...	...
−15·93	...	...	...	...	...	...	...	...	1	1
Total	90	54	83	100	86	122	137	98	53	823

There are 9 arrays representing 9 different temperatures. Taking a working mean at −1·93 we calculate the total and average excess over the working mean from each array, and for the aggregate of all 9. Each average is found by dividing the total excess by the number in the array; three decimal places are sufficient save in the aggregate, where four are needed. We have

[TABLE

TABLE 51

Array.	15.	17.	19.	21.	23.	25.	27.	29.	31.	Aggregate
Total excess	583	294	367	225	−43	+37	−369	−463·5	−306·5	+324
Mean excess	6·478	5·444	4·422	2·250	−·500	+·303	−2·693	−4·730	−5·783	+·3937

The sum of the products of these nine pairs of numbers, less the product of the final pair, gives the value of

$$S\{n_p(\bar{y}_p-\bar{y})^2\} = 12{,}370,$$

while from the distribution of the aggregate of all the values of y we have

$$S(y-\bar{y})^2 = 16{,}202,$$

whence is deduced the following table:

TABLE 52

Variance.	Degrees of Freedom.	Sum of Squares.	Mean Square.
Between arrays .	8	12,370	...
Within arrays .	814	3,832	4·708
Total . .	822	16,202	

The variance within the arrays is thus only about 4·7; the variance between the arrays will be made up of a part which can be represented by a linear regression, and of a part which represents the deviations of the observed means of arrays from a straight line.

To find the part represented by a linear regression, calculate

$$S(x-\bar{x})^2 = 4742 \cdot 21$$

and

$$S(x-\bar{x})(y-\bar{y}) = -7535 \cdot 38,$$

which latter can be obtained by multiplying the above total excess values by $x-\bar{x}$; then since

$$\frac{(7535 \cdot 38)^2}{4742 \cdot 21} = 11,974$$

we may complete the analysis as follows:

TABLE 53

Variance between Arrays due to	Degrees of Freedom.	Sum of Squares.	Mean Square.
Linear regression . .	1	11,974	...
Deviations from regression	7	396	56·6
Total . .	8	12,370	

It is useful to check the figure, 396, found by differences, by calculating the actual value of Y for the regression formula and evaluating

$$S\{n_p(\bar{y}_p - Y_p)^2\};$$

such a check has the advantage that it shows to which arrays in particular the bulk of the discrepancy is due, in this case to the observations at 23 and 25° C.

The deviations from linear regression are evidently larger than would be expected, if the regression were really linear, from the variations within the arrays. For the value of z, we have

TABLE 54

Degrees of Freedom.	Mean Square.	Natural Log.	$\frac{1}{2}$ Log$_e$.
7	56·6	4·0360	2·0180
814	4·708	1·5493	·7746
	Difference (z)	...	1·2434

while the 1 per cent. point is about ·488. There can therefore be no question of the statistical significance of the deviations from the straight line, although the latter accounts for the greater part of the variation.

Note that Sheppard's adjustment is not to be applied in making this test; a certain proportion both of the variation within arrays and of the deviations from the regression line is ascribable to errors of grouping, but to deduct from each the average error due to this cause would be unduly to accentuate their inequality, and so to render inaccurate the test of significance.

The example of regression worked out in Section 29·2 supplies a further illustration, to which the test given in this section is equally applicable.

45. The "Correlation Ratio" η

We have seen how, from the sum of the squares of the deviations of all observations from the general mean, a portion may be separated representing the differences between different arrays. The ratio which this bears to the whole is often denoted by the symbol η^2, so that

$$\eta^2 = S\{n_p(\bar{y}_p - \bar{y})^2\} \div S(y - \bar{y})^2,$$

and the square root of this ratio, η, is called the correlation ratio of y on x. Similarly, if Y is the hypothetical regression function, we may define R, so that

$$R^2 = S\{n_p(Y-\bar{y})^2\} \div S(y-\bar{y})^2,$$

then R will be the correlation coefficient between y and Y, and if the regression is linear, $R^2 = r^2$, where r is the correlation coefficient between x and y. From these relations it is obvious that η exceeds R, and thus that η provides an upper limit, such that no regression function can be found, the correlation of which with y is higher than η.

As a descriptive statistic the utility of the correlation ratio is extremely limited. It will be noticed that the number of degrees of freedom in the numerator of η^2 depends on the number of the arrays, so that, for instance in Example 42, the value of η obtained will depend, not only on the range of temperatures explored, but on the number of temperatures employed within a given range.

To test if an observed value of the correlation ratio is significant is to test if the variation between arrays is significantly greater than is to be expected, in the absence of differentiation, from the variation within the arrays; and this can be done from the analysis of variance (Table 52) by means of the Table of z. Attempts have been made to test the significance of the correlation ratio by calculating for it a standard error, but such attempts overlook the fact that, even with indefinitely large samples, the distribution of η for undifferentiated arrays does not tend to normality, unless the number of arrays also is increased without limit. On the contrary, with very large samples, when N is the total number of observations, $N\eta^2$ tends to be distributed as is χ^2 when n, the number of degrees of freedom, is equal to $(a-1)$, that is, to one less than the number of arrays.

46. Blakeman's Criterion

In the same sense that η^2 measures the difference between different arrays, so $(\eta^2-R^2)/(1-R^2)$ measures the aggregate deviation of the means of the arrays from the hypothetical regression line. The attempt to obtain a criterion of linearity of regression by comparing this quantity to its standard error results in the test known as Blakeman's criterion. In this test, also, no account is taken of the number of the arrays, and in consequence it does not provide even a first approximation in estimating what values of η^2-r^2 are permissible. Similarly with η^2 with zero regression, so with η^2-r^2, the regression being linear, if the number of observations is increased without limit, the distribution does not tend to normality, but that of $N(\eta^2-r^2)/(1-r^2)$ tends to be distributed as is χ^2 when $n=a-2$. Its mean value is then $(a-2)$, and to ignore the value of a is to disregard the main feature of its sampling distribution.

In Example 42 we have seen that with 9 arrays the departure from linearity was very markedly significant; it is easy to see that had there been 90 arrays, with the same values of η^2 and r^2, the departure from linearity would have been even less than the expectation based on the variation within each array. Using Blakeman's criterion, however, these two opposite conditions are indistinguishable.

As in other cases of testing goodness of fit, so in testing regression lines it is essential that if any parameters have to be fitted to the observations, this process of fitting shall be efficiently carried out.

Some account of efficient methods has been given in Chapter V. In general, save in the more complicated cases, of which this book does not treat, the necessary condition may be fulfilled by the procedure known as the Method of Least Squares, by which the measure of deviation

$$S\{n_p(\bar{y}_p - Y_p)^2\}$$

is reduced to a minimum subject to the hypothetical conditions which govern the form of Y.

In the cases to which it is appropriate this method is a special application of the Method of Maximum Likelihood, from which it may be derived, and which will be more fully discussed in Chapter IX.

47. Significance of the Multiple Correlation Coefficient

If, as in Section 29 (p. 156), the regression of a dependent variate y on a number of independent variates x_1, x_2, x_3 is expressed in the form

$$Y = b_1x_1 + b_2x_2 + b_3x_3,$$

then the correlation between y and Y is greater than the correlation of y with any other linear function of the independent variates, and thus measures, in a sense, the extent to which the value of y depends upon, or is related to, the combined variation of these variates. The value of the correlation so obtained, denoted by R, may be calculated from the formula

$$R^2 = \{b_1S(x_1y) + b_2S(x_2y) + b_3S(x_3y)\} \div S(y^2).$$

The multiple correlation, R, differs from the correlation obtained with a single independent variate in that it is always positive ; moreover, it has been recognised in the case of the multiple correlation that its random sampling distribution must depend on the number of independent variates employed. The exact treatment is in fact strictly parallel to that developed above (Section 45) for the correlation ratio, with a similar analysis of variance.

In the section referred to we made use of the fact that

$$S(y^2) = S(y-Y)^2 + \{b_1 S(x_1 y) + b_2 S(x_2 y) + b_3 S(x_3 y)\};$$

if n' is the number of observations of y, and p the number of independent variates, these three terms will represent respectively $n'-1$, $n'-p-1$, and p degrees of freedom. Consequently the analysis of variance takes the form ;

TABLE 55

Variance due to	Degrees of Freedom.	Sum of Squares.
Regression function . .	p	$b_1 S(x_1 y) + \ldots$
Deviations from the regression function	$n'-p-1$	$S(y-Y)^2$
Total . .	$n'-1$	$S(y^2)$

it being assumed that y is measured from its mean value.

If in reality there is no connexion between the independent variates and the dependent variate y, the values in the column headed " sum of squares " will be divided approximately in proportion to the number of degrees of freedom ; whereas if a significant connexion exists, then the p degrees of freedom in the regression function will obtain distinctly more than their share. The test, whether R is or is not significant, is in fact exactly the test whether the mean square ascribable to the regression function is or is not significantly greater than the mean square of deviations from the regression function, and may be carried out, as in all such cases, by means of the Table of z.

Ex. 43. *Significance of a multiple correlation.*—To illustrate the process we may perform the test whether the rainfall data of Example 24 was significantly related to the longitude, latitude, and altitude of the recording stations. From the values found in that example, the following table may be immediately constructed :

TABLE 56

Variance due to	Degrees of Freedom.	Sum of Squares.	Mean Square.	½ Log.
Regression formula	3	791·7	263·9	2·7878
Deviations . .	53	994·9	18·77	1·4661
Total .	56	1786·6		

The value of z is thus 1·3217 while the 1 per cent. point is about ·714, showing that the multiple correlation is clearly significant. The actual value of the multiple correlation may easily be calculated from the above table, for

$$R^2 = 791 \cdot 7 \div 1786 \cdot 6 = \cdot 4431,$$
$$R = \cdot 6657;$$

but this step is not necessary in testing the significance.

48. Technique of Plot Experimentation

The statistical procedure of the analysis of variance is essential to an understanding of the principles underlying modern methods of arranging field experiments. This section and the two following illustrate its application to these methods. Since they were written the cognate subject of experimental design has developed rapidly, and a much fuller account of the principles and logic of experimentation will be found in *The Design of Experiments*.

The first requirement which governs all well-planned experiments is that the experiment should yield not only a comparison of different manures, treatments, varieties, etc., but also a means of testing the significance of such differences as are observed. Consequently all treatments must at least be duplicated, and preferably further replicated, in order that a comparison of replicates may be used as a standard with which to compare the observed differences. This is a requirement common to most types of experimentation; the peculiarity of agricultural field experiments lies in the fact, verified in all careful uniformity trials, that the area of ground chosen for the experimental plots may be assumed to be markedly heterogeneous, in that its fertility varies in a systematic, and often a complicated manner from point to point. For our test of significance to be valid the differences in fertility between plots chosen as parallels must be truly representative of the differences between plots with different treatment; and we cannot assume that this is the case if our plots have been chosen in any way according to a prearranged system; for the systematic arrangement of our plots may have, and tests with the results of uniformity trials show that it often does have, features in common with the systematic variation of fertility, and thus the test of significance is wholly vitiated.

Ex. 44. *Accuracy attained by random arrangement.*—The direct way of overcoming this difficulty is to arrange the plots wholly at random. For example, if 20 strips of land were to be used to test 5 different treatments each in quadruplicate, we might take such an arrangement as the following, found by shuffling 20 cards thoroughly and setting them out in order:

TABLE 57

B	C	A	C	E	E	E	A	D	A
3504	3430	3376	3334	3253	3314	3287	3361	3404	3366
B	C	B	D	D	B	A	D	C	E
3416	3291	3244	3210	3168	3195	3330	3118	3029	3085

The letters represent 5 different treatments; beneath each is shown the weight of mangold roots obtained by Mercer and Hall in a uniformity trial with 20 such strips.

The deviations in the total yield of each treatment are

A	B	C	D	E
+290	+216	−59	−243	−204;

in the analysis of variance the sum of squares corresponding to "treatment" will be a quarter of the sum of the squares of these deviations. Since the sum of the squares of the 20 deviations from the general mean is 289,766, we have the following analysis:

TABLE 58

Variance due to	Degrees of Freedom.	Sum of Squares.	Mean Square.	Standard Deviation.
Treatment . .	4	58,726	14,681	121·1
Experimental error .	15	231,040	15,403	124·1
Total . . .	19	289,766	15,251	123·5

It will be seen that the standard error of a single plot estimated from such an arrangement is 124·1, whereas, in this case, we know its true value to be 123·5; this is an exceedingly close agreement, and illustrates the manner in which a purely random arrangement of plots ensures that the experimental error calculated shall be an unbiased estimate of the errors actually present.

Ex. 45. *Restrictions upon random arrangement.*—While adhering to the essential condition that the errors by which the observed values are affected shall be a random sample of the errors which contribute to our estimate of experimental error, it is still possible to eliminate much of the effect of soil heterogeneity, and so increase the accuracy of our observations, by laying restrictions on the order in which the strips are arranged. As an illustration of a method which is widely applicable, we may divide the 20 strips into 4 blocks, and impose the condition that each treatment shall occur once in each block; we shall then be able to separate the variance into three parts representing (i) local differences between blocks, (ii) differences due to treatment, (iii) experimental errors; and if the 5 treatments are arranged at random within each block, our estimate of experimental error will be an unbiased estimate of the actual errors in the differences due to treatment. As an example of a random arrangement subject to this restriction, the following was obtained :

A E C D B | C B E D A | A D E B C | C E B A D.

Analysing out, with the same data as before, the contributions of local differences between blocks, and of treatment, we find

TABLE 59

Variance due to	Degrees of Freedom.	Sum of Squares.	Mean Square.	Standard Deviation.
Local differences .	3	154,483	51,494	...
Treatment . .	4	40,859	10,215	...
Experimental error .	12	94,424	7,869	88·7
Treatment+error .	16	135,283	8,455	92·0

The local differences between the blocks are very significant, so that the accuracy of our comparisons is much improved, in fact the remaining variance is reduced almost to 55 per cent. of its previous value. The arrangement arrived at by chance has happened to be a slightly unfavourable one, the errors in the treatment values being a little more than usual, while the estimate of the standard error is 88·7 against a true value 92·0. Such variation is to be expected, and indeed upon it is our calculation of significance based.

It might have been thought preferable to arrange the experiment in a systematic order, such as

A B C D E | E D C B A | A B C D E | E D C B A,

and, as a matter of fact, owing to the marked fertility gradient exhibited by the yields in the present example, such an arrangement would have produced smaller errors in the totals of the 5 treatments. With such an arrangement, however, we have no guarantee that an estimate of the standard error derived from the discrepancies between parallel plots is really representative of the differences produced between the different treatments, consequently no such estimate of the standard error can be trusted, and no valid test of significance is possible.

That part of the fertility gradient which is not included in the differences between blocks may, however, be eliminated by regarding position within the blocks, *i.e.*, the ordinal numbers, 1 2, 3, 4, 5, or more simply −2, −1, 0, 1, 2, as an independent variate for each plot, from which the yield as dependent variate may be predicted by the regression. An analysis of covariance of the ordinal numbers (x) and the yields (y), as explained in Section 49·1, gives the following results :—

TABLE 59·1

Analysis of Covariance of Yield (y), and Order within Block (x)

	Degrees of Freedom.	x^2.	xy.	y^2.	y'^2_x.	Mean Square.
Blocks .	3	0	0	154483		
Treatments	4	5·5	− 268·25	40859	28678	7169·5
Error .	12	34·5	−1206·75	94424	52214	4746·7
Treatments and Error	16	40·0	−1475·00	135283	80892	5392·8

It will be seen that the precision of the experiment has been increased. The mean square for treatments plus error is now 5393; in contrast, using blocks only, it was 8455, while disregarding blocks it was 15251.

If we take as having unit value an experiment

giving comparable yields subject to a standard error of 10 per cent., the value of such an experiment as this, in quadruplicate, may be found by squaring one-tenth of the mean yield, multiplying by four (giving 431816), and dividing by the mean square obtained by each method of procedure. For randomisation without blocks we have then

$$\frac{431816}{15250\cdot8} = 28\cdot18$$

units of information. Using randomised blocks we have 51·07, while adjustment for ordinal position within the block raises the value to 80·07 units.

In this case, as in many others, the lower mean square is obtained at the expense of some reduction of the number of degrees of freedom on which the estimate of error is based. This makes the tests of significance somewhat less stringent. If n is the number of degrees of freedom for error, the loss of information due to this cause is found (*Design of Experiments*, xi.) to be the fraction $2/(n+3)$, so that, taking this factor into consideration, we may summarise the results as follows :—

TABLE 59·2

AMOUNTS OF INFORMATION ELICITED BY DIFFERENT METHODS

	Degrees of Freedom for Error.	Units of Information.	
		Crude.	Adjusted.
Randomisation of 20 plots .	15	28·18	25·05
Randomisation in 4 blocks .	12	51·07	44·26
Eliminating order in block .	11	80·07	68·63

Even when allowance is thus made for the degrees of freedom absorbed, it is clear that in this case both the use of blocks, and that of order within the block, have been exceedingly profitable. The latter, of course, is due to the exceptionally regular gradient of fertility which these data exhibit.

49. The Latin Square

The method of laying restrictions on the distribution of the plots and eliminating the corresponding degrees of freedom from the variance is, however, capable of some extension in suitably planned experiments. In a block of 25 plots arranged in 5 rows and 5 columns, to be used for testing 5 treatments, we can arrange that each treatment occurs once in each row, and also once in each column, while allowing free scope to chance in the distribution subject to these restrictions. Then out of the 24 degrees of freedom, 4 will represent treatment; 8, representing soil differences between different rows or columns, may be eliminated; and 12 will remain for the estimation of error. These 12 will provide an unbiased estimate of the errors in the comparison of treatments, provided that every pair of plots, not in the same row or column, belong equally frequently to the same treatment.

Ex. 46. *Doubly restricted arrangements.*—The following root weights for mangolds were found by Mercer and Hall in 25 plots; we have distributed letters representing 5 different treatments at random in such a way that each appears once in each row and column.

TABLE 60

						Total of Row.
	D 376 B 316 C 326 E 317 A 321	E 371 D 338 A 326 B 343 C 332	C 355 E 336 B 335 A 330 D 317	B 356 A 356 D 343 C 327 E 318	A 335 C 332 E 330 D 336 B 306	1793 1678 1660 1653 1594
Total	1656	1710	1673	1700	1639	8378

Analysing out the contributions of rows, columns, and treatments we have

TABLE 61

Differences between	Degrees of Freedom.	Sum of Squares.	Mean Square.	S.D.
Rows . . .	4	4240·24	...	...
Columns . .	4	701·84	...	...
Treatments . .	4	330·24	130·3	11·41
Remainder . .	12	1754·32		
Total . .	24	7026·64	292·8	17·11

By eliminating the soil differences between different rows and columns the mean square has been reduced to less than half, and the value of the experiment as a means of detecting differences due to treatment is therefore more than doubled. This method of equalising the rows and columns may with advantage be combined with that of equalising the distribution over different blocks of land, so that very accurate results may be obtained by using a number of blocks each arranged in, for example, 5 rows and columns. In this way the method may be applied even to cases with only 3 treatments to be compared. Further, since the method is suitable whatever may be the differences in actual fertility of the soil, the same statistical method of reduction may be used when, for instance, the plots are 25 strips lying side by side. Treating each block of 5 strips in turn as though they were successive columns in the former arrangement, we may eliminate, not only the difference between the blocks, but such differences as those due to a fertility gradient, which affect the yield according to the order of the strips in the block. When, therefore, the number of strips employed is the square of the number of treatments, each treatment can be not only *balanced* but completely *equalised* in respect to order in the block, and we may rely upon the (usually) reduced value of the standard error obtained by eliminating the corresponding degrees of freedom. Such a double elimination may be especially fruitful if the blocks of strips coincide with some physical feature of the field such as the ploughman's "lands," which often produce a characteristic periodicity in fertility due to variations in depth of soil, drainage, and such factors.

To sum up: systematic arrangements of plots in field trials should be avoided, since with these it is usually possible to estimate the experimental error in several different ways, giving widely different results, each way depending on some one set of assumptions as to the distribution of natural fertility, which may or may not be justified. With unrestricted random arrangement of plots the experimental error, though accurately estimated, will usually be unnecessarily large. In a well-planned experiment certain restrictions may be imposed upon the random arrangement of the plots in such a way that the experimental error may still be accurately estimated, while the greater part of the influence of soil heterogeneity may be eliminated.

It must be emphasised that when, by an improved method of arranging the plots, we can reduce the standard error to one-half, the value of the experiment is increased at least fourfold ; for only by repeating the experiment four times in its original form could the same accuracy have been attained. This argument really under-estimates the preponderance in the scientific value of the more accurate experiments, for, in agricultural plot work, the experiment cannot in practice be repeated upon identical conditions of soil and climate.

49·1. The Analysis of Covariance

It has been shown that the precision of an experiment may be greatly increased by equalising, among the different treatments to be compared, certain potential sources of error. Thus in dividing the area available for an agricultural experiment into blocks, in each of which all treatments are equally represented, the differences of fertility between the different blocks of land, which without this precaution would be a source of experimental error, have been eliminated from the comparisons, and, by the analysis of variance, are eliminated equally from our estimate of error. In the Latin square any differences in fertility between entire rows, or between entire columns, have been eliminated from the comparisons, and from the estimates of error, so that the real and apparent precision of the comparison is the same as if the experiment had been performed on land in which the entire rows, and also the entire columns, were of equal fertility.

A strictly analogous equalisation is widely applied in all kinds of experimental work. Thus in nutritional experiments the growth rates of males and females may be distinctly different, while nevertheless both sexes may be equally capable of showing the advantage of one diet over another. The effect of sex, on the growth rates compared, will, therefore, be eliminated by assigning the same proportion of males to each experimental treatment, and, what is more often neglected, eliminating the average difference between the sexes from the estimate of error. Notably different reactions are often found also in different strains or breeds of animals, and for this reason each strain employed should be used equally for all treatments. The effect of strain will then be eliminated from the comparisons, and may be easily eliminated by the analysis of variance from the estimate of error. It is sometimes assumed that all the animals in the same experiment must be of the same strain, and adequate replication is in consequence believed to be impossible for lack of a sufficient quantity of homogeneous material. The examples already discussed show that this requirement is superfluous, and adds nothing to the precision of the comparisons actually attained. Indeed, while adding nothing to the precision, this course detracts definitely from the applicability of the results; for results obtained from a number of strains are evidently applicable to a wider range of material than results only established for a single strain; and, working from highly homogeneous material, there is a real danger of drawing inferences, which, had we had a wider inductive basis, would have been seen to be insecure.

There are, however, many factors relevant to the precision of our comparisons, which, while they cannot be equalised, can be measured, and for which we may reasonably attempt to make due allowance. Such are the age and weight of experimental animals, the initial weight being particularly relevant in experiments on the growth rate. In field experiments with roots the yield is often notably affected by the plant number, and if we have reason to be willing to ignore any effect our treatments may have on plant number, it would be preferable to make our comparisons on plots with an equal number of plants. Again, although we cannot equalise the fertility of the plots used for different treatments, the same land may be cropped in a previous year under uniform treatment, and the yields of this uniformity trial will clearly be relevant to the interpretation of our experimental yields. This principle is of particular importance with perennial crops, for there is here continuity, not only of the soil, but of the individual plants growing upon it; and the much more limited facilities for confirming results on a new, or unused, plantation make it especially important to increase the precision of such material as we have.

Ex. 46·1. *Covariance of tea yields in successive periods.*—T. Eden gives data for successive periods each of fourteen pluckings from sixteen plots of tea bushes intended for experimental use in Ceylon. The yields are given in per cent. of the average for each period, but the process to be exemplified would apply equally to actual yields. We give below (Tables 61·1, 61·2) data for his second and third periods, which for our purpose may be regarded as preliminary and experimental yields respectively. The sixteen plots are arranged in a 4×4 square.

TABLE 61·1

PRELIMINARY YIELDS OF TEA PLOTS

88	102	91	88	369
94	110	109	118	431
109	105	115	94	423
88	102	91	96	377
379	419	406	396	1600

TABLE 61·2

EXPERIMENTAL YIELDS OF TEA PLOTS

90	93	85	81	349
93	106	114	121	434
114	106	111	93	424
92	107	92	102	393
389	412	402	397	1600

Let us suppose the area in the experimental period had been occupied by a Latin square in 4 treatments. Of the 15 degrees of freedom, 6 representing differences between rows and columns would then be eliminated, and the remaining 9 would be made up of 3 for differences between treatments, and 6 for the estimation of error. Since no actual treatment differences were applied, we shall use all 9 for the estimation of error. The experimental yields then give

[TABLE

T

TABLE 61·3

ANALYSIS OF EXPERIMENTAL YIELDS

	Degrees of Freedom.	Sum of Squares.	Mean Square.
Rows . . .	3	1095·5	...
Columns . .	3	69·5	...
Error . . .	9	875·0	97·22
Total . .	15	2040·0	136·00

Even after eliminating the large variance among rows, the residual variance is as high as 97·22; the standard error of a single plot is, therefore, about 9·86 per cent., and that for the total of four plots about 4·93 per cent.

It is, however, evident that a great part of this variance of yield in the experimental period has been foreshadowed in the yields of the preliminary period. A glance at the table will show that of the eight plots which were above the average in the experimental period, seven were above the average in the preliminary period. In fact, by choosing sets of plots which in the first period yielded nearly the same total for each set, and assigning these sets to treatments in the experimental period, we might have very materially reduced the experimental error of our treatment comparisons. The equalisation of the total preliminary yields has often been advocated, but seldom practised for reasons which will become apparent. The common-sense inference that sets of plots, giving equal total yields in the preliminary period, should under equal treatment give equal totals in the experimental period, implies that the expectation of subsequent yield of any plot is well represented in terms of the preliminary yield by a linear regression function. The important point is that the adjustments of the results of the experiment appropriate to any regression formula (of which the linear form is obviously the most important) may be made from the results of the experiment themselves without taking any notice, in the arrangement of the plots, of the previous yields. The method of regression also avoids two difficulties which are encountered in the equalisation of previous yields, namely, that the advantage of eliminating differences between rows and columns (or blocks) would often have to be sacrificed to equalisation, and that such equalisation as would be possible would always be inexact.

The adjustment to be made in the difference in yield between two plots, the previous yields of which are known, is evidently the difference to be expected in the subsequent yields, judged from the difference observed between plots treated alike. The appropriate coefficient of linear regression is given by the ratio of the covariance to the variance of the independent variate, which in this case is the variance in the preliminary yields ascribable, in our experimental arrangement, to error. To find this variance of the independent variate, the preliminary yields are analysed in exactly the same way as the experimental yields. A third table, this time an analysis of the covariance of the preliminary and the experimental yields, is constructed by using at every stage, products of the yields in these two periods in place of squares of yields at either one period.

TABLE 61·4

ANALYSIS OF PRELIMINARY YIELDS

	Degrees of Freedom.	Sum of Squares.
Rows . . .	3	745·0
Columns . .	3	213·5
Error . . .	9	567·5
Total . .	15	1526·0

The exact similarity of the arithmetic in constructing these three tables may be illustrated by taking out in parallel the contributions of "columns" to each table. In Tables 61·1 and 61·2 the mean of the column totals is 400, the deviations in the first columns are −21 and −11; denoting these by x and y, the squares and products of these pairs of numbers are written in parallel below :—

TABLE 61·5

x^2	xy	y^2
441	+231	121
361	+228	144
36	+12	4
16	+12	9
854	+483	278

Dividing these totals each by 4 (the number of plots contributing to each), we have the corresponding entries in the triple table :—

TABLE 61·6

SUMS OF SQUARES AND PRODUCTS

	Degrees of Freedom.	x^2	xy	y^2
Rows . . .	3	745·0	837·0	1095·5
Columns . .	3	213·5	120·75	69·5
Error . . .	9	567·5	654·25	875·0
Total . .	15	1526·0	1612·00	2040·0

in which the variances of the two variates, and their covariance are analysed in parallel columns.

Relationships expressed either by regression or by correlation, between the two variates, may now be determined independently for the different rows of the table. In particular we need the ratio 654·25/567·5 representing the regression of y on x, for plots treated alike, after eliminating the differences between rows and columns. This is evidently the correct allowance to be deducted from any experimental yield y, for each unit by which the corresponding x is in excess of the average.

The correction, being linear, may be applied to individual plots, or to the composite totals represented by rows, columns or treatments. More comprehensively, the result of applying the correction and analysing the variance of the adjusted yields, may be derived directly from the analysis of sums and products already presented. For, if b stand for the regression coefficient, comparisons of adjusted yields will be in fact comparisons of quantities $(y-bx)$. Now

$$(y-bx)^2 = b^2x^2 - 2bxy + y^2;$$

so that, to obtain the sum of squares for the adjusted yields in any line, we need only multiply the entries in the table already constructed by b^2, $-2b$ and unity, and add the products.

In the present example $b = 1 \cdot 1529$, $b^2 = 1 \cdot 3291$. giving :—

TABLE 61·7

ANALYSIS OF ADJUSTED YIELDS

	Degrees of Freedom.	Sum of Squares.	Mean Square.
Rows . . .	3	155·8	51·93
Columns . .	3	74·8	24·93
Error . . .	8	120·7	15·09
Total . .	14	351·3	25·09

It will be noticed that the total number of degrees of freedom has been diminished from 15 to 14, to allow for the one adjustable constant in the regression formula, and that this 1 degree has been subtracted from the particular line from which the numerical value of the regression has been estimated. In this line, in fact, b has been chosen so that

$$bS(x^2) = S(xy)$$

and consequently, so that

$$S(y-bx)^2 = S(y^2) - S^2(xy)/S(x^2);$$

showing that the entry in this line is always diminished by the contribution of 1 degree of freedom. In the other lines the entry may be either increased or diminished by the adjustment.

The value of b used in obtaining the adjusted yields is a statistical estimate subject to errors of random sampling. In consequence, although the quantities $y-bx$ are appropriate estimates of the corrected yields, they are of varying precision, as shown in Section 26; the sums of their squares in the lines of the table from which b has not been calculated do not therefore supply exact material for testing the homogeneity of deviations from the simple regression formula. This test we should wish to make if real differences of treatment had been given to our plots, in which case for each variate we should have 3 degrees of freedom assigned to treatments, and only 6 left for error, from which 6 the value of b would be calculated. In our example there are no real treatments, and we shall illustrate the test of significance by applying it to the rows, the significance of which is in reality of no consequence to the result of the experiment.

Taking those parts of Table 61·7 which refer to rows and error only, we obtain the reduced values of the sum of squares of the dependent variate y, respectively for the error and for the total, by deducting in each case from $S(y^2)$, the quantity

$$S^2(xy)/S(x^2)$$

derived from the same line. This gives for the error, the reduced value of the sum of squares of y, 120·7, as in Table 61·7; for the total we have $1970{\cdot}5-1694{\cdot}3 = 276{\cdot}2$, corresponding to 11 degrees of freedom. Subtracting the first from the second, we find the reduced sum of squares ascribable to the 3 degrees of freedom for rows to be 155·5, which is the value to be compared with the reduced sum of squares for error, in making an exact test. The whole process is shown in Table 61·71. (See also Table 59·1.) In this case it is obvious that the sum of squares of $(y-bx)$ would have provided an excellent approximation. As such, however, it is, always to some extent, and sometimes greatly, inflated by the sampling errors of b; and there is no difficulty in applying the exact test, which makes proper allowance for these sampling errors.

TABLE 61·71

TEST OF SIGNIFICANCE WITH REDUCED VARIANCE

	Degrees of Freedom.	x^2	xy	y^2	Degrees of Freedom.	Reduced y^2	Mean Square.
Rows . .	3	745·0	837·0	1095·5	3	155·5	51·83
Error . .	9	567·5	654·25	875·0	8	120·7	15·09
Total .	12	1312·5	1491·25	1970·5	11	276·2	

Comparing the analysis of the adjusted yields with that obtained without using the preliminary pluckings, the most striking change is the reduction of the mean square error per plot from 97·22 to 15·09, in spite of the reduction in the degrees of freedom, showing that the precision of the comparison has been increased over six-fold. A second point should also be noticed. The large difference in yield between different rows, which appears in the original analysis, has fallen to about one-seventh of its original value. It appears therefore that the greater part of this element of heterogeneity may be eliminated in favourable cases by the use of preliminary yields; but this does not diminish the importance, when such preliminary yields are available, of eliminating from the comparisons differences between the larger areas of land, blocks, rows, columns, etc. In fact, the elimination of rows and columns is more important in the adjusted yields, where it reduces the mean square from 24·08 to 15·09, than in the unadjusted yields, where it reduced it from 136 to 97·2. If, for example, we take an experiment with 10 per cent. error in the means of treatments, to have unit value, the elimination of rows and columns in the unadjusted yields only increased the value from 2·94 to 4·12, a net gain of 1·18 units; while the same elimination in the adjusted yields increases the value from 16·61 to 26·51, a net gain of 9·90 units, or nearly nine times as much. In practice, however, especially when the numbers of degrees of freedom are small, it is desirable to base such comparisons on the quantity of information realised, making due allowance for the number of degrees of freedom available in each of the cases to be compared as in Table 59·2.

An examination of the process exemplified in the foregoing example shows that it combines the advantages and reconciles the requirements of the two very widely applicable procedures known as regression and analysis of variance. Once the simple procedure of building up the covariance tables is recognised, there will be found no difficulty in applying the analysis to three or more variates and the complete set of their covariances, and so making allowance simultaneously for two or more measurable but uncontrolled concomitants of our observations. These observations are treated as the dependent variate, the variability of which may be partially accounted for in terms of concomitant observations, by the method of multiple regression. Thus, if we were concerned to study the effects of agricultural treatments upon the purity index of the sugar extracted from sugar-beet, a variate which might be much affected by concomitant variations in (*a*) sugar-percentage, and (*b*) root weight, an analysis of covariance applied to the three variates, purity, sugar percentage and root weight, for the different plots of the experiment, would enable us to make a study of the effects of experimental treatments on purity alone ; *i.e.*, after allowance for any effect they may have on root weight or concentration, without our needing to have observed in fact any two plots agreeing exactly in both root weight and sugar percentage.

In such a research it would again be open to the investigator to eliminate not merely the mean root weight of the plots, but, if he judged it profitable, also its square, so using a regression non-linear in root weight. Again, if he possessed not merely the mean root weight for the different plots, but the individual values of which the mean is the average, he could eliminate simultaneously mean root weight and mean square root weight, or, in other words, make his purity comparisons with corrections appropriate to equalising both the means and the variances of the roots from the different plots.

In considering, in respect to any given body of data, what particular adjustments are worth making, it is sufficient for our immediate guidance to note their effect upon the residual error. If, in Example 46·1, we compare Tables 61·3 and 61·7, it is apparent that we may divide the 9 degrees of freedom for error of unadjusted yields into two parts, one of which comprises the 1 degree of freedom eliminated by the regression equation, and the other the 8 degrees of freedom remaining after this equation has been used for adjusting the yields. This analysis of error is shown below in Table 61·8.

TABLE 61·8

ANALYSIS OF RESIDUAL ERROR

	Degrees of Freedom.	Sum of Squares.	Mean Square.
Regression	1	754·3	754·3
Error of adjusted yields . .	8	120·7	15·09
Error of unadjusted yields .	9	875·0	...

The great advantage of making due allowance for the preliminary yields is evidently due to the very large share of the residual error which is contained in the 1 degree of freedom specified by our regression formula. We need not test the significance of a regression before using it, but any advantage it may confer will be slight unless it is in fact significant.

The chief advantage of the analysis of covariance lies, however, not in its power of getting the most out of an existing body of data, but in the guidance it is capable of giving in the design of an observational programme, and in the choice of which of many possible concomitant observations shall in fact be recorded. The example of the tea yields shows that in that case the value for experimental purposes of a plantation was increased six-fold by the comparatively trifling additional labour of recording separately the yields from different plots for a period prior to the experiment. With annual agricultural crops, to crop the experimental area in the previous year is nearly to double the labour of the experiment. What is often more serious, a year's delay is incurred before the result is made available. Analysis of covariance on successive yields on uniformly treated land shows that the value of the experiment is usually increased, but seldom by more than about 60 per cent., by a knowledge of the yields of the previous year. It seems therefore to be always more profitable to lay down an adequately replicated experiment on untried land than to expend the time and labour available in exploring the irregularities of its fertility.

In most kinds of experimentation, however, the possibilities of obtaining greatly increased precision from comparatively simple supplementary observations are almost entirely unexplored, and, indeed, in many fields the possibility of making a critically valid use of such observations is scarcely recognised. The probability that methods of experimentation can be greatly improved, either by a great increase of precision, or by a proportionate decrease in the labour required, is naturally greatest in these fields.

An analysis of covariance always involves the primary classification of the analysis, in addition to the relation between a dependent and an independent variate. Sometimes the classification may be complex, as is a hierarchical classification in three or more stages; also there may be more than one dependent variate, and possibly a number of independent variates may need to be eliminated. An example involving these complications, and with the working procedure exhibited in detail, is referred to in the bibliography (with B. Day, 1937).

49·2. The Discrimination of Groups by Means of Multiple Measurements; Appropriate Scores

A valuable application of the technique of calculation used in multiple regression consists in finding which of all possible linear compounds of a set of measurements will best discriminate between two different groups. For example, a human mandible or jaw bone may be found in circumstances in which, apart from the evidence provided by its form, the sex of its possessor is unknown. The anthropologist desires, so far as is possible, to assign the right sex to such finds. If he has a number of mandibles of known sex, measurements of these may provide a clue. Some measurements, in fact, show significant differences, but, as these are likely to be highly correlated, the evidence they provide cannot be treated as independent. For the same reason other measurements, which by themselves provide no means of discrimination, may in conjunction with the rest aid considerably. Only when that particular linear function is determined which, better than any other, discriminates mandibles of the two sexes, can we recognise that some measurements are useless, while others are of real evidential value.

To illustrate the formal equivalence with multiple regression let us suppose we have N_1 male and N_2 female mandibles, on each of which measurements $x_1, \ldots, x_p$ can be made. The mean differences (male − female) will be represented by $d_1, \ldots d_p$; further, we represent the sums of squares and products of the measurements, ignoring sex, by

$$S_{ij} = S(x_i - \bar{x}_i)(x_j - \bar{x}_j)$$

Then it has been shown that the solutions $b_1, \ldots, b_p$ of the equations

$$S_{11}b_1+S_{12}b_2+\ldots+S_{1p}b_p=d_1$$
$$S_{1p}b_1+S_{2p}b_2+\ldots+S_{pp}b_p=d_p$$

will be proportional to the coefficients of that linear function,

$$X=b_1x_1+b_2x_2+\ldots+b_px_p,$$

which, as judged from the data, will most successfully discriminate mandibles of unknown sex.

If we had introduced a formal variate y, equal to $N_1/(N_1+N_2)$ for all males and to $-N_1/(N_1+N_2)$ for all females, the equations for the coefficients of multiple regression of y on $x_1, \ldots, x_p$ would in fact only differ from those written above by a factor $N_1N_2/(N_1+N_2)$ on the right. The value of the coefficient of multiple correlation of y with $x_1, \ldots, x_p$ is therefore given by

$$R^2=\frac{N_1N_2}{N_1+N_2}(b_1d_1+\ldots+b_pd_p).$$

Hotelling (1931) has shown that, if the variates x are normally distributed within groups, the significance of the correlation can be tested, in an analysis of variance test, with p, and $n-p+1$ degrees of freedom, where n is the number of degrees of freedom within groups. So that

$$e^{2z}=\frac{n-p+1}{p}\cdot\frac{R^2}{1-R^2}.$$

This, of course, is the basic test as to whether any significant discrimination has been achieved. We may also wish to test whether any proposed discriminant function,

$$X'=\beta_1x_1+\ldots+\beta_px_p,$$

specifying the ratios of the coefficients, but not their absolute values, is compatible with the observational facts. It has been shown that this can be easily done, merely by finding the correlation coefficient, within groups, between X and X′. If this is r, the value of R^2 in Hotelling's test may be multiplied by $(1-r^2)$, and used as before with 1 less degree of freedom to test the special form of discriminant proposed.

The value of z may now be obtained from

$$e^{2z} = \frac{n-p+1}{p-1} \cdot \frac{R'^2}{1-R'^2},$$

when $R'^2 = R^2(1-r^2)$ and the degrees of freedom are $n_1 = p-1$ and $n_2 = n-p+1$. The test thus rejects any proposed formula having r so small that the value of z given above is significant.

Instead of the differences between the means of the variates from two samples, the method may be applied equally to the regressions of the means of several samples on any variate characteristic of these samples. Thus Barnard has used the regressions of the means of certain measurements of Egyptian skulls on the approximate date of burial, to ascertain what linear function of the cranial measurements obtainable shows the most distinct change with time. An important application to plant selection has been made by Fairfield Smith to determine how the different observable characters of plant progenies should be combined in selecting for any particular end.

If, in a replicated variety trial, observables x_1, . . ., x_p are recorded from each plot, we may obtain sums of squares and products, first, for varieties, which we shall denote t_{ij} and next for errors e_{ij}. Subtracting the second from the first we obtain unbiased estimates of the varietal effects $g_{ij} = t_{ij} - e_{ij}$. If, now, the value of a variety, for which $x_1, \ldots, x_p$ were exactly known, is judged to be correctly assessed by the formula

$$a_1x_1+a_2x_2+ \ldots a_px_p,$$

where the coefficients a may be positive or negative. we may at once calculate

$$A_i = a_1g_{1i}+a_2g_{2i}+ \ldots +a_pg_{ip}$$

for each value of i. The appropriate scores, $b_1, \ldots, b_p$ for rating the selective value of any variety will then be found from the simultaneous equations

$$b_1t_{11}+ \ldots +b_pt_{1p} = A_1,$$
$$b_2t_{12}+ \ldots +b_pt_{2p} = A_2,$$

and so on.

On solving these we compare the values of the compound score

$$X = b_1\bar{x}_1+b_2\bar{x}_2+ \ldots +b_p\bar{x}_p$$

for each variety, X being the function of the observables most highly correlated with the true value of the variety.

The foregoing examples all illustrate the general principle that we may determine a set of adjustable coefficients in such a way as to maximise the ratio of the square of one chosen component to the sum of squares of a set of other components in an analysis of variance. The same principle may be applied to maximise the ratio which the sum of squares for n_1 degrees of freedom bears to that of a residue of n_2 degrees of freedom. After making the adjustment to obtain the maximal ratio, involving p adjustable constants, we shall, as the best available approximation, test the significance of n_1+p compared with n_2-p degrees of freedom.

When only a single component is to be maximised relative to the rest, the equations are linear, and the procedure of multiple regression may be used. Other cases may lead to equations of higher degree. Thus, given a two-way table of non-numerical observations we may ask what values, or scores, shall be assigned to them in order that the observations shall be as additive as possible.

Ex. 46·2. *The derivation of an additive scoring system from serological readings.*—Twelve samples of human blood tested with twelve different sera gave reactions represented by the five symbols −, ?, w, (+), and +, according to Table 61·9 on next page (G. L. Taylor, Galton Laboratory).

[TABLE

TABLE 61·9

NON-NUMERICAL TWO-WAY TABLE OF SEROLOGICAL READINGS

Sera

Cells	1	2	3	4	5	6	7	8	9	10	11	12
1	w	w	w	(+)	w	(+)	?	w	w	(+)	w	w
2	?	w	?	w	w	w	?	w	w	w	w	?
3	w	w	w	w	w	w	w	w	w	w	w	w
4	w	w	w	w	w	w	—	w	w	w	w	?
5	w	(+)	w	(+)	w	w	?	(+)	w	(+)	w	w
6	w	w	(+)	(+)	w	w	?	w	w	(+)	w	w
7	(+)	(+)	(+)	(+)	+	+	w	(+)	w	(+)	(+)	w
8	w	+	(+)	(+)	w	(+)	w	(+)	w	(+)	(+)	w
9	w	(+)	(+)	(+)	w	(+)	w	(+)	w	(+)	w	w
10	?	?	w	w	w	w	?	w	w	w	w	?
11	w	w	(+)	w	w	w	?	w	w	w	w	w
12	w	(+)	+	(+)	(+)	(+)	w	(+)	w	(+)	+	w

If we arbitrarily assign the value 0 to the symbol −, and the value 1 to the symbol +, the values corresponding to the symbols ?, w, and (+) may be given the algebraic values x, y and z. Then by counting the numbers of the different kinds of symbol in each row and column, we find the sum of squares corresponding to rows and columns to be :—

TABLE 61·901

MATRIX FOR ROWS AND COLUMNS

	x	y	z	1
x	718	2	−672	−106
y	2	1630	−1416	−218
z	−672	−1416	1944	216
1	−106	−218	216	118

where it is convenient to write the quadratic expression as a symmetrical 4×4 matrix. Thus the coefficient of x^2 is 718, while those of xy and yx are both 2, making together the term $4xy$. The whole has been multiplied by 144 to avoid fractions. Similarly, the total sum of squares for 143 degrees of freedom is found to be :—

TABLE 61·902

MATRIX FOR TOTAL

	x	y	z	1
x	1703	−1157	−468	−65
y	−1157	4895	−3204	−445
z	−468	−3204	3888	−180
1	−65	−445	−180	695

To find the values of x, y and z which will make the ratio of the first of these expressions to the second as large as possible, it is necessary to solve an equation of the 4th degree. If from each element of the first matrix a multiple (θ) of the corresponding element of the second matrix is subtracted, the determinant of the sixteen values so found when equated to zero gives the equation. What is wanted is this equation's largest solution.

It is not necessary to calculate the coefficients of the equation. It is usually more convenient to evaluate the determinant exactly for chosen values of θ, and to apply the method of divided differences to calculate the required solution. The following table shows the values obtained at six chosen values of θ, simplified by dividing by 3456 :

TABLE 61·91

TRIAL VALUES OF A DETERMINANT, AND THEIR DIVIDED DIFFERENCES

θ	Determinant.	First Divided Difference.	Second Divided Difference.	Third Divided Difference.	Fourth Divided Difference.
0	429106				
0·2	49982·376	−1,895618·12			
0·4	−598370·560	−3,241764·68	−3,365366·4		
0·6	−1,536668·072	−4,691487·56	−3,624307·2	−431568	
0·8	4,123941·552	28,303048·12	82,486339·2	143,517744	179,936640
1·0	30,181877	130,289677·24	254,966572·8	287,467056	179,936640

The second column is found by dividing the successive differences of the first column by 0·2, the interval between successive values of θ; the third column is likewise found from the second, the divisor in this case being the difference between values of θ separated by two steps, which in this table is constantly 0·4. Since, for any expression of the 4th degree, the fourth divided difference is constant, the exactitude of the values is checked in the last column, if enough values of θ are used.

It is apparent that the value required lies between 0·6 and 0·8. Since the fourth difference is constant whether the intervals are equal or unequal, positive or negative, the equation may be solved by choosing successive values of θ to continue the table so as to make the determinant approximate to zero. Thus in calculating the value for 0·7 a new line is added in which the third divided difference is increased by the fourth difference multiplied by 0·3, the multiplier being simply the new value less the value in the table four steps back. The new third difference is then multiplied by 0·1, the difference in θ taken three steps back, and added to the second difference. The factor by which the new second difference is multiplied is −0·1, since the new value of θ is ·1 less than that used two steps back. Finally, the new first difference is multiplied by −0·3 and added to the value of the determinant at 1·0 to find its value at 0·7. In the table on p. 294 (Table 61·92) this line has been filled in with exact values. In the subsequent lines sufficient figures have been retained for a very accurate determination. Notice that the value chosen for the third line is too high by 3 units in the fifth place of decimals, but that this circumstance does not interrupt the straightforward course of the work. For lower accuracy fewer figures would be needed in each column, and the process would be terminated in fewer steps. For machine calculation, however, the work shown is not heavy, and completely avoids the algebraic manipulation of the determinant.

TABLE 61·92

STEPS IN THE SOLUTION OF AN ALGEBRAIC EQUATION BY DIVIDED DIFFERENCES; FOURTH DIFFERENCE 179,936640 THROUGHOUT

θ	Determinant.	1st.	2nd.	3rd.
1·0	30,181877	130,289677·24	254,966572·8	287,467056
0·7	−231684·844	101,378539·48	289,111377·6	341,448048
0·708	− 18463·0046	26,652729·92	255,910306·7	360,881205
0·70869	+860·1817	28,004617·84	155,568230·5	344,451190
0·7086593	−2·7600	28,108851·19	158,096991·4	292,028323
0·7086593982	−·0002	28,104007·21	158,290581·8	293,586466

The value of θ so obtained is actually the fraction of the total sum of squares ascribable to rows and columns, when this fraction is maximised. To obtain the corresponding score values, x, y and z, the matrix for total sum of squares is multiplied by this value of θ, and subtracted from that for rows and columns, to give the following equations :—

$$-488{\cdot}8470x + 821{\cdot}9189y - 340{\cdot}3474z = 59{\cdot}9371$$
$$821{\cdot}9189x - 1838{\cdot}8878y + 854{\cdot}5447z = -97{\cdot}3534$$
$$-340{\cdot}3474x + 854{\cdot}5447y - 811{\cdot}2677z = -343{\cdot}5587,$$

of which the solution is

$$x = {\cdot}192959,$$
$$y = {\cdot}584453,$$
$$z = {\cdot}958163,$$

the values appropriate to the symbols ?, w, and (+) if zero is assigned to −, and unity to +. It will be observed that the numerical values, of which only the first two figures need be used, lie between 0 and 1 in the proper order for increasing reaction. This is not a consequence of the procedure by which they have been obtained, but a property of the data examined.

Without evaluating the scores we may test the significance of rows and columns directly from the value of θ, for only the ratio of the sums of squares is needed. An approximate test is supplied by adding 3 *degrees of freedom* for the 3 unknown adjusted, to the 22 for rows and columns, and subtracting 3 from the remainder. Thus we have :—

TABLE 61·93

ANALYSIS OF VARIANCE OF A NON-NUMERICAL TABLE

	Degrees of Freedom.	Sums of Square.	Mean Square.	½ Log$_e$
Rows and columns .	25	·70866	·028346	1·6723
Remainder . .	118	·29134	·002469	·4519
Total . .	143	1·00000		$z = 1·2204$

The differences between different rows and columns are thus very highly significant. We may infer that large differences exist in the strengths of the sera, or in the sensitivities of the different cells used. This is important, since it is only on this condition that the scores are worth anything.

49·3. The Precision of Estimated Scores

The numerical values obtained for the scores are, of course, subject to sampling errors. The notion of a standard error is not, however, very simply applicable to such scores, which cannot be used except in conjunction with the other scores of the system, including the two which have been assigned arbitrary values. This difficulty may be overcome comprehensively by developing a test whether the data differ significantly from expectation based on any given system of scores. Thus, retaining the score zero for a negative reading, we might have given to the readings ?, w, (+) and + the scores ·25, ·50, ·75 and 1·00, or equally 1, 2, 3 and 4. Then a test of significance exactly analogous to that made above will show whether such a system is sufficient to explain the whole of the apparent differentiation of rows and columns.

To perform the test, which is indeed of a kind for which extensive data, rather than a single table, should be used, we may denote the new variate by ξ. Then in Tables 61·901 and 61·902 (p. 287) we may make a new column by multiplying the four columns by 1, 2, 3 and 4 and adding; this gives the two sets of values :—

Rows and Columns.	Totals.
−1718	−2275
−1858	−2759
3192	4068
578	1285

If we multiply the four rows by 1, 2, 3 and 4 and add we shall obtain an analysis of variance for ξ; equally, if we multiply by the system of scores we have derived from the data, we shall have an analysis of covariance for X and ξ, where X stands for the system of scores previously derived. Similarly, we may find the analysis of variance for X, giving :—

TABLE 61·94

ANALYSIS OF COVARIANCE FOR ARBITRARY AND EMPIRICAL SCORES

	$S(\xi^2)$	$S(\xi X)$	$S(X^2)$
Rows and columns . .	6454	2219·039	770·496
Remainder	3097	912·280	316·762
Total . .	9551	3131·319	1087·258

If now we eliminate ξ according to the general procedure, by deducting from $S(X^2)$ the square of $S(\xi X)$ divided by $S(\xi^2)$, using the lines for remainder and total, and obtaining that for rows and columns by subtraction, we find :—

TABLE 61·95

ANALYSIS OF VARIANCE OF EMPIRICAL SCORES, ELIMINATING ARBITRARY SCORES

	Degrees of Freedom.	Sum of Squares.	Mean Square.	½ Log.
Rows and columns .	24	12·615	·5256	·8297
Remainder . .	118	48·033	·4071	·6982
Total . . .	142	60·648	z	·1315

The degrees of freedom have been reduced for rows and columns, since, after eliminating ξ, there are only two values adjustable; the value of z exceeds the 20 per cent. point, but falls far short of the 5 per cent. point. The table of data examined, with its very few − and + entries, is thus not sufficient to show that the linear series of scores is inadequate.

In this, as in Table 61·93, the z test is only approximate, though in both cases it is sufficient to answer the question at issue. In Table 61·93 the distribution of the fraction of sums of squares ·70866 depends on the three parameters 22 and 121 for original degrees of freedom, and 4, the degree of the equation solved, which is one more than the number of adjustable scores. In Table 61·95 the corresponding ratio, ·2080, likewise depends on the numbers 22, 120 and 3. The general solution of this problem of distribution has been found, but no exact tables are yet available.

The comprehensive method outlined in this section is applicable to a great variety of practical problems. It often happens that the statistician is provided with data on aggregates which it is required to allocate to different items. Thus, we may have data on the total consumption of different households, without knowing how this consumption is allocated between a man and his wife, or among children of different ages. If the composition of each household is known, the relative importance of each class of consumer may be obtained by minimising the deviation between the consumption recorded, and that expected, on assigned scores, from the composition of the family. Where continuous variables, such as age, are involved, it is preferable not to assign a separate unknown score to each age recorded, but to introduce the age, its square and possibly its cube, or higher powers, as independent variates, as in fitting curved regressions. Thus Day of the U.S. Forest Service has succeeded in allocating the cost of hauling logs of different diameters, from data giving only the composition by diameter of seventy different loads, each load involving the same haulage cost. An equation, quadratic in the diameter, was found sufficient to represent the curve of true cost.

IX

THE PRINCIPLES OF STATISTICAL ESTIMATION

50. The practical importance of using satisfactory methods of statistical estimation, and the widespread use in statistical literature of inefficient statistics, in the sense explained in Section 3, makes it necessary for the research worker, in interpreting his own results, or studying those reported by others, to discriminate between those conclusions which flow from the nature of the observations themselves, and those which are due solely to faulty methods of estimation.

Ex. 47.—As an example which brings out the main principles of the theory, and which does not involve data so voluminous that we cannot easily try out a variety of methods, we shall choose the estimation of linkage from the progeny of self-fertilised heterozygotes. Thus for two factors in maize, Starchy *v.* Sugary and Green *v.* White base leaf we may have (W. A. Carver's data) such observations as the following seedling counts :—

TABLE 62

Starchy.		Sugary.		Total.
Green.	White.	Green.	White.	
1997	906	904	32	3839

51. The Significance of Evidence for Linkage

It is a useful preliminary before making a statistical estimate, such as one of the intensity of linkage, to test if there is anything to justify estimation at all. We therefore test the possibility that the two factors are inherited independently. If such were the case the two factors, each segregating in a 3 : 1 ratio, would give the four combinations in the ratio 9 : 3 : 3 : 1, or with expectations, and corresponding contributions to χ^2, shown in Table 63.

TABLE 63

Expectation (m) .	2159·4	719·8	719·8	239·9	
Difference (d) .	−162·4	+186·2	+184·2	−207·9	
d^2/m . .	12·21	48·17	47·14	180·17	287·69

Since for 3 degrees of freedom the 1 per cent. point is only 11·34, the observed values are clearly in contradiction to the expectations. Such a result would, however, be produced either by linkage or by a departure from the 3 : 1 ratios ; the test may be made specific by analysing χ^2 into its components as in Section 22. For this purpose, designating the four observed frequencies by a, b, c, d, and their total by n, the deviations from expectation in the ratio of starchy and sugary will be measured by

$$x=(a+b)-3(c+d)=+95$$

that of the other factor by

$$y=(a+c)-3(b+d)=+87,$$

while to complete the analysis we need

$$z = a - 3b - 3c + 9d = -3145.$$

Then dividing the square of each discrepancy by its sampling variance, namely $3n$ for x and y, and $9n$ for z, we have the components

$x^2 \div 3n$ . . .	·784
$y^2 \div 3n$ . . .	·657
$z^2 \div 9n$ . . .	286·273
Total . .	287·714

agreeing with the former total as nearly as its limited accuracy will allow. The conclusion is evident that neither of the single factor ratios is abnormal, and that all but an insignificant fraction of the discrepancy is ascribable to linkage. The principles on which the deviations x, y, and z are constructed will be made more clear in Section 55.

52. The Specification of the Progeny Population for Linked Factors

When, as in the present case, the results are to be interpreted in terms of a definite theory, the specification of the population consists merely in following out the logical consequences of that theory. The theory we have to consider is that in both male and female gametogenesis, while each gamete has an equal chance of bearing the starchy or the sugary gene, and again of bearing the gene for green or white base leaf, yet the parental combinations Starchy White and Sugary Green are produced more frequently than the recombination classes Starchy Green and Sugary White. If the probability of the two latter classes is p in female gametogenesis and p' in male gametogenesis, the probability of the four types of ovules and of pollen will be

TABLE 64

	Starchy.		Sugary.	
	Green.	White.	Green.	White.
Ovules . .	$\frac{1}{2}p$	$\frac{1}{2}(1-p)$	$\frac{1}{2}(1-p)$	$\frac{1}{2}p$
Pollen . .	$\frac{1}{2}p'$	$\frac{1}{2}(1-p')$	$\frac{1}{2}(1-p')$	$\frac{1}{2}p'$

The theory further asserts that each grain of pollen will with equal probability fertilise each ovule, and that the seeds and seedlings produced will be equally viable. Then the probability that a seedling will be the double recessive Sugary White, which can only happen if both pollen and ovule carry these characters, will be $\frac{1}{4}pp'$. The probability of each of the other three classes of seedlings may be deduced at once, for the total probability of the two Sugary classes is $\frac{1}{4}$ irrespective of linkage, which leaves $\frac{1}{4}(1-pp')$ for the Sugary Green class. Similarly, the probability of the Starchy White class is $\frac{1}{4}(1-pp')$, leaving $\frac{1}{4}(2+pp')$ for Starchy Green.

Since these probabilities involve only the quantity pp', it is only of this and not of the separate values of p and p' that the data can provide an estimate. We shall therefore illustrate the problem of estimating the unknown quantity pp', which we may designate by θ. If p and p' were equal, then $\sqrt{\theta}$ would give the recombination fraction in both sexes, and if these are unequal it will still give their geometric mean. The data before us, however, throw direct light only on the value of θ. It is to be observed that in the case of coupling, when both dominant genes are received from the same grandparent, exactly the same specification is used, only it is $1-\sqrt{\theta}$ instead of $\sqrt{\theta}$ which is to be interpreted as the recombination fraction.

The statistical problem now takes the definite form: the probabilities of four events are

$$\tfrac{1}{4}(2+\theta),\ \tfrac{1}{4}(1-\theta),\ \tfrac{1}{4}(1-\theta),\ \tfrac{1}{4}\theta;$$

estimate the value of the parameter θ from the observed frequencies a, b, c, d.

53. The Multiplicity of Consistent Statistics

Nothing is easier than to invent methods of estimation. It is the chief purpose of this chapter to explain how satisfactory methods may be distinguished from unsatisfactory ones. The late development of this branch of the subject seems to be chiefly due to the lack of recognition of the number and variety of the plausible statistics which present themselves. We shall consider five of these.

In our example we may observe that the probability of the first and fourth class increases, and that of the two other classes diminishes as θ is increased. The expression

$$a-b-c+d$$

will therefore afford a convenient estimate of θ. To make a consistent estimate on these lines, we substitute the expected values

$$\frac{n}{4}(2+\theta,\ 1-\theta,\ 1-\theta,\ \theta),$$

for a, b, c, and d, and finding the result to be $n\theta$, we define our first estimate, T_1, by the equation

$$nT_1 = a-b-c+d.$$

Alternatively, we might take the expression for z in Section 51, which appears there as a measure of linkage for the purpose of testing its significance; substituting the expected values, as before, we obtain $n(4\theta-1)$, and may define a new estimate, T_2, by the equation

$$n(4T_2-1)=a-3b-3c+9d,$$

or

$$4nT_2=2a-2b-2c+10d.$$

Obviously any number of similar estimates may be formed by the same method.

Instead of considering the sum of the extreme frequencies a and d we might have considered their product. The ratio of the product ad to the product bc clearly increases with θ; on substitution we have an equation for a third estimate in the form

$$\frac{\theta(2+\theta)}{(1-\theta)^2}=\frac{ad}{bc},$$

a quadratic equation of which T_3 is taken to be the positive solution.

As a fourth statistic we shall choose that given by the method of maximum likelihood. This method consists in multiplying the logarithm of the number expected in each class by the number observed, summing for all classes and finding the value of θ for which the sum is a maximum.

Now,

$$a\log(2+\theta)+b\log(1-\theta)+c\log(1-\theta)+d\log\theta$$

may be seen, by differentiating with respect to θ, to be a maximum if

$$\frac{a}{2+\theta}+\frac{d}{\theta}=\frac{b+c}{1-\theta},$$

leading to the quadratic equation

$$n\theta^2-(a-2b-2c-d)\theta-2d=0,$$

of which the positive solution, T_4, satisfies the condition of maximum likelihood.

Finally, for any value adopted for θ, we shall be able to make a comparison of observed with expected frequencies, and to calculate the discrepancy, χ^2, between them. In fact χ^2 can be expressed in the form

$$\chi^2 = \frac{4}{n}\left(\frac{a^2}{2+\theta} + \frac{b^2}{1-\theta} + \frac{c^2}{1-\theta} + \frac{d^2}{\theta}\right) - n,$$

and the value for which this is a minimum will be the positive solution of the equation of the 4th degree

$$\frac{a^2}{(2+\theta)^2} + \frac{d^2}{\theta^2} = \frac{b^2+c^2}{(1-\theta)^2},$$

a statistic which we shall designate by T_5.

54. The Comparison of Statistics by means of the Test of Goodness of Fit

All the statistics mentioned, except the last, are easily calculated. The reader should calculate the first four, and verify that the value of the fifth given below approximately satisfies its equation. For each statistic we may calculate the numbers expected in the four classes of seedlings, and compare them with those observed. This is done in Table 65, where also the values of χ^2 derived from this comparison are given.

TABLE 65

COMPARISON OF FIVE STATISTICAL ESTIMATES OF LINKAGE

Method.	1.	2.	3.	4.	5.	
r	·057046	·045194	·035645	·035712	·035785	
Recombination per cent. .	23·88	21·26	18·880	18·898	18·917	Observed
Numbers expected	1974·25	1962·875	1953·711	1953·775	1953·845	1997
	905·00	916·375	925·539	925·475	925·405	906
	905·00	916·375	925·539	925·475	925·405	904
	54·75	43·375	34·211	34·275	34·345	32
χ^2 . . .	9·717	3·860	2·0158	2·0154	2·0153	...

In the actual values of the estimates the first three methods differ considerably, but the last three are closely alike; so closely that the expectations of methods (3) and (5) differ from those of (4) by only about one-fifteenth of a seedling in each class. In the comparisons between the numbers expected and those observed, the most important discrepancies are in the fourth class, where method (2) gives a large and method (1) a very large discrepancy. The contrast between the first three methods in the values of χ^2 is very striking. For 2 degrees of freedom—not 3 because on fitting a linkage value 1 degree should be eliminated—a value above 9·21 should only occur once in a hundred trials. The value given by method (2) is not in itself significant, but since its value is nearly double that of methods (3), (4), and (5) we may be sure that the test of goodness of fit, if correct for the latter, must be highly erroneous for method (2), as well as for method (1). The general theorem which this illustrates is that the test of goodness of fit is only valid when efficient statistics are used in fitting a hypothesis to the data; in this case, as will be seen in the next section, methods (3), (4), and (5) are efficient, while methods (1) and (2) are not.

55. The Sampling Variance of Statistics

A more searching examination of the merits of various statistics may be made by calculating the sampling variance of each. Since the subject of sampling variance is usually treated by somewhat elaborate mathematical methods, it will be as well to give a number of simple formulæ by which the majority of ordinary cases may be treated.

First, if x is a linear function of the observed frequencies, such as

$$k_1a+k_2b+k_3c+k_4d,$$

then, designating the theoretical probability of any class by p, the mean value of x will be

$$nS(pk).$$

The random sampling variance of x is given by the formula

$$\frac{1}{n}V(x)=S(pk^2)-S^2(pk), \qquad \text{(A)}$$

and if the mean value of x is zero, the variance of x becomes simply

$$nS(pk^2).$$

Further, if a second linear function of the frequencies, y, is specified by coefficients, k', then the covariance of x and y is

$$nS(pkk').$$

In view of this theorem the choice of the linear functions used for analysing χ^2 in Section 51 will no longer appear arbitrary, and the values taken for their sampling variance will be apparent. For the values of p are

$$\frac{1}{16}(9, 3, 3, 1),$$

and for x the values of k are

$$1, 1, -3, -3,$$

giving

$$S(pk)=0, \quad S(pk^2)=3,$$

so that the variance is $3n$, the value adopted. For y we evidently have the same values, with the additional fact that the mean value of xy is zero. For z again

$$S(pk)=0, \quad S(pk^2)=9,$$

while the mean values of xz and yz are each zero. In analysing χ^2 into its components we always use linear functions of the frequencies, the mean value of each being zero, and such that all the covariances shall vanish.

It should be noted that the mean of xy is only zero in the absence of linkage. When linkage is present the values of p are

$$\tfrac{1}{4}(2+\theta,\ 1-\theta,\ 1-\theta,\ \theta),$$

giving for the covariance of x and y,

$$nS(pkk')=n(4\theta-1),$$

and for the correlation between them,

$$\tfrac{1}{3}(4\theta-1).$$

A statistic used for estimation will not be a linear function of the frequencies, for it must tend to a finite value as the sample is increased indefinitely; it will, however, often be of the form

$$T=\frac{1}{n}(k_1a+k_2b+k_3c+k_4d),$$

as in our example are T_1 and T_2.

For such cases a convenient formula is

$$nV(T)=S(pk^2)-\theta^2 \qquad \text{(B)}$$

the statistic being supposed to be consistent. Now for T_1, k is always $+1$ or -1, and we have at once

$$V(T_1)=\frac{1-\theta^2}{n};$$

while for T_2, with $k=\tfrac{1}{2},\ -\tfrac{1}{2},\ -\tfrac{1}{2},\ 2\tfrac{1}{2}$, and $p=\tfrac{1}{4}(2+\theta,\ 1-\theta,\ 1-\theta,\ \theta)$ it is easy to find

$$V(T_2)=\frac{1+6\theta-4\theta^2}{4n}.$$

These two sampling variances are very different; if θ is small (close linkage in repulsion), the variance of T_2 is only a quarter of that of T_1, and we may say that T_2 utilises four times as much of the available information as does T_1. This advantage diminishes, but persists over the whole range of repulsion linkages, for at $\theta = \frac{1}{4}$ the ratio of the variances is as five to three. The variances become equal at $\theta = \frac{1}{2}$, at which value the coupling recombination, $1-\sqrt{\theta}$, is about ·29, and for closer linkage than this, in the coupling phase, T_1 is the better statistic.

The standard error to which either estimate, T, is subject is, of course, found by taking the square root of the variance; it will be of more practical interest to find the standard error of the recombination fraction, $\sqrt{\theta}$. For this purpose the above variances are divided by 4θ, before taking the square root. Putting $\theta = \cdot 0357$, in the variances, we then have the two estimates of the recombination percentage,

$$23\cdot 88 \pm 4\cdot 268 \text{ and } 21\cdot 26 \pm 2\cdot 348,$$

from the first of which we might judge roughly that the recombination per cent. lay between 15·3 and 32·4, while the second indicates the much closer limits 16·6 to 26·0.

For any function of the frequencies, whether the sample number n appears explicitly or not, we can obtain the approximation to the sampling variance appropriate to the theory of large samples in the form

$$\frac{1}{n} V(T) = S\left\{p\left(\frac{\partial T}{\partial a}\right)^2\right\} - \left(\frac{\partial T}{\partial n}\right)^2, \quad . \quad . \quad (C)$$

a formula which involves the differential coefficients of the function in question with respect to each observed frequency, and to the total, n. After differentiation the expectation pn is substituted for each frequency a. If we apply formula (C) to the function

$$F = \log (ad) - \log (bc) = \log \{T_3(2+T_3)\} - 2 \log (1-T_3),$$

the values of $\partial F/\partial a$ are

$$\frac{1}{a}, \quad -\frac{1}{b}, \quad -\frac{1}{c}, \quad \frac{1}{d},$$

while, since n does not appear explicitly, $\partial F/\partial n = 0$. Hence, substituting pn for a, and the known values of p in terms of θ, we have

$$\frac{n}{4} V(F) = \frac{1}{2+\theta} + \frac{2}{1-\theta} + \frac{1}{\theta} = \frac{2(1+2\theta)}{\theta(1-\theta)(2+\theta)}.$$

To obtain the variance of T_3 we must divide this by the square of dF/dT_3, putting T_3 equal to θ after differentiation ; but

$$\frac{dF}{dT_3} = \frac{1}{2+T_3} + \frac{2}{1-T_3} + \frac{1}{T_3},$$

hence

$$nV(T_3) = \frac{2\theta(1-\theta)(2+\theta)}{1+2\theta}.$$

For the variance of the statistic which satisfies the conditions of maximum likelihood a very simple and direct general method is available. The expression obtained by direct differentiation, and which, equated to zero, gave the equation for T_4 in Section 53, was

$$\frac{a}{2+\theta} - \frac{b+c}{1-\theta} + \frac{d}{\theta}.$$

If this is differentiated again with respect to θ, and the expected values substituted for a, b, c, and d, we obtain

$$-\frac{n}{4}\left(\frac{1}{2+\theta} + \frac{2}{1-\theta} + \frac{1}{\theta}\right);$$

and this is simply equated to $-1/V(T_4)$, giving

$$nV(T_4) = \frac{2\theta(1-\theta)(2+\theta)}{1+2\theta},$$

the same expression as we have obtained for the sampling variance of T_3. This expression is of great importance for our problem, for it has been proved that no statistic can have a smaller sampling variance, in the theory of large samples, than has the solution of the equation of maximum likelihood. This group of statistics (to which the minimum χ^2 solution also always belongs), which agree in their sampling variance with the maximum likelihood solution, are therefore of particular value, and are designated *efficient* statistics, on the ground that for large samples they may be said to make use of the whole of the relevant information available, whereas less efficient statistics such as T_1 and T_2 utilise only a portion of it.

The expression for the minimum variance

$$\frac{2\theta(1-\theta)(2+\theta)}{(1+2\theta)n}$$

represents, therefore, an intrinsic property of the data, irrespective of the methods of estimation actually used. For large samples we may interpret its reciprocal

$$I = \frac{(1+2\theta)n}{2\theta(1-\theta)(2+\theta)}$$

as a numerical measure of the total amount of information, relevant to the value of θ, which the sample contains; and it is evident that each seedling observed contributes a definite amount of information, measured by

$$\frac{1+2\theta}{2\theta(1-\theta)(2+\theta)},$$

relevant to the estimation of the value of θ. This consideration affords a basis for the exact treatment of sampling problems even for small samples, for once we know how to calculate the amount of information in the data, the amount extracted by any proposed method of analysis may be evaluated likewise, though this may be difficult, and a comparison of the two quantities gives an objective measure of the efficiency of the method proposed in conserving the relevant information available.

The actual fraction of the information utilised by inefficient statistics in large samples is obtained by expressing the random sampling variance of efficient statistics as a fraction of that of the statistic in question. Thus for T_1 and T_2 we have the fractions,

$$E(T_1) = V(T_4) \div V(T_1) = \frac{2\theta(2+\theta)}{(1+2\theta)(1+\theta)},$$

which rises to unity at $\theta = 1$, but is less at all other values; and

$$E(T_2) = V(T_4) \div V(T_2) = \frac{8\theta(1-\theta)(2+\theta)}{(1+2\theta)(1+6\theta-4\theta^2)},$$

which rises to unity at $\theta = \frac{1}{4}$, falling to zero if $\theta = 0$, or $\theta = 1$.

Fig. 11 shows the course of these fractions expressed as a percentage, for all values of the recombination percentage, $\sqrt{\theta}$ for repulsion, and $1-\sqrt{\theta}$ for coupling. It will be seen that for our actual value of about 19 per cent. in repulsion, the efficiency of T_1 is about 13 per cent., while that of T_2 is about 44 per cent. The use of T_1 wastes about seven-eighths of the information utilised by T_3, T_4, and T_5, while the use of T_2 wastes more than half of it. In other words, T_1 is only as good an estimate as should be obtained from a count of 503 seedlings, while T_2 is as good as should be obtained from 1661 out of the 3839 actually counted.

The standard error of the efficient estimates of recombination value is 1·545 per cent., giving probable limits of 15·8 to 22·0 for the true value. The use of inefficient statistics is therefore liable to give not merely inferior estimates of the value sought, but

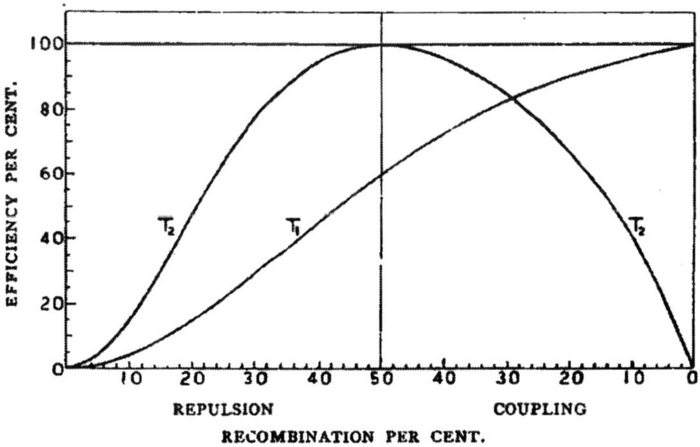

FIG. 11.—Efficiency of T_1 and T_2 for all values of θ. T_3, T_4, and T_5 having 100 per cent. efficiency throughout the range, are represented by the upper line.

estimates which are distinctly contradicted by the data from which they are derived. The value 23·88 per cent. obtained for T_1 differs from the better estimates by more than three times the standard error of the latter. It is highly misleading to derive such an estimate from data which themselves prove it to be erroneous.

The second respect in which the use of inefficient statistics is liable to be misleading is in the use of the χ^2 test of goodness of fit. Using T_1, we should naturally be led to conclude that the simple hypothesis of linked factors was in ill accord with the observations and that the results must be complicated by some such additional factor as differential viability. Finding only 32 double recessives against an expectation of 55, it would be natural to draw the conclusion that this genotype suffered from a low viability; whereas the data rightly interpreted give no significant indication of this sort. In the second place, whether the discrepancy were ascribed to differential viability or not, its existence would provide a very good reason for distrusting the linkage value obtained from such data; if, on the contrary, satisfactory methods of estimation are used, the grounds for this distrust are seen to fall away.

56. Comparison of Efficient Statistics

It has been seen that the three efficient statistics tested give closely similar results. This is in accordance with a general theorem that the correlation between any two efficient statistics tends to $+1$, as the sample is indefinitely increased. The conclusions drawn from their use will therefore ordinarily be equivalent. It appears from Fig. 11 that, for special values of θ, T_1 and T_2 also rank as efficient.

T_2 is efficient when θ is $\frac{1}{4}$, or in the absence of linkage. This accords with the use of z in Section 51 for testing the significance of linkage, for we are then testing the hypothesis that the factors are unlinked, and the test may be applied simply by seeing whether or not z^2 exceeds (say) $36n$. Any test based upon an efficient estimate of linkage compared to its standard error must agree with this. It is by no means uncommon to find statistics such as T_2 which provide excellent tests of significance, yet which become highly inefficient in estimating the magnitude of a significant effect. An outstanding example of this is the use of the third and fourth moments to measure the departure from normality of a frequency curve. The third and fourth moments provide excellent tests of the significance of the departure from normality, but when the distribution is one of the Pearsonian types differing considerably from the normal, the third and fourth moments are very inefficient statistics to use in estimating the form of the curve. This is the more noteworthy as the method of moments is ordinarily used for this purpose. The fact is that the efficiency of each of these statistics rises to 100 per cent. only for the normal form, just as that of T_2 reaches 100 per cent. only for zero linkage; but that the efficiency depends on the form of the curve, just as that of T_2 depends on the value of θ, and falls rapidly away as we leave the special region of high efficiency.

The statistic, T_1, is fully efficient when $\theta = 1$, that is, for very high linkage in the coupling phase; and therefore, in the theory of large samples, should give an estimate equivalent to T_3, T_4, and T_5. This extreme case, $\theta = 1$, is interesting in bringing out a limitation of the theory of large samples, which it is sometimes important to bear in mind; for the theory is valid only if none of the numbers counted, *a*, *b*, *c*, and *d*, is very small. Now for high linkage in coupling the recombination types, *b* and *c*, may be very scarce. It is true that for any proportion of crossing-over, however small, it is possible theoretically to take a sample so big that *b* and *c* will be large enough numbers; and in such cases the theory of large samples is justified. But it is also true for a sample of any given size, that linkage may be so high that seedlings of types b and c will be few; then, it is easy to see that some of the efficient statistics will fail. If, for example, either b or c is zero, T_3 will necessarily be unity, indicating complete linkage, whereas two or three seedlings in the other recombination class will show that crossing-over has really taken place. In the same way T_5 also fails, for it makes the recombination fraction proportional to $\sqrt{b^2+c^2}$, while T_1 and T_4 make it proportional to $b+c$. In general, the equation for minimising χ^2 is never satisfactory when some of the classes are thinly occupied, as one might expect from the nature of χ^2; the method therefore fails whenever the number of classes possible is infinite, as it usually is when we are concerned with the distributions of continuous variates. The two remaining efficient statistics T_1 and T_4 give equivalent estimates

$$\frac{b+c}{n}$$

for the recombination fraction, when the linkage is very high. Of course, as shown by Fig. 11, for any incomplete linkage the efficiency of T_1 is slightly below 100 per cent., so that the exact value of T_4 is slightly preferable. T_1, however, does provide a distinctly better estimate than T_3 or T_5 if b and c are small.

57. The Interpretation of the Discrepancy χ^2

The statistic obtained by the method of maximum likelihood stands in a peculiar relation to the measure of discrepancy, χ^2, and an examination of this relation will serve to illuminate the method, using degrees of freedom, which we have adopted in Chapter IV, and throughout the book. It has been stated that although in the distribution of a given number of individuals among four classes there are 3 degrees of freedom, yet if, as in the present problem, the expected numbers have been calculated from those observed by means of an adjustable parameter (θ), then only 2 degrees of freedom remain in which observation can differ from hypothesis. Consequently the value of χ^2 calculated in such a case is to be compared with the values characteristic of its distribution for 2 degrees of freedom. This principle has been disputed, but the common-sense considerations upon which it was based have since received complete theoretical verification. In the present instance we can in fact identify the 2 degrees of freedom concerned. For the observed numbers in each class will be entirely specified if we know:

(i) The number in the sample;
(ii) The ratio of starchy to sugary plants;
(iii) The ratio of green to white base leaf;
(iv) The intensity of linkage.

Now if the expected series agrees in items (i) and (iv), it can only differ in items (ii) and (iii) and these will be completely given by the two quantities x and y defined by

$$x = a+b-3c-3d,$$
$$y = a-3b+c-3d,$$

specifying the ratios by linear functions of the frequencies.

The mean values of x and y are zero, and the random sampling variance of each is $3n$. In the absence of linkage their deviations will be independent, but if linkage is present the mean value of xy has been found to be

$$-3n\frac{1-4\theta}{3},$$

and the correlation between x and y to be

$$\rho=-\frac{1-4\theta}{3}.$$

The simultaneous deviation of x and y from zero will therefore be measured (compare Section 30) by

$$Q^2=\frac{1}{1-\rho^2}\left\{\frac{x^2-2\rho xy+y^2}{3n}\right\}$$
$$=\frac{3}{8n(1-\theta)(1+2\theta)}\left\{x^2+y^2+\frac{2}{3}(1-4\theta)xy\right\}.$$

This expression, which of course depends upon θ, is a quadratic function of the frequencies; in this it resembles χ^2, and on comparing term by term the two expressions it appears that

$$\chi^2=Q^2+\frac{1}{I}\left\{\frac{a}{2+\theta}-\frac{b+c}{1-\theta}+\frac{d}{\theta}\right\}^2,$$

where I is the quantity of information contained in the data as defined in Section 55.

This identity has two important consequences: first, that $\chi^2 = Q^2$ for the particular value of θ given by the equation of maximum likelihood, and for no other value. At this point, then, even for finite samples, the deviations between observation and expectation represent precisely the deviations in the two single factor ratios.

The second point is, that for any value of θ, χ^2 is the sum of two positive parts of which one is Q^2, while the other measures the deviation of the value of θ considered from the maximum likelihood solution; this latter part is the contribution to χ^2 of errors of estimation, while the discrepancy of observation from hypothesis, allowing any value of θ, is measured by Q^2 only.

Fig. 12 shows the values of χ^2 and Q^2 over the region covering the three efficient solutions.

The contact of the graphs at the maximum likelihood solution makes it evident why the solution based

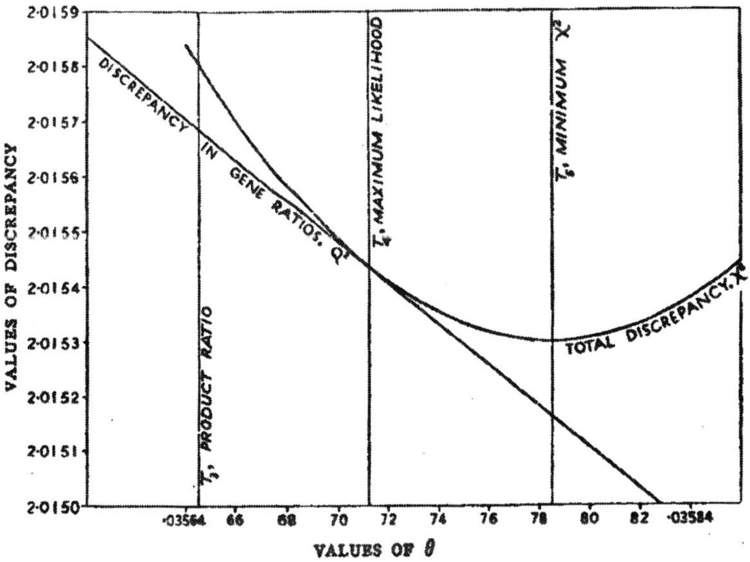

FIG. 12.—Graphs of χ^2 and Q^2 for varying θ in the neighbourhood of the efficient estimates.

on minimum χ^2 should be of no special interest, although χ^2 is a valid measure of discrepancy between observation and hypothesis. As the hypothetical value, θ, is changed the value of Q^2 changes, and, although this change is very minute, it gives the line a sufficient slope to make an appreciable shift in the point of contact.

If we set aside the portion ascribable to errors of estimation, which satisfactory methods of estimation will always reduce to a trifling amount, it is apparent that the measure of discrepancy, χ^2, in our chosen problem, merely measures the deviation from expectation of the two single factor ratios, and its significance must therefore be judged by comparison with expectation for 2 degrees of freedom. Such a comparison will give an objective test dependent only on the data, and independent of our methods of treating it, if and only if the error of estimation measured from the maximum likelihood solution is sufficiently small. This, of course, where the theory of large samples is applicable, will be true if any efficient statistic is used; it will always be true for the method of maximum likelihood.

57·1. Fragmentary Data

It very frequently happens, in a statistical enumeration, that only a portion of the whole sample is completely classified, the remaining members showing various degrees of incompleteness in their classification. Since the treatment of such data appears extremely troublesome, it is proper to lay great stress upon completeness of classification, whenever this is possible. In many cases, however, some degree of incompleteness is unavoidable, and the problem of framing an adequate statistical treatment, which shall utilise the whole of the information actually available, should be fairly faced. It will be shown that if approached in the right manner, and on the basis of a comprehensive theory of estimation, such problems offer no insuperable difficulties. We may again find a good example in the estimation of linkage, remembering that the type of difficulty to be discussed occurs in statistical work of all kinds.

Ex. 48. Tedin, working with two linked factors in *Pisum*, **Ar** and **Oh**, obtained, by selfing the double heterozygote, a progeny of 216 plants which could be classified as 99 **OhAr** 71 **ohAr** and 46 **ar**. The factor **Oh** could not be discriminated in the last group of plants, and, as is inevitable with moderate numbers and high linkage in repulsion, the proportions of this progeny give little information as to linkage value. From 63 of the **OhAr** group progenies were raised by self-fertilisation, which enabled their parents to be classified; 3 were homozygous for **Ar** but not for **Oh**, 8 for **Oh** and not for **Ar**, while 52 were heterozygous for both factors. Further, all of these 52 showed repulsion. Finally, of 47 plants of the **ohAr** group the progenies raised showed only 3 to be heterozygous for **Ar**, the remaining 44 being homozygous.

We may now set out the distribution of those 110 plants which in the end were completely classified alongside a table showing the relative frequencies with which plants completely classified should fall into the several classes, the recombination proportion being represented by p.

TABLE 66

	Ar Ar	**Ar ar**	**ar ar**
OhOh	0	8	—
Ohoh	3	0 52	—
ohoh	44	3	—

TABLE 67

	Ar Ar	Ar ar	ar ar
OhOh	p^2	$2p(1-p)$	$(1-p)^2$
Ohoh	$2p(1-p)$	$2p^2$ $2(1-p)^2$	$2p(1-p)$
ohoh	$(1-p)^2$	$2p(1-p)$	p^2

Next we have 60 plants, from which progenies were not grown, but which could be classified by their appearance as follows :—

TABLE 68

	Ar Ar Ar ar	ar ar
OhOh Ohoh	36	0
ohoh	24	0

TABLE 69

	Ar Ar Ar ar	ar ar
OhOh Ohoh	$2+p^2$	$1-p^2$
ohoh	$1-p^2$	p^2

and finally 46 plants, of which the classification is still less complete :—

TABLE 70

	Ar Ar	Ar ar	ar ar
OhOh, Ohoh, ohoh	0		46

TABLE 71

	Ar Ar	Ar ar	ar ar
OhOh, Ohoh, ohoh	3		1

If now it may be assumed that those plants, which, within any class, are incompletely specified, are a random sample of the members of that class, we may apply the method of maximum likelihood, as in Section 53, by multiplying the logarithm of the expectation in any class by the number recorded in that class, and adding all classes together, *irrespective of the completeness of classification*. When the expectations of any two classes are the same, the numbers in such classes may therefore be pooled, and we obtain

$$(8+3+3)\log\{2p(1-p)\}+52\log\{2(1-p)^2\}+44\log(1-p)^2$$
$$+36\log(2+p^2)+24\log(1-p^2)$$
$$+46\log(1)$$

as the logarithm of the likelihood, which is to be maximised. Any constant factor, such as 2, in the expectations makes a constant contribution to this quantity, independent of p, and may therefore be ignored. In particular the expectation in the **arar** class being entirely independent of p, the number in that class makes no contribution whatever to our knowledge of the linkage, and the whole class must be ignored. With these simplifications, and using the fact that the logarithm of a product is the sum of the logarithms of its factors, the expression to be maximised is reduced to

$$14 \log p + 206 \log (1-p) + 36 \log (2+p^2) + 24 \log (1-p^2).$$

By differentiating this expression with respect to p, we obtain the equation of maximum likelihood in the form

$$\frac{14}{p} - \frac{206}{1-p} + \frac{72p}{2+p^2} - \frac{48p}{1-p^2} = 0;$$

the first two terms are due to plants completely classified, and may be expected to contain the bulk of the desired information, the latter pair including the supplementary information due to the 60 **Ar** plants less completely classified. From the former only we should judge that p was nearly $14 \div 220$, or between 6 and 7 per cent. The exact estimate of the method of maximum likelihood may be most rapidly approached by substituting likely values for p and interpolating. Thus putting p equal to ·06 and ·07 we obtain :—

TABLE 72

	$p = \cdot 06.$	$p = \cdot 07.$	$p = \cdot 0638.$
$14/p$ . . .	233·33	200·00	219·436
$-206/(1-p)$.	$-219·15$	$-221·51$	$-220·038$
$72\,p/(2+p^2)$.	2·16	2·51	2·292
$-48\,p/(1-p^2)$.	$-2·89$	$-3·38$	$-3·075$
Total $\frac{\partial L}{\partial p}$.	+13·45	$-22·38$	$-1·385$

The result of substituting ·06 being 13·45, while with ·07 we obtain $-22·38$, the true value which gives zero must be near to ·06+·01 (13·45÷35·83), or ·0638. The effect of substituting this value is shown in the final column, which serves both as a check to the previous work, and as a basis, if such were needed, for a more accurate solution. The improved value is ·06345, from which as an exercise in the method the student may rapidly obtain a still more accurate value.

57·2. The Amount of Information : Design and Precision

The standard error to be attached to such an estimate is derived directly from the amount of information in the data. In cases in which the data are fragmentary, we proceed as usual in differentiating the left-hand side of the equation of maximum likelihood, and in changing the sign of the terms, but in substituting the expected for the observed frequencies note should be taken of the basis on which these are expected, as well as of the expectation in the classes which do not appear in our sample. Thus in the classification of the first year the expectations from 216 plants are $54(2+p^2)$ **OhAr** and $54(1-p^2)$ **ohAr** ;

these will make contributions to the information available of

$$54(2+p^2)\left(\frac{2p}{2+p^2}\right)^2+54(1-p^2)\left(\frac{-2p}{1-p^2}\right)^2$$

or

$$216p^2\left\{\frac{1}{2+p^2}+\frac{1}{1-p^2}\right\}$$

$$=216\,\frac{3p^2}{(2+p^2)(1-p^2)} \qquad \text{(A)}$$

and this, a very trifling amount numerically, is the amount of information available from the first year's classification.

If we now consider the 47 **ohAr** plants from which progenies were grown, we have expectations $47(1-p)^2 \div (1-p^2)$**ArAr** and $47\times 2p(1-p)\div(1-p^2)$ **Arar**. The *additional* information which these will contribute will be

$$47\,\frac{1-p}{1+p}\left(\frac{-1}{1-p}\right)^2+94\,\frac{p}{1+p}\left(\frac{1}{p}\right)^2-47\left(\frac{1}{1+p}\right)^2$$

the expected frequency in each portion being multiplied by the square of its logarithmic differential, and a like term deducted for the total ; this gives

$$47\left\{\frac{1}{1-p^2}+\frac{2}{p(1+p)}-\frac{1}{(1+p)^2}\right\}$$

$$=47\,\frac{2}{p(1-p)(1+p)^2}.$$

The additional information per plant of this group is therefore

$$\frac{2(1-p)}{p(1-p^2)^2} \qquad \text{(B)}$$

Finally, the observed distribution of the 63 **ArOh** plants into 52 **ohAr/Ohar**, 11 **OhOh/Arar** or **Ohoh/**

ArAr, and o **OhOh/ArAr** or **OhAr/ohar** must be replaced by the expectations

$$\frac{63}{(2+p^2)}\left\{2(1-p)^2,\ 4p(1-p),\ 3p^2\right\}.$$

The additional information per plant in this group is therefore

$$\frac{1}{2+p^2}\left\{2(1-p)^2\left(\frac{-2}{1-p}\right)^2+4p(1-p)\left(\frac{1}{p}-\frac{1}{1-p}\right)^2+3p^2\left(\frac{2}{p}\right)^2\right\}-\left(\frac{2p}{2+p^2}\right)^2,$$

or $$\frac{1}{2+p^2}\left\{8+\frac{4(1-2p)^2}{p(1-p)}+12\right\}-\frac{4p^2}{(2+p^2)^2},$$

which may be reduced to

$$\frac{4(2+2p-p^2)}{p(1-p)(2+p^2)^2} \quad . \quad . \quad . \quad \text{(C)}$$

At 6·345 per cent. recombination the numerical contribution per plant under (A), (B) and (C) are ·006051, 29·76 and 35·58. The second year's classifications thus give nearly 5000 and 6000 times as much information per plant as the first year's classification. On the actual numbers available the total information is 3642. The reciprocal of this, ·0002746 is the variance of the recombination fraction ; whence 2·746 is the variance of the recombination percentage, and 1·657 per cent. is the standard error.

The advantage of examining the amount of information gained at each stage of the experiment lies in the fact that the precision attainable in the majority of experiments is limited by the amount of land, labour and supervision available, and much guidance may be gained as to how these resources should best be allocated, by considering the quantity of information to be anticipated. In the experiment in question, for example, it appears that progenies from **OhAr** plants are somewhat more profitable than those from **ohAr** plants.

If, on the contrary, our object is merely to assign a standard error to a particular result, we may estimate the amount of information available directly by differentiating the expression for $\partial L/\partial p$ in the equation of maximum likelihood, using the actual numbers recorded in the classes observed. We should then obtain

$$\frac{14}{p^2}+\frac{206}{(1-p)^2}-\frac{72(2-p^2)}{(2+p^2)^2}+\frac{48(1+p^2)}{(1-p^2)^2};$$

this gives 3725 as the total amount of information upon which our estimate has been based, and 1·638 as the standard error of the estimate of the recombination percentage. It should be noted that an estimate obtained thus is in no way inferior to one obtained from the theoretical expectations; only that it gives no guidance as to the improvement of the conduct of the experiment. It might be said that owing to chance the experiment has given a somewhat higher amount of information than should be expected from the numbers classified.

The difference between the amount of information actually supplied by the data and the average value to be expected from an assigned set of observations is of theoretical interest, and being often small requires the rather exact calculations illustrated above. For the purpose of merely estimating the precision of the result attained a much briefer method may be indicated. The values obtained in Table 72 show that for a change of ·01 in p, the value of $\partial L/\partial p$ falls by 35·83; from this the amount of information may be estimated at once to be 3583 units, and the standard error to be 1·67 per cent., a sufficiently good estimate for most purposes.

In some cases this very crude approximation will not be good enough. It really estimates the amount of information appropriate to a value about 6·5 per cent., half-way between the two trial values. We want its value at 6·345 per cent. the actual value obtained from our estimate. An improved value may easily be obtained where three trial values have been used. From $p = \cdot 06$ and $p = \cdot 0638$, we have

$$\frac{13\cdot 45 + 1\cdot 385}{0\cdot 0038} = 3904$$

at $p = \cdot 0619$.

From $p = \cdot 0638$ and $p = \cdot 07$

$$\frac{-1\cdot 385 + 22\cdot 38}{0\cdot 0062} = 3386$$

at $p = \cdot 0669$.

Whence for $p = \cdot 06345$ we should take

$$\frac{\cdot 00155 \times 3386 + \cdot 00345 \times 3904}{\cdot 005} = 3743,$$

corresponding to a standard error 1·635 per cent., a result of amply sufficient accuracy, obtained without the evaluation of the algebraical expressions for quantity of information.

57·3. Test of Homogeneity of Evidence used in Estimation

When diverse data throw light on what is theoretically the same quantity, the evidence from different sources may be combined, as in the last Section, to provide a single estimate based on the whole of the evidence. The need for such methods can scarcely be overlooked. In practical research, however, it is often of equal or greater importance to test whether the different sources of information fully concur in the estimate towards which they lead, or whether, on the contrary, this is a compromise between bodies of evidence which are significantly discrepant. We shall now show how a χ^2 test of homogeneity may be applied, making use of the same computational procedure as that employed in finding the combined estimate.

In tetrasomic inheritance each chromosome is capable of pairing, not with a single mate, but with any other of the set of four homologous chromosomes to which it belongs. If different parts of it pair with different partners it is possible for the two homologous genes carried by a single gamete to have been in origin identical. The proportion of such gametes will be designated by a, in respect of any particular factor. It is thus possible for a plant containing one dominant gene, out of the four present, to transmit two such genes in the same gamete. The frequencies with which it transmits 0, 1 and 2 dominant genes being then $2+a$, $2-2a$, and a out of 4. The corresponding frequencies for a duplex plant (carrying two dominant genes) will be $1+2a$, $4-4a$, and $1+2a$, out of 6.

For a gene determining top-necrosis of potato plants grafted with a scion infected with virus X, Cadman gives data from four sources: the backcross and intercross progenies of simplex plants, and the backcross and intercross progenies from duplex plants. These are as shown in Table 73.

From these data we may estimate the magnitude of a, and test the homogeneity of the evidence. A standard form of calculation is shown in Table 74.

Values of a, ·120 and ·122, are sufficiently closely approximate to give both an improved joint estimate

TABLE 73

	Necrotic.	Non-necrotic.	Total.
Simplex plants: Backcross .	762	842	1604
Simplex plants: Intercross .	122	41	163
Duplex plants: Backcross .	144	38	182
Duplex plants: Intercross .	122	10	132

TABLE 74

	a = ·120.	a = ·122.	I.	D^2/I.	D^2/I.
Simplex backcross					
$842/(2+a)$	397·1698	396·7955			
$-762/(2-a)$	−405·3191	−405·7508			
D	−8·1493	−8·9553	403·0	·1990	·5131
Simplex intercross—					
$82/(2+a)$.	38·6792	38·6428			
$-244(2+a)/\{16-(2+a)^2\}$.	−44·9590	−45·0346			
D	−6·2798	−6·3918	56·0	·7296	
Duplex backcross—					
$76/(1+2a)$	61·2903	61·0932			
$-288/(5-2a)$	−60·5042	−60·5551			
D	+·7861	+·5381	124·0	·0023	1·0984
Duplex intercross—					
$40/(1+2a)$	32·2581	32·1543			
$-488(1+2a)\{36-(1+2a)^2\}$	−17·5588	−17·6206			
D	+14·6993	+14·5337	82·8	2·5511	
Total	+1·0563	−·2753	665·8	−·0001	−·0001
			χ^2	3·4819	1·6114
			n	3	1

of a, 12·16 per cent., and the amount of information, I, provided by the several parts of the data. These are given sufficiently nearly by dividing the difference between the discrepancies found for these two estimates by ·002. (Table 74.)

The amount of information is estimated for a = 12·1 per cent., near to the true value. At the true value $\chi^2 = D^2/I$, as shown in section 57; in this case we add the contributions from the separate parts of the data, subtracting that for the data as a whole, which is almost negligible. In the table the values of D used are for a = ·122; the reader may be interested to make the test using those for a = ·120.

It should be noted that the exact equivalence, demonstrated in Section 57, requires that I from each batch of data should be calculated as the amount of information expected from the total number of observations in each batch. *E.g.* for the simple backcross I would be $1604/(4-a)^2$. This process gives amounts of information slightly different from those used in Table 74, namely, for the four sections, 402·5, 56·71, 123·0, and 61·302, or 643·5 in all. The corresponding values of D^2/I are then ·1992, ·7204, ·0023, and 3·4457, with a total χ^2 of 4·3675. These last values check exactly with the contributions to χ^2 found by calculating the expected numbers in each of the eight classes enumerated. The discrepancy between the two methods of calculating χ^2 is due to errors of random sampling, and tends to zero as the size of the sample is increased; both methods therefore tend to give the theoretical χ^2 distribution for large samples of homogeneous material, and there appears to be no good reason for preferring one to the other. The method of this Section is available, however, when estimation is based on measurements and not on frequencies, so that no alternative value based on frequencies can be calculated.

The test is applied both for all three degrees of freedom among the four kinds of data, and for the one degree of freedom contrasting simplex with duplex parents. On both tests the homogeneity is satisfactory, though we should perhaps wish to repeat the test with a larger amount of information in all than the 665·8 units here available.

58. Summary of Principles

In any problem of estimation innumerable methods may be invented arbitrarily, all of which will tend to give the correct results as the available data are increased indefinitely. Each of these methods supplies a formula from which a statistic, intended as an estimate of the unknown, can be calculated from the observed frequencies. These statistics are of very different value.

A test of five such statistics in a simple genetical problem has shown that a particular group of them give closely concordant results, while the estimates obtained by the remainder are discrepant. This discrepancy is particularly marked in the misleading values found for χ^2.

An examination of the sampling errors shows that the concordant group have in large samples a variance equal to that of the maximum likelihood solution, and therefore as small as possible. These are efficient statistics; the variances of the inefficient statistics are larger, and may be so large that their values are quite inconsistent with the data from which they are derived.

Efficient statistics give closely equivalent results if the samples are sufficiently large, but when the theory of large samples no longer holds, such statistics, other than that obtained by the method of maximum likelihood, may fail.

The measure of discrepancy, χ^2, may be divided into two parts, one measuring the real discrepancy between observation and hypothesis, while the other measures merely the discrepancy between the value adopted and that given by the method of maximum likelihood. Using this fact, the homogeneity of data drawn from various sources may be tested in the process of obtaining the estimate.

The amount of information supplied by the data is capable of exact measurement, and the fraction of the information available which is utilised by any inefficient statistic can thereby be calculated. The same method may, though more laboriously, be applied to compare efficient statistics when the sample of data is small.

The method of maximum likelihood is directly applicable to fragmentary data, of which part is less completely classified than the remainder. Each fraction then contributes to the total amount of information utilised, according to the completeness with which it is classified. The knowledge of the amount of information supplied by the different fractions may be profitably utilised in planning the allocation of labour, and other resources, to observations of different kinds.

It will be readily understood that the thorough investigation which we have given to three somewhat slight genetical examples is not all necessary to their practical treatment. Its purpose has been to elucidate principles which are applicable to all problems involving statistical estimation. In many cases one need do no more than solve, at least to a good approximation the equation of maximum likelihood, and calculate the sampling variance of the estimate so obtained.

SOURCES USED FOR DATA AND METHODS

A. C. AITKEN (1931). Note on the computation of determinants. Trans. Fac. Act, xiii. 12-15.

A. C. AITKEN (1932). On the evaluation of determinants, the formation of their adjugates and the general solution of simultaneous linear equations. Proc. Edin. Math. Soc., Ser. II, iii. 207-219.

F. E. ALLAN. (1930). The general form of the orthogonal polynomials for simple series, with proofs of their simple properties. Proc. Roy. Soc. Edin., l. 310-320.

M. M. BARNARD (1935). The secular variations of skull characters in four series of Egyptian skulls. Annals of Eugenics, vi. 352-371.

T. BAYES (1763). An essay towards solving a problem in the doctrine of chances. Phil. Trans., liii. 370-418.

J. W. BISPHAM (1923). An experimental determination of the distribution of the partial correlation coefficient in samples of thirty. Metron, ii. 684-696.

J. BLAKEMAN (1905). On tests for linearity of regression in frequency distributions. Biometrika, iv. 332.

C. I. BLISS (1935). The calculation of the dosage-mortality curve. Annals of Applied Biology, xxii. 134-167, particularly Appendix, 164, by R. A. Fisher.

C. I. BLISS (1935). The comparison of dosage-mortality data. Annals of Applied Biology, xxii. 307-333.

M. BRISTOL-ROACH (1925). On the relation of certain soil algæ to some soluble organic compounds. Ann. Bot., xxxix. 149-201.

J. BURGESS (1895). On the definite integral, etc. Trans. Roy. Soc. Edin., xxxix. 257-321.

C. H. CADMAN (1942). Autotetraploid inheritance in the potato: some new evidence. Journal of Genetics, xliv. 33-52.

W. A. CARVER (1927). A genetic study of certain chlorophyll deficiencies in maize. Genetics, xii. 415-440.

W. G. COCHRAN (1940). Note on an approximate formula for the significance levels of *z*. Ann. Math. Stats., xl. 93-96.

C. G. COLCORD and LOLA S. DEMING (1936). The 0·1 per cent. level of *z*.

B. B. DAY (1937). A suggested method for allocating logging costs to log sizes. Journal of Forestry, xxxv. 69-71.

T. EDEN (1931). Studies in the yield of tea. I. The experimental errors of field experiments with tea. Journal of Agricultural Science, xxi. 547-573.

W. P. ELDERTON (1902). Tables for testing the goodness of fit of theory to observation. Biometrika, i. 155.

E. C. FIELLER (1940). The biological standardisation of insulin. Supplement to the Journal of the Royal Statistical Society, vii. 1-53.

R. A. FISHER. *See* Bibliography, p. 340.

J. G. H. FREW (1924). On *Chlorops Tæniopus* Meig. (The gout fly of barley.) Annals of Applied Biology, xi. 175-219.

GEISSLER (1889). Beiträge zur Frage des Geschlechts verhältnisses der Geborenen. Zeitschrift des K. Sachsischen Statistischen Bureaus.

J. W. L. GLAISHER (1871). On a class of definite integrals. Phil. Mag., Series IV, xlii. 421-436.

H. GRAY (1935). Athletic performance as a function of growth: speed in sprinting. Journal of Pediatrics, vi. 14-21.

M. GREENWOOD and G. U. YULE (1915). The statistics of antityphoid and anticholera inoculations, and the interpretation of such statistics in general. Proc. Roy. Soc. Medicine; Section of epidemiology and State medicine, viii. 113.

R. P. GREGORY, D. DE WINTON, and W. BATESON (1923). Genetics of *Primula Sinensis*. Journal of Genetics, xiii. 219-253.

J. A. HARRIS (1913). On the calculation of intraclass and interclass coefficients of correlation from class moments when the number of possible combinations is large. Biometrika, ix. 446-472.

J. A. HARRIS (1916). A contribution to the problem of homotyposis. Biometrika, xi. 201-214.

F. R. HELMERT (1875). Ueber die Berechnung des wahrscheinlichen Fehlers aus einer endlichen Anzahl wahrer Beobachtungsfehler. Zeitschrift für Mathematik und Physik, xx. 300-303.

A. H. HERSH (1924). The effects of temperature upon the heterozygotes in the bar series of *Drosophila*. Journal of Experimental Zoology, xxxix. 55-71.

H. HOTELLING (1931). The generalisation of Student's ratio. Annals of Mathematical Statistics, ii. 360-378.

J. S. HUXLEY (1923). Further data on linkage in *Gammarus Chevreuxi* and its relation to cytology. British Journal of Exp. Biology, i. 79-96.

M. N. KARN (1934). An investigation of the records of height and weight taken in school medical inspections in the county borough of Croydon. Annals of Eugenics, vi. 83-107.

T. L. KELLEY (1923). Statistical method. Macmillan and Co.

J. LANGE (1931). Crime and destiny. Allen and Unwin. (Translated by C. Haldane.)

LAPLACE (1820). Théorie analytique des probabilités. Paris. 3rd Edition.

K. MATHER (1938). The measurement of linkage in heredity. Methuen & Co. Ltd., London.

" MATHETES " (1924). Statistical study on the effect of manuring on infestation of barley by gout fly. Annals of Applied Biology, xi. 220-235.

W. B. MERCER and A. D. HALL (1911). The experimental error of field trials. Journal of Agricultural Science, iv. 107-132.

J. R. MINER (1922). Tables of $\sqrt{1-r^2}$ and $1-r^2$. Johns Hopkins Press, Baltimore.

F. MOSTELLER and J. W. TUKEY (1949). The uses and usefulness of binomial probability paper. Journal of the American Statistical Association, xliv. 174-212.

A. A. MUMFORD and M. YOUNG (1923). The interrelationships of the physical measurements and the vital capacity. Biometrika, xv. 109-133.

K. PEARSON (1900). On the criterion that a given system of deviations from the probable in the case of a correlated system of variables is such that it can be reasonably supposed to have arisen from random sampling. Phil. Mag., Series V, l. 157-175.

K. PEARSON and A. LEE (1903). Inheritance of physical characters. Biometrika, ii. 357-462.

J. RASMUSSON (1934). Genetically changed linkage values in *Pisum*. Hereditas, xix. 323-340.

N. SHAW (1922). The air and its ways. Cambridge University Press.

W. F. SHEPPARD (1907). Table of deviates of the normal curve. Biometrika, v. 404-406.

W. F. SHEPPARD (1938). Tables of the Probability Integral, completed and edited by the British Association Committee for the calculation of Mathematical Tables. British Association Mathematical Tables, vii.

H. FAIRFIELD SMITH (1936). A discriminant function for plant selection. Annals of Eugenics, vii. 240-250.

"Student" (1907). On the error of counting with a hæmacytometer. Biometrika, v. 351-360.

"Student" (1908). The probable error of a mean. Biometrika, vi. 1-25.

"Student" (1925). New tables for testing the significance of observations. Metron, V, No. 3, 105-120.

P. V. SUKHATMÉ (1938). On Fisher and Behrens' test of significance for the difference in means of two normal samples. Sankyha, iv. 39-48.

H. TEDIN and O. TEDIN (1928). Contributions to the Genetics of *Pisum*. V, Seed coat colour, linkage and free combination. Hereditas, xi. 11-62.

O. TEDIN (1931). The influence of systematic plot arrangement upon the estimate of error in field experiments. Journal of Agricultural Science, xxi. 191-208.

T. N. THIELE (1903). Theory of observations. C. & E. Layton, London, 143 pp.

J. F. TOCHER (1908). Pigmentation survey of school children in Scotland. Biometrika, vi. 129-235.

W. L. WACHTER (1927). Linkage studies in mice. Genetics, xii. 108-114.

H. WORKING and H. HOTELLING (1929). The application of the theory of error to the interpretation of trends. Journal of the American Statistical Association, xxiv. 73-85.

F. YATES (1934). Contingency tables involving small numbers and the χ^2 test. Supplement to Journal of the Royal Statistical Society, i. 217-235.

G. U. YULE (1917). An introduction to the theory of statistics. C. Griffen and Co., London.

G. U. YULE (1923). On the application of the χ^2 method to association and contingency tables, with experimental illustrations. Journal of the Royal Statistical Society, lxxxv. 95-104

BIBLIOGRAPHY

THE following list includes the statistical publications of the Author up to November 1949, together with a few other mathematical publications.

1912

On an absolute criterion for fitting frequency curves. Messenger of Mathematics, xli. 155-160.

1915

Frequency distribution of the values of the correlation coefficient in samples from an indefinitely large population. Biometrika, x. 507-521.

1918

The correlation between relatives on the supposition of Mendelian inheritance. Transactions of the Royal Society of Edinburgh, lii. 399-433.

1919

The genesis of twins. Genetics, iv. 489-499.

1920

A mathematical examination of the methods of determining the accuracy of an observation by the mean error and by the mean square error. Monthly Notices of the Royal Astronomical Society, lxxx. 758-770.

1921

Some remarks on the methods formulated in a recent article on "the quantitative analysis of plant growth." Annals of Applied Biology, vii. 367-372.

On the mathematical foundations of theoretical statistics. Philosophical Transactions of the Royal Society of London. A, ccxxii. 309-368.

Studies in crop variation. I. An examination of the yield of dressed grain from Broadbalk. Journal of Agricultural Science, xi. 107-135.

On the "probable error" of a coefficient of correlation deduced from a small sample. Metron, i, pt. 4, 1-32.

1922

On the interpretation of χ^2 from contingency tables, and the

1922—(*contd.*)

calculation of P. Journal of the Royal Statistical Society, lxxxv. 87-94.

The goodness of fit of regression formulæ, and the distribution of regression coefficients. Journal of the Royal Statistical Society, lxxxv. 597-612.

The systematic location of genes by means of crossover ratios. American Naturalist, lvi. 406-411.

[*with* W. A. MACKENZIE.] The correlation of weekly rainfall. Quarterly Journal of the Royal Meteorological Society, xlviii. 234-245.

[*with* H. G. THORNTON and W. A. MACKENZIE.] The accuracy of the plating method of estimating the density of bacterial populations. Annals of Applied Biology, ix. 325-359.

On the dominance ratio. Proceedings of the Royal Society of Edinburgh, xlii. 321-341.

1923

[*with* W. A. MACKENZIE.] Studies in crop variation. II, The manurial response of different potato varieties. Journal of Agricultural Science, xiii. 311-320.

Statistical tests of agreement between observation and hypothesis. Economica, iii. 139-147.

Note on Dr Burnside's recent paper on errors of observation. Proceedings of the Cambridge Philosophical Society, xxi. 655-658.

1924

The distribution of the partial correlation coefficient. Metron, iii. 329-332.

[*with* SVEN ODÈN.] The theory of the mechanical analysis of sediments by means of the automatic balance. Proceedings of the Royal Society of Edinburgh, xliv. 98-115.

The influence of rainfall on the yield of wheat at Rothamsted. Philosophical Transactions of the Royal Society of London, B, ccxiii. 89-142.

On a distribution yielding the error functions of several well-known statistics. Proceedings of the International Mathematical Congress, Toronto, 1924, pp. 805-813.

The conditions under which χ^2 measures the discrepancy between observation and hypothesis. Journal of the Royal Statistical Society, lxxxvii. 442-449.

A method of scoring coincidences in tests with playing cards. Proceedings of the Society for Psychical Research, xxxiv. 181-185.

1925

Sur la solution de l'équation intégrale de M. V. Romanovsky. Comptes Rendus de l'Académie des Sciences, clxxxi. 88-89.

[*with* P. R. ANSELL.] Note on the numerical evaluation of a Bessel function derivative. Proceedings of the London Mathematical Society, xxiv. 54-56.

The resemblance between twins, a statistical examination of Lauterbach's measurements. Genetics, x. 569-579.

Statistical methods for research workers. Oliver & Boyd, Edinburgh, xvi+350. (Editions 1925, 1928, 1930, 1932 1934, 1936, 1938, 1941, 1944, 1946.)

Theory of statistical estimation. Proceedings of the Cambridge Philosophical Society, xxii. 700-725.

1926

On the capillary forces in an ideal soil; correction of formulæ given by W. B. Haines. Journal of Agricultural Science, xvi. 492-505.

Periodical health surveys. Journal of State Medicine, xxxiv. 446-449.

Applications of "Student's" distribution. Metron, v. pt. 3, 90-104.

Expansion of "Student's" integral in powers of n^{-1}. Metron, v. pt. 3, 109-112.

On the random sequence. Quarterly Journal of the Royal Meteorological Society, lii. 250.

The arrangement of field experiments. Journal of the Ministry of Agriculture, xxxiii. 503-513.

Bayes' theorem and the fourfold table. The Eugenics Review, xviii. 32-33.

1927

[*with* H. G. THORNTON.] On the existence of daily changes in the bacterial numbers in American soil. Soil Science, xxiii. 253-257.

[*as* SECRETARY.] Recommendations of the British Association Committee on Biological Measurements. British Association, Section D, Leeds, 1927, pp. 13.

[*with* T. EDEN.] Studies in crop variation. IV, The experimental determination of the value of top dressings with cereals. Journal of Agricultural Science, xvii. 548-562.

Triplet children in Great Britain and Ireland. Proceedings of the Royal Society of London, B, cii. 286-311.

1927—(*cont.*)

[*with* J. WISHART.] On the distribution of the error of an interpolated value, and on the construction of tables. Proceedings of the Cambridge Philosophical Society, xxiii. 912-921.

On some objections to mimicry theory: statistical and genetic. Transactions of the Entomological Society of London, lxxv. 269-278.

1928

The possible modification of the response of the wild type to recurrent mutations. American Naturalist, lxii. 115-126.

[*with* L. H. C. TIPPETT.] Limiting forms of the frequency distribution of the largest or smallest member of a sample. Proceedings of the Cambridge Philosophical Society, xxiv. 180-190.

Further note on the capillary forces in an ideal soil. Journal of Agricultural Science, xviii. 406-410.

[*with* BHAI BALMUKAND.] The estimation of linkage from the offspring of selfed heterozygotes. Journal of Genetics, xx. 79-92.

[*with* E. B. FORD.] The variability of species in the Lepidoptera, with reference to abundance and sex. Transactions of the Entomological Society of London, lxxvi. 367-384.

Two further notes on the origin of dominance. American Naturalist, lxii. 571-574.

The general sampling distribution of the multiple correlation coefficient. Proceedings of the Royal Society of London, A, cxxi. 654-673.

[*with* T. N. HOBLYN.] Maximum- and Minimum-correlation tables in comparative climatology. Geografiska Annaler, iii. 267-281.

On a property connecting the χ^2 measure of discrepancy with the method of maximum likelihood. Bologna. Atti del Congresso Internazionale dei Matematici, vi. 94-100.

1929

A preliminary note on the effect of sodium silicate in increasing the yield of barley. Journal of Agricultural Science, xix. 132-139..

[*with* T. EDEN.] Studies in crop variation. VI, Experiments on the response of the potato to potash and nitrogen. Journal of Agricultural Science, xix. 201-213.

The over-production of food. The Realist, i. pt. 4, 45-60.

Tests of significance in harmonic analysis. Proceedings of the Royal Society of London, A, cxxv. 54-59.

The statistical method in psychical research. Proceedings of the Society for Psychical Research, xxxix. 189-192.

Moments and product moments of sampling distributions. Proceedings of the London Mathematical Society (Series 2), xxx. 199-238.

The evolution of dominance; reply to Professor Sewall Wright. American Naturalist, lxiii. 553-556.

The sieve of Eratosthenes. The Mathematical Gazette, xiv. 564-566.

1930

The distribution of gene ratios for rare mutations. Proceedings of the Royal Society of Edinburgh, l. 205-220.

The evolution of dominance in certain polymorphic species. The American Naturalist, lxiv. 385-406.

[*with* J. Wishart.] The arrangement of field experiments and the statistical reduction of the results. Imperial Bureau of Soil Science: Technical Communication No. 10. 24 pp.

Inverse probability. Proceedings of the Cambridge Philosophical Society, xxvi. 528-535.

The moments of the distribution for normal samples of measures of departure from normality. Proceedings of the Royal Society of London, A, cxxx. 16-28.

The genetical theory of natural selection. Oxford: at the Clarendon Press, 1930, xiv+272.

1931

The evolution of dominance. Biological Reviews, vi. 345-368.

[*with* J. Wishart.] The derivation of the pattern formulæ of two-way partitions from those of simpler patterns. Proceedings of the London Mathematical Society (Series 2), xxxiii. 195-208.

The sampling error of estimated deviates, together with other illustrations of the properties and applications of the integrals and derivatives of the normal error function. British Association: Mathematical Tables, vol. 1. xxvi-xxxv.

1932

[*with* F. R. Immer and O. Tedin.] The genetical interpretation of statistics of the third degree in the study of quantitative inheritance. Genetics, xvii. 107-124.

Inverse probability and the use of likelihood. Proceedings of the Cambridge Philosophical Society, xxviii. 257-261.

The bearing of genetics on theories of evolution. Science Progress, xxvii. 273-287.

1933

The concepts of inverse probability of fiducial probability referring to unknown parameters. Proceedings of the Royal Society of London, A, cxxxix. 343-348.

On the evidence against the chemical induction of melanism in Lepidoptera. Proceedings of the Royal Society of London, B, cxii. 407-416.

Selection in the production of the ever-sporting stocks. Annals of Botany, clxxxviii. 727-733.

Number of Mendelian factors in quantitative inheritance. Nature, cxxxi. 400.

The contribution of Rothamsted to the development of statistics. Rothamsted Experimental Station, Harpenden. Report for 1933, pp. 43-50.

1934

Two new properties of mathematical likelihood. Proceedings of the Royal Society of London, A, cxliv. 285-307.

[*with* C. DIVER.] Crossing-over in the land snail *Cepæa nemoralis* L. Nature, cxxxiii. 834.

Professor Wright on the theory of dominance. The American Naturalist, lxviii. 370-374.

Probability, likelihood and quantity of information in the logic of uncertain inference. Proceedings of the Royal Society of London, A, cxlvi. 1-8.

[*with* F. YATES.] The 6×6 Latin squares. Proceedings of the Cambridge Philosophical Society, xxx. 492-507.

Randomization, and an old enigma of card play. Mathematical Gazette, xviii. 294-297.

The effect of methods of ascertainment upon the estimation of frequencies. Annals of Eugenics, vi. 13-25.

The amount of information supplied by records of families as a function of the linkage in the population sampled. Annals of Eugenics, vi. 66-70.

The use of simultaneous estimation in the evaluation of linkage. Annals of Eugenics, vi. 71-76.

1935

The logic of inductive inference. Journal of the Royal Statistical Society, xcviii. 39-82.

On the selective consequences of East's (1927) theory of heterostylism in *Lythrum*. Journal of Genetics, xxx. 369-382.

Some results of an experiment on dominance in poultry, with special reference to polydactyly. Proceedings of the Linnean Society of London, Session 147, pt. 3, 71-88.

1935—(*cont.*)

The detection of linkage with "Dominant" abnormalities. Annals of Eugenics, vi. 187-201.

Dominance in poultry. Philosophical Transactions of the Royal Society of London, B, ccxxv. 195-226.

The mathematical distributions used in the common tests of significance. Econometrica, iii. 353-365.

The sheltering of lethals. American Naturalist, lxix. 446-455.

The detection of linkage with recessive abnormalities. Annals of Eugenics, vi. 339-351.

The fiducial argument in statistical inference. Annals of Eugenics, vi. 391-398.

The design of experiments. Oliver & Boyd, Edinburgh, xii+236 (Editions 1935, 1937, 1942, 1946.)

1936

Has Mendel's work been rediscovered? Annals of Science, i. 115-137.

Heterogeneity of Linkage data for Friedreich's Ataxia and the spontaneous antigens. Annals of Eugenics, vii. 17-21.

Tests of significance applied to Haldane's data on partial sex linkage. Annals of Eugenics, vii. 87-104.

The use of multiple measurements in taxonomic problems. Annals of Eugenics, vii. 179-188.

[*with* S. Barbacki.] A test of the supposed precision of systematic arrangements. Annals of Eugenics, vii. 189-193.

The coefficient of racial likeness. Journal of the Royal Anthropological Institute, lxvi. 57-63.

Uncertain Inference. Proceedings of the American Academy of Arts and Sciences, lxxi. 245-258.

[*with* K. Mather.] A linkage test with mice. Annals of Eugenics, vii. 303-318.

1937

The relation between variability and abundance shown by the measurements of the eggs of British-nesting birds. Proceedings of the Royal Society of London, B, cxxii. 1-26.

Professor Karl Pearson and the Method of Moments. Annals of Eugenics, vii. 303-318.

On a point raised by M. S. Bartlett on fiducial probability. Annals of Eugenics, vii. 370-375.

[*with* B. Day.] The comparison of variability in populations having unequal means. An example of the analysis of covariance with multiple dependent and independent variates. Annals of Eugenics, vii. 333-348.

1937—(*cont.*)

The wave of advance of advantageous genes. Annals of Eugenics, vii. 355-369.

[*with* H. GRAY.] Inheritance in man: Boas's data studied by the method of analysis of variance. Annals of Eugenics, viii. 74-93.

[*with* E. A. CORNISH.] Moments and cumulants in the specification of distributions. Revue de l'Institut International de Statistique, 1937, iv. 1-14.

1938

Dominance in Poultry: Feathered Feet, Rose Comb, Interna Pigment and Pile. Proceedings of the Royal Society, B, cxxv. 25-48.

[*with* F. YATES.] Statistical Tables. Oliver & Boyd, Edinburgh.

The mathematics of experimentation. Nature, 142, 442.

Quelques remarques sur l'estimation statistique. Biotypologie, vi. 153-159.

On the statistical treatment of the relation between sea-level characteristics and high-altitude acclimatization. Proceedings of Royal Society, B, cxxvi. 25-29.

The statistical utilization of multiple measurements. Annals of Eugenics, viii. 376-386.

Statistical Theory of Estimation. Calcutta University Readership Lectures. Published by the University of Calcutta.

1939

" Student." Annals of Eugenics, ix. 1-9.

The precision of the product formula for the estimation of linkage. Annals of Eugenics, ix. 50-54.

Presidential Address. Proceedings of the Indian Statistical Conference, Calcutta, 1938. Statistical Publishing Society, Calcutta.

Selective forces in wild populations of *Paratettix texanus*. Annals of Eugenics, ix. 109-122.

The comparison of samples with possibly unequal variances. Annals of Eugenics, ix. 174-180.

[*with* J. HUXLEY and E. B. FORD.] Taste-testing the anthropoid apes. Nature, cxliv. 750.

The sampling distribution of some statistics obtained from non-linear equations. Annals of Eugenics, ix. 238-249.

Stage of development as a factor influencing the variance in the number of offspring, frequency of mutants and related quantities. Annals of Eugenics, ix. 406-408.

1940

Scandinavian influence in Scottish ethnology. Nature, cxlv. 500.

On the similarity of the distributions found for the test of significance in harmonic analysis, and in Stevens's problem in geometrical probability. Annals of Eugenics, x. 14-17.

An examination of the different possible solutions of a problem in incomplete blocks. Annals of Eugenics, x. 52-75.

[*with* W. H. DOWDESWELL and E. B. FORD.] The quantitative study of populations in the Lepidoptera. 1. *Polyommatus icarus* Rott. Annals of Eugenics, x. 123-135.

The estimation of the proportion of recessives from tests carried out on a sample not wholly unrelated. Annals of Eugenics, x. 160-170.

A note on fiducial inference. Annals of Mathematical Statistics, x. 383-388.

The precision of discriminant functions. Annals of Eugenics, x. 422-429.

[*with* K. MATHER.] Non-lethality of the mid factor in *Lythrum salicaria*. Nature, cxlvi. 521.

1941

The theoretical consequences of polyploid inheritance for the mid style form of *Lythrum salicaria*. Annals of Eugenics, xi. 31-38.

Average excess and average effect of a gene substitution. Annals of Eugenics, xi. 53-63.

The asymptotic approach to Behrens' integral with further tables for the *d* test of significance. Annals of Eugenics, xi. 141-172.

The negative binomial distribution. Annals of Eugenics, xi. 182-187.

1942

The likelihood solution of a problem in compounded probabilities. Annals of Eugenics, xi. 306-307.

The theory of confounding in factorial experiments in relation to the theory of groups. Annals of Eugenics, xi. 341-353.

1943

Some combinational theorems and enumerations connected with the numbers of diagonal types of a Latin Square. Annals of Eugenics, xi. 395-401.

[*with* A. S. CORBET and C. B. WILLIAMS.] The relation between the number of species and the number of individuals in a random sample of an animal population. Journal of Animal Ecology, xii. 42-58.

1943—(*contd.*)

[*with* K. MATHER.] The inheritance of style-length in *Lythrum salicaria*. Annals of Eugenics, xii. 1-23.

1944

[*with* S. B. HOLT.] The experimental modification of dominance in Danforth's short-tailed mutant mice. Annals of Eugenics, xii. 102-120.

Allowance for double reduction in the calculation of genotype frequencies with polysomic inheritance. Annals of Eugenics, xii. 169-171.

1945

A system of confounding for factors with more than two alternatives, giving completely orthogonal cubes and higher powers. Annals of Eugenics. xii. 283-290.

The logical inversion of the notion of the random variable. Sankhyā, vii. 129-132.

1946

A system of scoring linkage data, with special reference to the pied factors in mice. Amer. Nat., lxxx. 497-592.

The fitting of gene frequencies to data on Rhesus reactions. Annals of Eugenics, xiii. 150-155, and addendum, Note on the calculation of the frequencies of Rhesus allelomorphs. Annals of Eugenics, xiii. 223-224.

1947

The Rhesus factor. A study in scientific method. Amer. Scientist, xxxv. 95-103.

The theory of linkage in polysomic inheritance. Phil. Trans. Roy. Soc. B., no. 594, ccxxxiii. 55-87.

The analysis of covariance method for the relation between a part and the whole. Biometrics, iii. 65-68.

[*with* V. C. MARTIN.] Spontaneous occurrence in *Lythrum salicaria* of plants duplex for the short-style gene. Nature, clx. 541.

[*with* E. B. FORD.] The spread of a gene in natural conditions in a colony of the moth *Panaxia dominula* L. Heredity, i. 143-174.

Number of self-sterility alleles. Nature, clx. 797.

[*with* M. F. LYON and A. R. G. OWEN.] The sex chromosome in the house mouse. Heredity, i. 355-365.

1948

Conclusions fiduciaires. Annales de l'Institut Henri Poincaré, x. 191-213.

1948—(*cont.*)

[*with* Daniel Dugué.] Un résultat assez inattendu d'arithmetique des lois de probabilite. Comptes rendus des séances de l'Academie des Sciences, ccxxvii. 1205-1206.

A quantitative theory of genetic recombination and chiasma formation. Biometrics, iv. 1-13.

1949

The linkage problem in a tetrasomic wild plant, *Lythrum salicaria.* Proceedings of the Eighth International Congress of Genetics (Hereditas Suppl. Vol. 1949).

[*with* W. H. Dowdeswell and E. B. Ford.] The quantitative study of populations in the *Lepidoptera.* 2. *Maniola jurtina* L. Heredity, 3, 67-84.

A preliminary linkage test with *agouti* and *undulated* mice. Heredity, 3, 229-241.

Note on the test of significance for differential viability in frequency data from a complete three-point test. Heredity, 3, 215-219.

INDEX